More Than Blue, More Than Yankee

More Than Blue, More Than Yankee

COMPLEXITY AND CHANGE IN NEW ENGLAND POLITICS

EDITED BY
AMY FRIED AND ERIN O'BRIEN

University of Massachusetts Press
Amherst and Boston

Copyright © 2024 by University of Massachusetts Press
All rights reserved
Printed in the United States of America

ISBN 978-1-62534-830-2 (paper); 831-9 (hardcover)

Designed by Jen Jackowitz
Set in Adobe Garamond Pro
Printed and bound by Books International, Inc.

Cover design by adam b. bohannon
Cover art by Milos, *Map of New England region of United States of America*, AdobeStock.

Library of Congress Cataloging-in-Publication Data

Names: Fried, Amy, 1957– editor. | O'Brien, Erin, 1975– editor.
Title: More than blue, more than Yankee : complexity and change in New England politics / edited by Amy Fried and Erin O'Brien.
Description: Amherst : University of Massachusetts Press, 2024. | Includes bibliographical references and index.
Identifiers: LCCN 2024032662 (print) | LCCN 2024032663 (ebook) | ISBN 9781625348302 (paperback) | ISBN 9781625348319 (hardcover) | ISBN 9781685751012 (ebook) | ISBN 9781685751029 (epub)
Subjects: LCSH: Party affiliation—New England. | Political culture—New England. | Political participation—New England. | New England—Politics and government.
Classification: LCC JK2295.N53 M67 2024 (print) | LCC JK2295.N53 (ebook) | DDC 306.20974—dc23/eng/20240819
LC record available at https://lccn.loc.gov/2024032662
LC ebook record available at https://lccn.loc.gov/2024032663

British Library Cataloguing-in-Publication Data
A catalog record for this book is available from the British Library.

For those who helped me through my 2022–2023 chemo
AF

For my dad, Dr. William F. O'Brien
EO'B

CONTENTS

List of Illustrations ix

Preface xi

PART I. Introduction

CHAPTER 1

Introduction: More Than Blue, More Than Yankee

AMY FRIED, UNIVERSITY OF MAINE
ERIN O'BRIEN, UNIVERSITY OF MASSACHUSETTS BOSTON

3

CHAPTER 2

From Red to Blue: New England in American Political Development

AMY FRIED, UNIVERSITY OF MAINE
DOUGLAS B. HARRIS, LOYOLA UNIVERSITY MARYLAND

14

PART II. The Politics of the New England States

CHAPTER 3

Connecticut Sings the Blues: Suburbia, Mavericks, and Policy Innovation

SCOTT L. MCLEAN, QUINNIPIAC UNIVERSITY

37

CHAPTER 4

Maine: Pushed From Away, The Pine Tree State Sways But Does Not Break

JAMES P. MELCHER, UNIVERSITY OF MAINE FARMINGTON
AMY FRIED, UNIVERSITY OF MAINE

59

CHAPTER 5

Pols, Preachers, & Pragmatists: Massachusetts Politics in the Twenty-First Century

JEROLD DUQUETTE, CENTRAL CONNECTICUT STATE UNIVERSITY

81

CHAPTER 6

How New Hampshire Politics Turned Wicked Weird

CHRISTOPHER J. GALDIERI, SAINT ANSELM COLLEGE

104

CHAPTER 7
Rhode Island: More Than Yankee, Less Than True Blue
MAUREEN MOAKLEY, UNIVERSITY OF RHODE ISLAND
125

CHAPTER 8
Vermont Politics in the Modern Age: From Red to Blue
PAUL PETTERSON, CENTRAL CONNECTICUT STATE UNIVERSITY
147

PART III. Issues in New England Politics

CHAPTER 9
Civic Participation in New England
RACHAEL COBB, SUFFOLK UNIVERSITY
167

CHAPTER 10
Presidential Politics and Influence, New England Style(s)
DANTE J. SCALA, UNIVERSITY OF NEW HAMPSHIRE
185

CHAPTER 11
Demographic Change and Political Power in New England
LUIS JIMÉNEZ, UNIVERSITY OF MASSACHUSETTS BOSTON
206

CHAPTER 12
Gendering Yankee Ingenuity: Electing Women in New England
JANE JAKYUNG HAN, UNIVERSITY OF MASSACHUSETTS BOSTON
ERIN O'BRIEN, UNIVERSITY OF MASSACHUSETTS BOSTON
228

CHAPTER 13
Conclusion
AMY FRIED, UNIVERSITY OF MAINE
ERIN O'BRIEN, UNIVERSITY OF MASSACHUSETTS BOSTON
252

Index 259

LIST OF ILLUSTRATIONS

FIGURE 1.1. Trump Popular Vote Share, 2020 Presidential Election.
FIGURE 2.1. Democratic Congressional Representation in New England and the South, 1896–2023.
FIGURE 2.2. Democratic Representation in the House in New England and the Northeast, 1896–2023.
FIGURE 3.1. Connecticut Party Registration Percentages, 1958–2022.
FIGURE 3.2. Suburban Connecticut Voters: Party Identifiers plus Leaners, 2008–2022.
TABLE 4.1. Partisan Affiliation of Maine Election Winners, 1998–2022.
TABLE 6.1. Votes for president in New Hampshire, 1992–2020.
TABLE 6.2. Votes for US Senate and US House of Representatives, 1966–2022.
TABLE 6.3. Votes for Governor of New Hampshire, 1996–2022.
TABLE 7.1. Partisan Affiliation of Rhode Island Election Winners, 1998–2022.
FIGURE 7.1. Presidential Election Results by Municipality, 2016.
TABLE 9.1. Days Prior to Election Voter Must Register by New England State.
TABLE 10.1. Democratic Nominees' Vote Share in Presidential Elections, 2000–2020.
TABLE 10.2. Presidential Nomination Results in New England States, 2000–2016.
FIGURE 11.1. New England's changing demographics, 1975–2020.
TABLE 11.1. Percent Below Poverty in New England for Selected Demographic Groups, 1990–2020.
TABLE 11.2. Median Household Income in New England in 2020 dollars, 1990–2020.
TABLE 12.1. New England Women's Representation in Congress and Statewide Executive Office, 2023.
TABLE 12.2. New England Women's Representation in State Legislature, 2022.
FIGURE 12.1. Percentage of Female State Legislators Across New England, 1921–2023.
TABLE 12.3. Logistic Regression Coefficients – District Level.
TABLE 12.4. Pooled OLS Regression Coefficients – State Level.

PREFACE

Old-time Yankeeism may not reign in New England anymore, but our collaboration on this book was cemented in a classic New England locale—the Mt. Washington Hotel in New Hampshire. The place is historically important because it's where the meetings took place that, via the Bretton Woods Agreement, created the post-war international economic order. It also happened to be the site of the New England Political Science Association Annual Meeting, which both of us were attending. One of our favorite conferences for its collegiality and quality, for many years it has held a roundtable on New England politics.

In working on the project, both of us benefited a great deal from this scholarly community, as many of the chapter authors are regular attendees of this conference and present regionally oriented scholarly work (as well as other research) there.

For us, this was an opportunity to create a book that would endure as a good read and reference work on the political developments of this region, which somehow has received little attention from political scientists and pundits. As we conceptualized the project, found authors, developed a prospectus, wrote and edited, we also found that we gained a fantastic friendship.

For Amy, there was a big bump along the road when she was diagnosed with low-grade serous ovarian cancer. However, having the book to work on and our regular co-editor meetings when symptoms eased after each chemotherapy session helped her feel herself and keep going. She thanks everyone who supported her through all of that and has helped her along the way. The number one person in that category is her husband Dave. Amy's children and their people (Sarah and her husband Scott; Caleb and his partner Lily), sister Heidi and niece Ruthie came and lovingly helped. She is so thankful for so many friends (especially Karen Horton, Deb Rogers, Laura Cowan, Richard May, Sandy Caron, Lauri Schindler, Marie Hayes, and Alan Rosenwasser), the old friends who reached out, as well as many others in her broader community who brought or bought meals and visited. Erin's humor, tales, and smarts added to her morale. She also thanks the medical professionals who oversaw her care, from her oncologists to their nurses to her acupuncturist, and those at the Dempsey Center in Maine who provide services and keep it running. Amy also thanks co-authors Doug Harris and

Jim Melcher for their friendship and for their work with her, as she navigated her chemo-affected schedule.

For Erin, the book was originally dedicated to the "2004 Boston Red Sox." This is because I grew up in a thoroughly Red Sox home via some superb socialization by my father, Dr. William F. O'Brien. A Westfield, Massachusetts native, my dad was a life-long Red Sox fan and baseball player—he was the opening day starting pitcher as a freshman for Le Moyne College and named our dog "Fenway" in 1980s Newport News, Virginia. As this book came to completion, my lovely, fit father cruelly passed. He is the best man I'll ever know—deeply moral, inviting, an advocate and friend to those who struggle, and my biggest fan. When one goes to our house on Cape Cod, where my father lived, the first thing that greets you upon entering is a medium-height bookcase with the three previous books I have written or edited prominently displayed on top. That's emblematic of how my father made me feel—seen and prioritized. How wonderful is that? I'll now add this fourth book to the display, and it is dedicated to you, Dad. Thank you for always being in my corner, pushing me, and loving me. YOU are so very special. I miss you in ways hard to fully articulate and remain deeply grateful that you're my dad.

Before embarking on this project, Amy and I knew each other professionally and admired one another's research and approach to the discipline. We became trusted friends over the course of this project. Our weekly Zooms took on a familiar pattern: updates on Amy's health, Reilley barks, discussion of trips and other excitements, as well as advice on issues we might be struggling with or wanted trusted insight on—usually unrelated to work. Amy was extraordinarily brave in facing her diagnosis and subsequent treatments. I admire her fortitude, the trust she showed in me to share highs and lows and thank her for the ways she took the reins immediately after my father passed. Tremendous thanks as well to the scholars who wrote the chapters, made our suggested edits, and even cut figures and tables when we requested without audible groan. We both thank Brian Halley, our editorial editor at University of Massachusetts Press, as well as the superb team at the press who saw this book through peer review, production, marketing, and sales. University press publishing is so very vital, and your professional devotion to it is a tremendous service to the polity and, in particular, the New England region.

More Than Blue, More Than Yankee

PART I
INTRODUCTION

CHAPTER 1

INTRODUCTION

More Than Blue, More Than Yankee

Amy Fried and Erin O'Brien
Professor of Political Science | Associate Professor of Political Science
University of Maine | University of Massachusetts Boston

We cannot grasp changes in American politics without understanding the politics of New England. Its Yankee, mercantile character had a major influence on the early development of the United States. In the 1830s, French observer Alexis de Tocqueville viewed "the destiny of America embodied in the first Puritan who landed on those shores" (Tocqueville 1988, 278) and saw New England's local institutions as key to the nation's political culture and development. Tocqueville praised the New England township and town meeting as promoting the spirits of liberty and order and helping citizens learn "to rule society" and to develop "clear, practical ideas about the nature of his duties and the extent of his rights" (Tocqueville 1988, 70).

Moreover, New England has supplied esteemed and effective leaders from the founding period, including John Adams, John Hancock, Roger Sherman, Josiah Bartlett, William Lloyd Garrison, Lucy Stone, Franklin Pierce, Chester Arthur, Henry Cabot Lodge, Calvin Coolidge, John F. Kennedy, John Chafee, Michael Dukakis, George Mitchell, George H. W. Bush, Tip O'Neill, Edward Brooke, Olympia Snowe, John Kerry, Elizabeth Warren, Bernie Sanders, and Ayanna Pressley, to name but a few.

However, when we turn to regional electoral influence on national politics, pundits and scholars have paid a great deal of attention to the American South's transformation after World War II from a staunchly Democratic area to a region in which Republicans dominate (Key 1949; Richardson 2020). Far less has been written about political shifts in New England and why these matter. This volume addresses precisely these issues.

If little had changed politically in New England, the relative absence of political examinations about the area would make sense. But this is not true. Consider what has happened with New Englanders and national politics since World War II. New England went from two-thirds of its states supporting the Republican candidate for president in 1948 to having Democratic candidates win statewide in every New England state from 2008 through 2020. Indeed, in 2020 Joe Biden decisively won the region—especially when we consider that the vast majority of the counties Trump won were in low-population centers concentrated in far northern Vermont and New Hampshire as well as rural Maine. The Electoral College tally bolsters this take—Biden's thirty-two electoral votes to Trump's sole electoral vote pick-up in Maine's Second Congressional District. Congressional elections show this pattern, too. Only one state in the region, Rhode Island, had two Democratic senators in early 1949. New England was down to "five Republicans in the United States Senate" in 1980 along with "nine Republican members of the House of Representatives elected from the five New England states—[but with] at least one from each state" (Gregg 2018). In the 118th Congress, which was seated in January 2023, just one member of New England's entire delegation to the US Congress was a Republican—Maine's Susan Collins.

Inklings of this major shift in New England politics began even before Franklin D. Roosevelt's presidency, with the 1928 presidential candidacy of Democrat Al Smith, a Catholic who galvanized New England voters in Boston and Providence. This brought Smith the electoral votes of Massachusetts and Rhode Island, which had not voted Democratic in a presidential race since 1912. As Amy Fried and Douglas B. Harris note in chapter 2, party-building by President Roosevelt and state leaders such as Maine's Ed Muskie was crucial in creating the organizational infrastructure and ties between the electorate and Democratic parties and leaders which later dominated politically. Moreover, changes in the national Republican Party, particularly its embrace of social conservatism and use of racialized messages (particularly from the Reagan era on) undermined the GOP and boosted the Democratic Party in the region. Inklings of willingness to vote for Democrats begot patterns of New Englanders preferring to do so.

More than Blue

Simultaneously this transformation in party politics belies fascinating political variation among the New England states. Contrary to the takes of most political observers outside New England, the region is by no means uniform in politics, policy, or political cleavages. New Hampshire's "first in the nation" presidential primary makes it the only New England state to attract national influence and attention when deciding the major parties' nominee. Though, as Dante Scala points out in chapter 10, this influence is in danger as Democrats changed their primary schedule, reducing New Hampshire's impact. But New Hampshire, true to its state motto, is not going down without a fight. In January 2024, New Hampshire Democrats held the "first in the nation primary" even as the Democratic National Committee awarded no delegates in the contest. Maine is the only New England state, and one of only two US states, that does not adhere to a "winner-take-all" rule in the Electoral College. It also elected Paul LePage, the self-named "Trump Before Trump" governor, who served from 2011 to 2019—clearly not adhering to the image of liberal or moderate Republican governors winning in today's New England. Rhode Island politics is synonymous with the advantages and problems of a highly compact state, ranging from coziness and sense of community to parochialism and corruption . . . rewarded. Former Providence Mayor Buddy Cianci, for instance, was twice elected and twice forced to resign because of felony convictions. Rhode Island House Speaker Gordon Fox was convicted of taking a $52,000 bribe, "spending $108,000 of campaign funds on himself and filing a false return," and then going to three years in prison (Patkinkin 2021). The norm of Rhode Island corruption, or the unfair perception of it, as Maureen Moakley argues in chapter 7, stands in marked contrast to the politics of progressive purity that propels one of only two Senate Independents, former New Yorker Bernie Sanders, in Vermont. Massachusetts features a taste for Democratic dominance in elected office—but a propensity to elect Republican governors. Jerold Duquette's chapter 5 explains that pattern is now interrupted by the capture of the Massachusetts Republican Party structure by Trump Republicans (akin to some of the forces in Maine). Connecticut remains solidly blue but is undergoing a transition in what parts of the state vote red and blue as Scott McLean demonstrates in chapter 3. New England is "more than blue."

A map of the 2020 presidential election popular vote created by John Heppen drives home this point. Figure 1.1 provides the percentage of the vote won by former president Trump in each of the counties within the New England states. The darker the shade, the higher percentage of the vote that Trump won. What this map makes evident is that there is some taste for Trump in New England and that it varied considerably among states and among counties. Winner-take-all electoral rules (except for Maine in presidential elections) obfuscate the partisan variation that exists within New England. The shorthand that New England is a bunch of liberals is bolstered by the electoral count but complicated by Trump's vote share across the region. New England does not perform as one; as our title indicates, it is "more than blue."

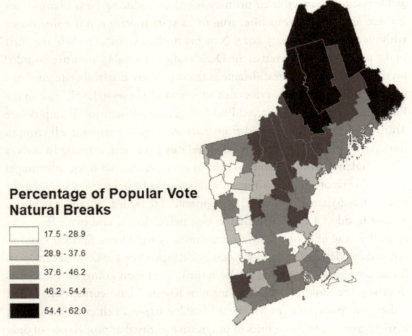

FIGURE 1.1. Trump Popular Vote Share, 2020 Presidential Election. Figure prepared for this volume by John Heppen, University of Wisconsin River Falls.

The chapters of this volume detail considerable state variation in preference for the Democratic Party, as well as urban-rural schisms in electoral behavior among New Englanders. What emerges is, yes, a top-line transformation in party politics from Republican to Democratic influence but also libertarian migration to New Hampshire in the "Free State Project" as well as wild state house swings in party control in the Granite State (chapter 6), suburban Connecticut voters recently tilting Democratic but open for courting from adept suitors (chapter 3), a potent rural-urban party divide in Maine (chapter 4), and Vermont moving left as people migrated to the state, while its more rural areas remain more socially and politically conservative (chapter 8). Massachusetts and Rhode Island, chapters 5 and 7, respectively, are strengthening in Democratic dominance to the near extinction of electorally competitive Republicans. Indeed, the only current party competition one can consistently count on in these states is whether progressive or moderate Democrats control the Democratic Party apparatus—with the latter usually at the reins though less uniformly ensconced in power, as Duquette points out in chapter 5 on Massachusetts. The power of the Democratic Party bosses, or the Democratic Party apparatus, to control candidate selection has weakened considerably.

So while New England has seen a partisan shift equally seismic as the American South, the chapters that follow demonstrate how too each New England state is "more than blue" in ways often unique to it. Party transformation collectively defines the region but the extent of this transformation, and the forces that animate it today, are too a product of particularistic state politics within the region, as the contributors to this collection make clear.

More than Yankee

Our volume also makes clear that today's New England politics are "more than Yankee." The term "New England Yankee" conjures forth Protestant descendants from English shores who were shrewd, plain-spoken, pragmatists with scrappy ingenuity. In an analysis of the regional identity of New England, one author (Conforti 2001, 115) notes that, as far back as the 1820s, New Englanders who moved to central and western New York were called a "Yankee exodus," with a character that was "intelligent, ingenious, acute, versatile," "sober, orderly [and] moral" as well as "ardent, enterprising, resolute, patient, active, industrious and persevering." Several decades later, Yankeeism was believed to involve "a commercial shrewdness," a people "on the move and on the make" (Conforti 2001, 151). More recently New England Yankees pride themselves on self-reliance and their "character [is] common sense, dry wit, a deep connection to the natural world, and an acceptance of hardship" (Tryba 2013). The deliberative participatory ideal of citizens plainly speaking their mind, and truly considering the perspectives of their neighbors, in a town meeting is a hallmark of New England Yankee lore and identity (Bryan 2003).

Scala's description in chapter 10 of the iconic New Hampshire resident participating in the presidential primary process: "the laconic citizen in the plaid shirt, stoically listening to the flashy presidential candidate from somewhere else, then cutting him or her down to size with a wry comment" epitomizes political Yankeeism. Yet, along with this compelling image comes exclusion. Yankeeism is a type which conjures up whiteness and, to a lesser extent, maleness. And, as historical fact, not all whites are even included. As Vanderbeck (2006, 646) notes, "This Yankee whiteness has historically served to marginalize both nonwhite and other 'white' identities within the region."

"Yankee" has thus not been a term those within and outside of New England associate with *all* those living in the region—consciously or subconsciously.

Yet, as this volume demonstrates repeatedly, the region and its states have diversified over time. In chapter 11, Luis Jiménez, first offers a sweeping history of the waves of immigration to New England and then tells the stories of Blacks, Latinx, and Asian Americans in modern New England. He documents demographic change in the region as well as uneven successes at political incorporation stemming, primarily, from discrimination as well as from differential organizational challenges in uniting these groups around shared political interests.

Although Vermont, Maine, and New Hampshire are three of the four whitest states in the nation, Massachusetts, Connecticut, and Rhode Island are at, or just slightly above, the average for all American states (World Population Review 2023). Thus, the states vary in the degree to which they appear "more than Yankee." The racial diversity of Massachusetts and Connecticut is especially influential as the population of these two states is more than double the other four states combined. This demographic diversity is fairly recent though. For instance, 89.8 percent of Massachusetts residents were white in 1990. Thirty-two years later, in 2022, that figure is 70.1 percent (US Census Bureau 1992, 2023). Significantly, immigration accounts for much of the increased diversity in New England though the top countries of origin differ across the six states. All this leads to unique state politics where demographic change—real and imagined—influences politics and policy.

Rachael Cobb's chapter on civic participation (chapter 9) in New England picks up on this theme of imagined demographic change, particularly how the perception of shifts is integral in explaining the variation in voter access among the New England states. Maine, for instance, has a culture of clean election reform and electoral tinkering aimed at expanding the right to vote. It is also one of the whitest states in the nation and region. Cobb problematizes the folklore surrounding the still popular New England town meeting form of government by presenting evidence that they forbid dissent, undermine majority rule, and "require conformity." In March 2023, the Massachusetts Supreme Judicial Court seemed to channel Cobb's critiques when it ruled citizens had the "right to be rude" in town meetings, rendering civility requirements in town meeting mute (DiMatteo 2023; Faneuf and Ochavillo 2023). Three-fourths of New England towns and cities still use the town meeting, making it very Yankee, but the Norman Rockwell lore it still enjoys may be misplaced. Yet not all the positive associations with Yankeedom are discounted in the chapter on civic participation. Not only Alexis de Tocqueville but also scholar Daniel Elazar (1966) and journalist Colin Woodard (2011) characterized New Englanders as highly participatory, civil in their politics, with citizens holding fairly positive attitudes toward government programs and regulations. Cobb documents high participation in state and national elections (if not local) and an examination of Maine by James Melcher and Amy Fried demonstrates the state's continued commitment to codifying and improving clean election laws. Duquette sees Massachusetts as a relative island of political civility with a populace not at war with government while Christopher Galdieri's documentation of "New Hampshire Weird" makes clear New Hampshire is just too weird to draw representative lessons for the rest of the nation. McLean's chapter on Connecticut, however, shows how American government can fix representational patterns that give disproportionate voice to rural voices. Its 1965 Constitution shifted the prior norm of all Connecticut towns having two representatives regardless of town size to one that is population based, making "one person one vote" a reality.

Jane JaKyung Han and Erin O'Brien evaluate the "more than Yankee" theme from a representational perspective in their over one-hundred-year accounting of women and women of color in electoral office in the New England states. Women, at least at New England's founding, were not usually considered among Yankee politicians having only won the right to vote nationally in 1920. Using advanced statistical analysis, they find that it is the New England states with low legislative professionalism that are most friendly to female candidates and female electoral victories. Additionally, the healthier the electoral competition between Democrats and Republicans in a state, the more likely women are to win. Thus, when New England states are "more than blue," as captured by electoral competition, their elected leaders are also more representative of the population.

Collectively then, the chapters that follow document broad shifts in New England politics, placing it in the context of other transformations in the nation, while grappling with complexity and heterogeneity within the region. Our volume also assesses how, and to what degree, New England remains committed to democratic ideals like civility across political differences and participatory democracy. We compare New England to other regions in the United States, especially in Fried and Harris's chapter 2, while also assessing the places where politics in New England speaks in the shared vernacular of one region (drop those r's, got to a tag sale, and grab the clicker) or in the localism of its six states ("Ayuh" is yes in Maine, "flatlanders" is anyone unlucky enough not to be born in Vermont, and drinking an "Awful Awful" happens in Rhode Island). This is a book about New England politics that explores regionalism across American politics, emphasizes nuance within New England, and, potentially, suggests an antidote to anti-government sentiments that now dominate the national stage.

Plan of the Book

Our book proceeds in three parts. Part I frames the book's primary contribution—a modern, scholarly examination of how and why the New England region transformed from "New England Republican" following World War II to a Democratic electoral stronghold as reliable as the South is for the GOP. All the chapters consider one, or both, of the twin themes of "more than blue" and "more than Yankee." Anchoring around these analytic themes presents the reader a comprehensive and linked understanding of the region. In chapter 2, Fried and Harris provide a foundational analysis of New England politics in American political development from the early republic through 2020. This chapter provides regional comparisons in congressional representation between New England and five other parts of the country, the non-New England Northeast, the Greater South, the Interior West, the Midwest, and the West Coast.

Part II offers six stand-alone chapters on each of the New England states from political scientists who largely live, teach, and research in the region. They breathe New England politics. Each state chapter covers the same topics in unique voices and presentations. The state chapters provide readers a political history focused on key moments of political change post-WWII and into the new millennium. Chapters trace electoral trends, key races, and the "brand" or types of Democrats and Republicans that emerge in each state. The defining political tensions in each state are documented and explained. For instance, in Massachusetts, Duquette argues that the biggest divide is between "insiders and outsiders," and this distinction roughly falls along racial and gender lines—with the old, more predominantly Yankee, Irish, and Italian power brokers being challenged by an increasingly diverse and more progressive Democratic Party. In Maine, Melcher and Fried emphasize Mainers' distaste for political meddling from groups "from away," particularly when it comes to issues involving guns and hunting, as well as the growing divisions between the state's two congressional districts. One of New Hampshire's key dividing lines, as documented by Galdieri, is among longtime Granite Staters and relatively new transplants from Massachusetts who live in New Hampshire but commute to work back in the Bay State. The latter are responsible for the purpling of New Hampshire. In Vermont, Paul Petterson finds the state's politics has changed as newcomers moved to the state, even as the independent flavor of the state remains strong. In Rhode Island, Moakley indicates divides are similar to Massachusetts—between old school politics and a more professionalized approach. McLean argues the rise of the persuadable suburban voter has recalibrated Connecticut politics and that the state still has a cultural taste for maverick politicians who buck more extreme factions of their party. Part II thus provides in-depth state analysis but with linked topics across chapters, enabling readers to become individual state aficionados while drawing meaningful comparisons across the states on shared metrics or considerations.

With the knowledge of the individual states in tow, and foundational knowledge of New England in US political development clear, the chapters of Part III are organized around conceptual themes core to understanding and assessing New England politics. As noted, Cobb's chapter on civic participation in New England addresses questions including: Does New England provide a model for a failing American republic when it comes to political civility, civic education, and voter access? Do just some New England states comport with said model? Scala's chapter on presidential politics and influence New England-style shows that, while the region is Democratic in presidential general elections, Republicans in New Hampshire often play a powerful role in testing and winnowing candidates seeking their party's presidential nomination. The 2024 Republican primary, for instance, saw Florida Governor Ron DeSantis drop out two days before New Hampshire residents went to the polls.

And finally, in the last two substantive chapters, Jiménez, as well as Han and O'Brien look at diversity, demography, and electoral power in the New England states. Jiménez's nuanced portrait of uneven political incorporation is a true primer on racial and ethnic diversity in New England and the impediments to electoral power most pronounced in the New England states. The chapter on women and politics in New England also finds real variation among the six states in political incorporation in elected office—though this time for women and women of color. Perhaps counterintuitively for those who believe the Democratic Party is always better at advancing women in the modern era, the scholars find that New England states with lower party competition—examined with an exhaustive database of all state legislative elections from 1990 to 2022—are less likely to run female candidates and see women win. And, problematically, the New England states with less prestigious legislative positions—as measured by professionalism of the state legislature—are those states where women win more frequently. So, the objectively less prestigious and monetarily enriching the job, the more likely that a woman holds that seat in New England.

Collectively, these chapters offer the reader a clear-eyed political analysis of New England. They remind that New England too has had a major party transformation equal and opposite of the South. It makes clear where the region acts as one, where neighbors do not align, as well as the core sources of tension in each state. Romantic notions of civic ideals and citizen government stand to political analysis. The diversifying faces of New Englanders and, to a lesser extent, the diversification of electoral officeholders in the region, are addressed in all their nuance. We hope the reader comes to appreciate that New England is more than blue and more than Yankee though these influences remain resonant.

And, like any good New Englander, we hope you root for the Sox, eat only real clam chowder—the New England kind—and insist your pancake's syrup is from a tree.

Works Cited

Bryan, Frank. 2003. *Real Democracy: The New England Town Meeting and How It Works*. Chicago: University of Chicago Press.

Conforti, Joseph A. 2001. *Imagining New England: Explorations of Regional Identity from the Pilgrims to the Mid-Twentieth Century*. Chapel Hill and London: University of North Carolina Press.

DiMatteo, Ali. 2023. "SJC Rules 'Civility' Cannot Be Required in Public Meetings." Massachusetts Municipal Association. March 20, 2023. https://www.mma.org/sjc-rules-civility-cannot-be-required-in-public-meetings/.

Elazar, Daniel J. 1966. *American Federalism: A View From the States*. New York: Thomas Y. Crowell Company.

Faneuf, Dave and Vanessa Ochavillo. 2023. "Mass. High Court Affirms Right to Be 'Rude' in Public Meetings." WBUR. March 8, 2023. https://www.wbur.org/news/2023/03/08/southborough-massachusetts-court-rules-rude-meetings.

Key, V. O. 1949. *Southern Politics in State and Nation*. New York: Alfred A. Knopf.

Patinkin, Mark. 2021. "RI Named One of the Six Most Corrupt States? How Dare They." *Providence Journal*. August 14, 2021. https://www.providencejournal.com/story/news/columns/2021/08/14/ri-named-one-six-most-corrupt-states-how-dare-they/8125554002/.

Richardson, Heather Cox. 2020. *How the South Won the Civil War: Oligarchy, Democracy, and the Continuing Fight for the Soul of America*. New York: Oxford University Press.

Tocqueville, Alexis de. 1988. *Democracy in America*. Translated by George Lawrence. New York: Harper Perennial.
Tryba, Lynn. 2013."New Hampshire's Real Life Yankees: Granite States Who Embody What It Is to Be a Yankee." *New Hampshire Magazine*. September 17, 2013. https://www.nhmagazine.com/new-hampshires-real-life-yankees/.
United States Census Bureau. 1992. "1990 Census of Population, General Population Characteristics, Massachusetts—1990 CP-1–23." U.S. Department of Commerce, Economics and Statistics Administration. https://www2.census.gov/library/publications/decennial/1990/cp-1/cp-1-23.pdf.
United States Census Bureau. 2023. "QuickFacts, Massachusetts." https://www.census.gov/quickfacts/MA.
Vanderbeck, Robert M. 2006. "Vermont and the Imaginative Geographies of American Whiteness." *Annals of the Association of American Geographers* 96, no. 3: 641–59.
Woodard, Colin. 2011. *American Nations: A History of the Eleven Rival Regional Cultures of North America*. New York: Viking.
World Population Review. 2023. "US States by Race 2023." https://worldpopulationreview.com/states/states-by-race.

CHAPTER 2

FROM RED TO BLUE

New England in American Political Development

Amy Fried | Douglas B. Harris
Professor of Political Science | Professor of Political Science
University of Maine | Loyola University Maryland

Introduction

After Representative Chris Shays lost his seat representing Connecticut's Fourth District in 2008, he noted that something broader changed in New England and in the GOP generally. Three years prior, in the midst of a congressional effort to intervene in an end-of-life decision in Florida, Shays had been blunt in criticizing his party: "This Republican Party of Lincoln has become a party of theocracy . . . There are a number of people who feel that the government is getting involved in their personal lives in a way that scares them" (Nagourney 2005). And with his 2008 loss, Shays told a reporter that his party's positioning had electoral consequences, saying, "I don't see us winning with social conservatism . . . The party will not be rebuilt without moderates being a part of it" (Applebome 2008).

Throughout his ten House terms, Shays—a moderate, somewhat independent Republican—was a throwback to a long-standing GOP tradition in his state and region. But party transformations beyond New England made the Republican Party become less appealing to the voters Shays needed. As national Republicanism became more Southern in character and more entwined with evangelicals, it sharply contrasted with New England Republicans, who were socially liberal and fiscally moderate, embracing Yankee pragmatism and backing governmental protections of individuals and the environment. Moreover, Shays was right about his party's near-inability to win national offices in New England, as very few Republicans did so after his loss. By 2008, what his party once stood for had been reshaped by conservative leaders and movements—redefining it, and, consequently, changing regional support patterns.

New England has been transformed into a reliable regional base for Democrats. What explains this transformation? Partisan political configurations may be stable, with particular parties and underlying issue and economic divisions dominating, and then eventually giving way to new political patterns (Burnham 1982). Scholars of critical elections and realignments identified five such "party systems" or realigning eras between the 1780s and the 1960s (Key 1955; Burnham 1982; Sundquist, 1983) with later scholars left to argue whether and when a sixth such party system took hold. Amid such realignments, regional partisan change sometimes occurs involving new allegiances, coalitions, policies, and ideological commitments—all of which affects who holds regional and national political power.

It is for these reasons that political observers have paid a great deal of attention to the American South's transformation from a staunchly Democratic area—the "solid South"—to a region in which Republicans dominate and is now the GOP's base. Scholars contend that the South began its party transformation as Democrats increasingly embraced civil rights during the New Deal and Great Society, and Republican Party leaders, by the 1960s, directed appeals to Southern white voters and built party organizations around this Southern strategy.[1] Later in the twentieth century, President Ronald Reagan combined conservative social issues and economic appeals to build a new Republican Party coalition with the South at its center (Ginsberg and Shefter 1988). Later GOP leaders and movements, including House Speaker Newt Gingrich, the Tea Party, and Donald Trump made the Republican Party more extremist in tone, even questioning and strategically fomenting distrust in democratic institutions and processes (Fried and Harris 2021).

While partisan transformations in the South receive considerable scholarly attention, this chapter focuses on analogous, if under-examined, shifts in New England politics that moved it from a Republican-dominated area to a competitive one and then to a region that is strongly Democratic. To be sure, New England is "more than blue," as the individual states did not move in lockstep and Republicans in the region sometimes find success with (nearly always) moderate gubernatorial candidates. However, Democrats unquestionably dominate federal elections in New England. Only one Republican serves among New England's entire congressional delegation in the 118th Congress—Maine's Susan Collins. New England's swing in party support has been at least as dramatic as what occurred in the former confederacy.

---

[1] Though some changes happened during the New Deal era (Schickler 2016), key shifts occurred in the 1960s including the signing of the 1964 Civil Rights Act and the 1965 Voting Rights Act, the reapportionment revolution, and Nixon's southern strategy (Black and Black 2008; Kondik 2021; Lublin 2004; McKee 2010).

One stage of New England's shift toward Democratic dominance was initiated nearly a century ago when what had been a predominantly Southern party took significant steps toward growing northward. Non-Yankee population groups key to Franklin D. Roosevelt's coalition, particularly Irish and Italian immigrants and Jewish voters, were critical to New England's political transformation. And, in individual states, Democratic political leaders, such as Ed Muskie of Maine, also broadened their party's base.

This chapter illuminates the political development of a Democratic "more than Yankee" New England. First, we discuss transformations in New England presidential voting patterns, pointing to national dynamics, strategies, and state leadership. Second, we trace the rise of Democratic Senators and House members in New England relative to the nation's other regions. As we argue and demonstrate, party organizations are built things—party coalitions must be found, nurtured, and sustained. The net effect of such changes was to turn a predominantly Republican region into a mostly Democratic one.

From Republican to Democrat: New England's Partisan Flip

New England's partisan politics changed from a region dominated by Republicans to a more competitive region during the New Deal and, again, to a Democratic bastion by the twenty-first century. Responding to the key demographic and partisan shifts of the twentieth century—from Roosevelt to Reagan and beyond—this is a story of partisan transformation that is less told but no less important than the analogous party transformation, from Democrat to Republican, in the American South.

FEDERALIST-WHIG-REPUBLICAN NEW ENGLAND

For a long time, New England was among the *least Democratic* parts of the nation. From the start of competitive elections for the presidency, New England stood out for its extraordinary levels of support for Federalists and then for Whig candidates. John Adams rode to victory in 1796 by adding New York, Maryland, and Delaware to his New England home base to best Thomas Jefferson.[2] Further, when Jefferson unseated Adams four years later, New England still held strong for the Federalist Adams. New England,

---

[2] The discussion that follows is from the authors' examination of the presidential electoral maps and electoral results from 1796 to the 2020, which can be found at John Woolley and Gerhard Peters' "The American Presidency Project" at UC Santa Barbara, https://www.presidency.ucsb.edu/statistics/elections/1789.

excepting Vermont, would similarly vote for Federalist Charles Pinckney and DeWitt Clinton in their respective defeats against James Madison in 1808 and 1812. Even during the 1816 Electoral College landslide of James Monroe, Maine, Massachusetts, and Connecticut joined only Delaware in supporting Federalist Rufus King just four years before the "Era of Good Feelings"—a term frequently used to describe the Democratic-Republicans party's rise to preeminence—left the Federalists to history and Monroe to win, effectively unopposed, in 1820. Thus, in an era when small government and states' rights Jeffersonianism dominated the national Democratic Party, New England was among the last holdouts the Federalists could count on to resist a coming Democratic dominance.

Andrew Jackson and his more democratized Democrats fared little better in New England even as they were reshaping the nation's electoral map and processes. In 1824, as Jackson would go on to win pluralities of the electoral and popular vote, it was again New England (along with New York and Delaware) that threw their support to John Quincy Adams (whom the House of Representatives would select as president). Jackson's subsequent campaign against the "corrupt bargain" elite deals that put Adams in the White House would lead to a resounding national victory but find no home (and thus zero won states) in New England. Even in his overwhelming reelection in 1832, with New England's neighboring New Yorker Martin Van Buren on the ticket as his vice presidential running mate, Jackson would win only Maine and New Hampshire, losing Massachusetts, Connecticut, and Rhode Island to Henry Clay and Vermont to the Anti-Mason candidate William Wirt.

Such it was in the early republic. New England was Federalist or Whig and eventually Free Soil, and it was consistently the least hospitable region of all to Democratic presidential candidates who, based in the South, were, among other things, committed to states' rights and slavery protections. When late Jacksonian era Democrats, seeking regional expansion, selected northern candidates, including New Hampshire's Franklin Pierce, the party was able to win some New England states (though Pierce failed to win his neighboring states of Massachusetts and Vermont). But, for the most part, "New England and the South were aligned almost solidly on opposing sides" in most electoral fights because of differing commitments to centralizing versus decentralizing the Union on questions related to commerce, infrastructural development, and, of course, slavery (Reichley 1992, 114).

The North (most prominently in New England) and the South would continue to "mirror" one another, especially as slavery emerged as the issue that would eventually precipitate the Civil War and launch the third-party system (of the five aforementioned party systems) when Democrats and Republicans began their historically enduring inter-party battle. James L. Sundquist noted the competitive nature of this emerging polarized politics, saying: "As abolitionist societies grew in the North, so did 'Southern rights' societies below the Mason-Dixon line" (1983, 58–9). Thus while a new party system was developing around slavery, abolitionism "flourished primarily in New England" (Sundquist 1983, 53). And even the non-New England states where abolition movements were prominent felt New England's influence in terms of the "westward path of New England migration—from upstate New York and northern Pennsylvania through Ohio's Western Reserve to Michigan and those parts of Indiana and Illinois lying north of the 41st parallel" (Sundquist 1983, 53–4). Those migrants also carried with them a religious culture: "Abolition was a church-centered movement" and "the common root cause would be found in the doctrine and philosophy of . . . particular New England churches" (Sundquist 1983, 54). When the Free Soil Party ran candidates in the elections of 1848 and 1852, both tickets had New Englanders on them, including John Quincy Adams' son Charles as the vice presidential candidate to Martin Van Buren and New Hampshire's John P. Hale atop the ticket in 1852.[3]

After the Republican Party came into existence (running its first presidential nominee in 1856) and until the 1930s, nearly all New England states voted Republican in each presidential election. Indeed, save for one atypical election year and a few state-by-state exceptions over the years, New England's support for the GOP was mostly uniform due to the lingering resentments of the Civil War and to Republicans' continuing support of nationalizing, coordinative efforts as they related to commerce. The atypical election year was 1912 when Theodore Roosevelt's return as a third party "Bull Moose" candidate split the Republican coalition and allowed Woodrow Wilson to best Teddy Roosevelt and incumbent William Howard Taft; Wilson won five New England states (Vermont stuck with Taft).[4] Other than those five exceptions in 1912, Connecticut voted Democrat four times (1876, 1884, 1888, and 1892—three of those for Grover Cleveland), New Hampshire voted for Wilson again in 1916, and Massachusetts and Rhode Island, tellingly, voted

---

[3] The Free Soilers did not fare well overall, but the 1848 ticket reached double digit popular vote totals in nine states (four in New England) and the 1852 ticket did so in four states (three New England states).

[4] Taft, the incumbent, won only two states that year—Vermont and Utah.

Democrat, for Al Smith, a Catholic, in 1928, even while Smith was on his way to a landslide loss to Herbert Hoover in 1928. In the nineteen presidential elections from 1856 to 1928, New England's 114 statewide contests produced 102 Republican victories and 12 Democratic ones. If anything, the post-Wilson 1920s returned New England, for a while, to its Republican roots. Except for notable victories in Massachusetts and Rhode Island in 1928, Democrats would lose every statewide contest for the presidency and hold only consistently small minorities of New England's House and Senate seats, respectively.

IMMIGRANTS AND PIVOTAL PARTISAN CHANGE BY 1928

Political scientist V.O. Key, Jr. argued in 1955 that the New Deal coalition that Franklin Roosevelt put together in 1932 was glimpsed in 1928's "activation" of urban immigrant (often Catholic) voters toward Democratic nominee, Al Smith. Perhaps it was the Democrats' confirmed status as a national minority that made them more risk acceptant by 1928 when they nominated a Tammany Hall-affiliated northerner, Al Smith, for president. Overall, the risk did not pay off as Smith, the first Roman Catholic to be a major party nominee, performed worse in the Electoral College than even John Davis had in 1924. Although Smith had a better popular vote total than Davis had, Davis scored 25.6 percent of the electoral vote and Smith just 16.4 percent of the electoral vote having lost key Southern states.

But amid that failure there was a silver lining for Democrats—they had picked up Massachusetts and Rhode Island, which had last gone to the Democrats in 1912 when the Taft–Teddy Roosevelt split allowed Woodrow Wilson a sizable Electoral College victory. Smith's Catholicism and his opposition to Prohibition may have been off-putting to many voters in the Midwest and the South, but his candidacy helped to mobilize first-time immigrant voters, many of them Catholic, to vote Democrat in 1928 (Andersen 1979, 100). Early hints of these broad changes among immigrant voting patterns occurred when both Massachusetts and Rhode Island flipped into the Democrats' column for Smith.

It was this 1928 "glimmer" that Key focused on as evidence of a coming partisan realignment that would become 1932's New Deal. Key noted that not only had Smith actually won Massachusetts and Rhode Island but that he had "made gains in all the New England states." If Smith's candidacy cost Democrats crucial Southern support that they usually relied on, these inroads outside the South, particularly in cities in the Northeast populated by recent immigrants, were something on which to build. What had tipped over the edge in Massachusetts and Rhode Island (where large cities like Boston and Providence provided a larger portion of the Democratic gains) would also prove beneficial as these trends continued in Philadelphia, New York, Baltimore, and other northeastern cities. It was, however, to start in New England. Although the "rise in Democratic strength was especially notable in Massachusetts and Rhode Island," the trend was region-wide and, overall, Key concluded, "the Roosevelt revolution of 1932 was in large measure an Al Smith revolution of 1928, a characterization less applicable to the remainder of the country" (Key 1955, 4). Franklin Roosevelt's highly successful New Deal coalition was to graft more liberal elements—mainly ethnic and urban liberals—onto the party's traditional Southern base.

STEPS TOWARD DEMOCRATS: CHANGES DURING THE NEW DEAL

During the New Deal and in the ensuing decades, New England became an important battleground for Democrats looking to grow the party. The Southern dominance of the Democratic Party was insufficient to win nationally without some broader geographical reach. By the time of the McKinley elections in 1896 and 1900, the Democrats' "solid South" plus a few mountain states in the west could produce no more than 40 percent of the Electoral College vote. And, winning just the South, as Democrats did in 1924, could produce little more than a quarter of the electoral vote. The Democrats had to grow westwardly, northward, or in the Midwest—the South alone could not yield victory.

Building on gains among immigrants, FDR won additional gains among immigrants and added middle-class voters and many others disaffected by Republicans' handling of the Great Depression to win in 1932. After his initial victory in 1932, Roosevelt influenced Democratic congressional leadership selection and activated important urban New England constituencies into the Democratic Party such that the "Democratic Party as remade by Franklin Roosevelt in the New Deal was grounded politically in the big cities of the North" (Mileur 2005, 413).

But the changes would come slowly. Even during FDR's 1932 landslide of 57.4 percent of the popular vote and nearly 90 percent of the electoral vote, he continued the Democrats' tradition of losing New England as voters retained their Republican loyalties. Roosevelt lost only six states to Herbert Hoover that year, but four of them were in New England (Vermont, New Hampshire, Maine, and Connecticut). His 1936 reelection built on the 1932 landslide, but the two states FDR lost were, again, Vermont and Maine. Even during years of historic Democratic victory, Republicans could count on some support in New England. Indeed, Maine and Vermont are the only two states to have never voted for FDR in all four of FDR's presidential bids. It would take effort and strategic focus from national, state, and local Democratic leaders to further shift the region.

Roosevelt's repeated electoral successes gave him the opportunity to remake the Democratic Party. In 1936, for example, FDR directed his 1932 campaign manager and then DNC chairman, Jim Farley, an Irish-Catholic, to repeal the Democrats' rule requiring presidential candidates to win two-thirds of the delegates to secure the nomination. Often viewed as beneficial to the Southern base, the two-thirds rule effectively anchored the party to the South, weakened its nominees, and sent the party into several divisive multiple ballot contests in the past. Changing the rule allowed for a majority to select a nominee, meeting FDR's aims to broaden the party: "It involved overhauling the party, opening up its ranks to an increasingly pluralistic array of groups and forces, and making it possible for the party in future years to nominate the kinds of presidential candidates who could appeal to these new elements without being subject to a minority veto at the convention" (Bass 1988, 314). This victory, then, was a step toward the "nationalization of the party . . . for the most part at the expense of the south" (Bass 1988, 314). This effort, along with Roosevelt's (mostly unsuccessful) effort to purge the party of the most recalcitrant Southerners "by intervening in Democratic primaries and backing liberal challengers to wayward [mostly southern] incumbents," had the potential to free the party from its Southern anchor and move it in a leftward ideological direction and a northward (and westward) geographic one (Dunn 2010, 6).

FDR's efforts also included working behind the scenes to influence the congressional leadership of his party. Although presidents generally steer clear (or at least try to be seen as having steered clear) of the internal selection of congressional party leaders, FDR's allies "helped" the House select New Deal allies rather than opponents when leadership vacancies occurred. Two key events, in 1937 and 1940, helped to engineer the "Austin-Boston" alliance that would help FDR achieve these ends and catapult New England into the top House Democratic leadership for the first time since Massachusetts' Joseph Varnum left the Speaker's chair in 1811.

The death of Speaker Joseph Byrns of Tennessee in 1936 allowed Majority Leader William Bankhead to succeed to that office, leaving the Majority leadership open to be filled the following year. Texan Sam Rayburn, an accomplished and capable New Deal champion, would run for the open floor leadership post against New Yorker and New Deal critic, John O'Connor (the only member on whom FDR's purge effort would succeed in 1938). FDR clearly favored Rayburn. Whereas O'Connor had argued that his candidacy offered the party regional balance (Speaker Bankhead was from Alabama), Boston's John McCormack gave crucial support to Rayburn's bid for Majority Leader. McCormack, as "the first New Englander to declare for Rayburn," provided key cross-regional support for Rayburn's 184–127 victory over O'Connor (Champagne et al. 2009, 115–7, 122). Three years later, when Rayburn succeeded to the Speakership after Bankhead's death, Rayburn returned the favor by supporting McCormack over Virginian Clifton Woodrum for Majority Leader. With Rayburn's support and support from the White House and its operatives, especially from Secretary of the Interior Harold Ickes and Secretary of Commerce Harry Hopkins, McCormack bested Woodrum 141 to 67.

With McCormack's victory, the famed Austin-Boston alliance in the House Democratic leadership was born (Champagne et al. 2009, 122–124; Nelson 2017, 250–1). The alliance helped FDR, Truman, and Kennedy finesse the regional differences that plagued the party. The two decades long alliance between Rayburn and McCormack was significant in and of itself, but the two also had a penchant for promoting their own protégés, thus perpetuating Texas's and Massachusetts's influence in the House for decades to come. McCormack became Speaker following Rayburn's death in 1961 and served throughout the remainder of the decade. And his fellow Bostonian and protégé, Tip O'Neill would also climb the House's leadership ladder from whip to floor leader to Speaker throughout the Carter years and most of the Reagan administration before turning the Speakership over to his then-Majority Leader, Jim Wright of Texas, thus capping off nearly a half-century of that alliance's reign and influence.

Franklin Roosevelt's imprint on the twentieth century Democratic Party was unmatched. Although FDR failed to win New England in his 1932 landslide and never won Maine or Vermont, his candidacy and presidency helped to transform New England politics: New Deal politics activated the Catholic immigrants of Boston and Providence; FDR elevated the "Austin-Boston" alliance into top congressional leadership; and he paved the way for a more liberal, and national policy-focused Democratic Party that would grow in favor throughout New England. In all, FDR helped turn a Republican region into a Democratic haven.

MUSKIE AND REAGAN: POST-FDR COALITION-BUILDERS AND NEW ENGLAND POLITICS

While Roosevelt played a critical role in helping to shift New England politics, he was not the only coalition-builder to affect the region's transformation. Another president, Republican Ronald Reagan, set into motion developments that, despite their initial success nationally, would ultimately undermine the GOP's support in New England. However, before Reagan's time, Democrats were party-building in New England. Maine leader Ed Muskie, for example, was critical in building his state's Democratic Party.

Nationally, Muskie is known best for his leadership as US Senator on environmental issues, his failed vice presidential and presidential runs in 1968 and 1972, and his service as Secretary of State for President Carter. But it was Muskie's surprising win of the governorship of Maine in 1954 that brought him to national prominence.

How unexpected was Muskie's win? Maine was such a one party-dominated state in the first half of the twentieth century that "the most important election in this period was the Republican primary" (Maisel and Ivry 1997, 15). And, as Muskie described it fourteen years afterward, "We won against hopeless odds. We had no resources . . . We had to talk to Republicans who had never even seen a live Democrat in their lives . . . We had to do it against an establishment, a machine . . . which had a century to entrench itself, and we did it." (Rooks 2018, 4). Moreover, Maine Democrats were limited in their demographic and geographic reach. Prior to the mid-1950s, the Democratic Party "was basically a loose-knit collection of urban fiefdoms sustained by the votes of Franco and Irish mill workers," as well as voters in northern Maine's rural Francophone St. John Valley (Maiman 2002, 44–45).

At the same time, neither party had been particularly active in reaching out to Maine's voters. Don Nicholl, a reporter who became a Muskie aide described Republicans "as really afflicted with dry rot . . . with no strong grassroots support" (Beam 1992, 6). And before Eisenhower became president, the Democratic Party in Maine "essentially functioned as a conduit for federal patronage, mostly local postmasterships and rural mail carrier jobs" (Maiman 2022, 44–45). In his accounting of state parties, political scientist David Mayhew rated Maine a "1" on a 1–5 scale of party organizational strength (Mayhew 1986, 151–3). These weak and rudimentary party forms created opportunities for Muskie and his team to reach out to previously overlooked parts of the population and to build a winning electoral coalition.

One of the campaign innovations adopted by Muskie and Democratic leaders was the development of a party platform based on responses it solicited from the public. Unveiled the day before the state convention in an event in which Maine people and the press could discuss it, the platform garnered positive media coverage for breaking with the typical approach of insiders crafting platforms behind closed doors. Moreover, the platform had a non-ideological tone and included consensus issues like land conservation and highway improvements. Notably, one message emphasized the need for two competitive political parties. At the same time, Democrats engaged in institutional party-building. Democratic Party chair Frank Coffin more than doubled the number of party municipal committees during the Muskie campaign, brought in national speakers and did extensive outreach to previously ignored areas, including to, Coffin said, "the countryside [and] groups that hadn't seen a Democrat since long before the Civil War" (Rooks 2018, 16). Led by an increasingly skilled, rhetorically accessible candidate, the Muskie campaign carried a statewide message through television and radio.

Ed Muskie's win in 1954 clearly transformed party competition in Maine. Before his victory, just one of the previous ten elected Maine governors was a Democrat. Since then (1959–2023), nine individuals have been elected governor; these included two Republicans, two Independents and five Democrats. Moreover, breaking one-partyism and developing a Democratic Party organization situated this New England state to be able to respond to national trends and party strategies that were to develop in the coming decades which shifted the South toward Republicans and New England toward Democrats. From 1992–2020, every Democratic presidential candidate won statewide in Maine, a stunning shift from a state that had never backed Franklin D. Roosevelt.

As this chapter noted at the start, the Democratic Party's embrace of civil rights in the latter decades of the twentieth century is key to understanding party transformation in New England. President Harry Truman and, later, Presidents John F. Kennedy and Lyndon Johnson, backed desegregation, civil rights, and voting rights. They also backed robust public efforts for retirement and health security, with programs aimed at buttressing the middle class and countering poverty. Starting in the late 1950s, moderate Republicans were increasingly pushed aside by the far-right figures of their time. The 1964 presidential nominee Senator Barry Goldwater lost to Johnson in a landslide. However, the South moved toward Republicans during this period, backing its presidential candidates increasingly consistently. By 1980—after the upheavals of the Vietnam War, cultural conflicts, stagflation, and tax revolts fractured the Democratic Party—Goldwater backer and coalition-builder Ronald Reagan won the presidency.

Reagan won big nationally and in New England in both his 1980 and 1984 runs. However, the Reagan coalition, and the GOP after Reagan, included elements that were not a good fit for New England, a region that is more secular than the South.[5] Religion mattered politically in several ways. First, evangelical Christians became a far more organized force in the Reagan years after largely avoiding politics and were assiduously courted by Reagan (who is credited as turning "southerners into evangelicals" in terms of their voting habits) and later GOP leaders (Ginsberg and Shefter 1988). Second, the social issues explicitly motivating evangelical Christians—abortion, women's rights, and LGBTQ+ rights—over time mapped more and more onto developing regional and partisan divides, with Republicans becoming highly socially conservative and Democrats liberally inclined. As these and other social issues moved the political agenda from predominantly economic issues to issues of social concern—race, life and reproductive choice, and law and order crime issues—the South moved toward the GOP. New England, by contrast, continued its tradition of electing mostly moderate Republicans who were pro-choice, comparatively feminist and, particularly in coming decades, pro-LGBTQ+ rights. Third, less explicit religiously based issue commitments also mattered for regional and political differences. As one scholar notes, "Not only in the South but nationwide, higher levels of racism are associated with higher probabilities of identifying as a white Christian; and conversely, adding Christianity to the average white person's identity moves him or her toward more, not less, affinity for white supremacy" (Jones 2020, 186–7). Fourth, orientations toward religion and race also mattered for views toward social welfare programs. Reagan's invocation of the "welfare queen" was part of what has been called the Long Southern Strategy, which Republicans used to attract white voters, particularly in the South. But "poor whites" in the South did not have that label applied to them so as to "not

---

[5] By 2018 the Southeast and Southwest were the regions of the country with the largest percentage of individuals who were "'very religious'"—a classification based on how important people say religion is to them and how often they attend religious services" while New England had the lowest rate (Norman, 2018). Moreover, the denominational composition of Christians varied; for example, nearly three times as many southerners are evangelical Christians compared to New Englanders (34% vs 12%), while the percentage of Catholics in New England is nearly double than in the South (30% vs 15%) and weekly church attendance is much higher in the South than in New England (Pew Research Center, 2014).

tarnish the whiteness brand." Rather, "Railing against entitlements did more than just inflate whiteness by contrasting it to undeserving blackness; it also pulled at the southern white purse strings to which racism has always been tied" (Maxwell and Shields 2019, 11). While New England certainly cannot be said to be free of racism, its still-cherished abolitionist history generally mitigated against overt racialized party appeals.

Since Reagan, the Republican Party has become even more wed to far-right messages and has moved in an anti-government, even anti-democratic direction, which swept in conspiracy theorists, while undermining governance (Fried and Harris 2020, 2021). Partisan polarization is increasingly racialized and asymmetric, with Republicans more extreme than Democrats (Mann and Ornstein 2012; Tesler 2016). These dynamics have further solidified New England's regional shift and wedded it to the Democratic Party.

Overall, New England states' support for the respective parties in presidential elections went through a dramatic change. If the Democratic Party's presidential wins in New England ebbed and flowed, as have the party's fortunes, the overall trajectory is clearly upward. From the late nineteenth century and throughout all but the last decade of the twentieth century, Republican presidential candidates repeatedly won most New England states.[6] But, in 1992 and after, New England swung hard in favor of Democratic presidential candidates. Overall, Democrats went from generally winning zero New England states at the end of the nineteenth and the beginning of the twentieth century and being as reliably Republican as any region to producing New England sweeps for Democrats for almost the entirety of the early twenty-first century. Now New England is as reliably Democratic in presidential contests as any region in the nation.

Regional Party Patterns in Congressional Representation

Similar shifts took place in regard to congressional representation, too. Tracking these broader transformations for the last century and a quarter, we present data on the changing percentage of Democratic US House members and Senators in New England from 1896 to 2023 in light of the analogous transformations in five other geographical regions, particularly in contrast

---

[6] This was generally true outside of a few big Democratic national landslides (like 1912, FDR's last three elections, and 1964) when a majority of New England states would go toward the Democrats.

to the South and the non-New England states of the Northeast.[7] Following recent works reflecting contemporary regional patterns of politics, our analysis is based on the definitions used by David Hopkins (2017) [and subsequently by Kyle Kondik (2021)], though we separate out the New England states from the rest of the Northeast. The resulting regions[8] are constituted as follows:

New England: Connecticut, Maine, Massachusetts, New Hampshire, Rhode Island, and Vermont.
(Non-New England) Northeast: Delaware, Maryland, New Jersey, New York, and Pennsylvania.
Greater South: Alabama, Arkansas, Florida, Georgia, Kentucky, Louisiana, Mississippi, North Carolina, Oklahoma, South Carolina, Tennessee, Texas, Virginia, and West Virginia.
Interior West: Alaska, Arizona, Colorado, Idaho, Kansas, Montana, Nebraska, Nevada, New Mexico, North Dakota, South Dakota, Utah, and Wyoming.
Midwest: Illinois, Indiana, Iowa, Michigan, Minnesota, Missouri, Ohio, and Wisconsin.
West Coast: California, Hawaii, Oregon, and Washington.

A first pattern that emerges is the steady increase in New England's Democratic Party throughout the twentieth century and into the twenty-first century. This near-complete partisan transformation is depicted in Figure 2.1 as New England Democratic representation in the House ranged from 3.3 percent in 1896 to 100 percent by 2023 and New England Democratic

---

[7] A comparison of regional party patterns over time requires, first, imposing a somewhat artificial delineation of which states belong to which region. We do this with some caution, first, because scholars and other authorities differ over regional definitions. The U.S. Census Bureau divides the United States into four regions. Without a standard scholarly definition of U.S. regions, historical groupings (like "states of the former Confederacy") or other operationalizations are employed. Schantz (1992), for example, identified eight regions (New England, Middle Atlantic, South, Border, Midwest, Plains, Rocky Mountains, and Pacific Coast) (357, n6). Jerome Mileur (1992) identified as many as eleven. Moreover, there is reason to expect that partisan regional patterns will shift over time making some once-useful groupings less meaningful in another era. Maryland, for example, is more of a Northeastern state and West Virginia acts as much like a southern state than as the "border" states where they, in older studies, they might be categorized.
[8] To be sure, these regional groupings are, to some extent, as artificial as states in different regions, for example, Maryland and Northern Virginia, might be thought to have much in common and there are within state differences that make, for example, eastern Washington state seem much like Idaho or parts of southern Ohio akin to Kentucky or West Virginia, culturally and politically speaking. Still, these regional breakdowns make intuitive sense and have the added advantage of allowing comparisons between our findings and other recent studies. Plus, the electoral college awards "winner-take-all" votes in most states and there are regional similarities in voting patterns.

representation in the Senate went from 0 to 91.7 percent in the same timeframe. The overall steady increase in Democratic gains in New England were punctuated by spikes in Democratic gains during key elections of the twentieth and twenty-first centuries; notably, the gains made were generally maintained in subsequent years, producing a steady accumulation of New England Democrats in the House and to a lesser degree in the Senate. The first spike in House representation occurred when Republicans split during the 1912 election between Taft and Teddy Roosevelt winning not only Wilson the presidency but allowing Democrats to take over half of New England's House seats. The gains made in that atypical year were not maintained at those levels, but Democrats won generally between 11 and 18 percent of the House seats and between 14 and 16 percent of the Senate seats throughout the remainder of the 1910s and 1920s.

With the Great Depression costing Republicans support throughout the nation, Democratic gains in New England accelerated in the 1930 midterm elections to about a quarter of the House seats, nearly doubling in 1932 (to 40 percent and 30.8 percent in the House and Senate, respectively), and achieving a majority of New England's House seats and a 50/50 split with Republicans for New England's Senate seats by the 1934 midterms. When the New Deal's political fortunes cooled in 1938 and thereafter, New England Democrats settled into a new era's pattern of winning between a quarter and a third of New England's House and Senate seats in the 1940s and 1950s—less than at the height of the New Deal but more than prior to 1930.

Democratic gains spiked again in 1958 after the second midterm election of the Eisenhower administration, when the Democrats won over two-thirds (67.9 percent) of the House seats and nearly half (46.2 percent) of the Senate seats. After 1958 Democrats never again fell below half of the region's House delegation and almost uniformly had a majority of the Senate seats as well.[9] Thereafter, Democrats held about two-thirds of New England's House seats and generally over half of its Senate seats throughout the 1960s, 1970s, and 1980s.

New England Democrats once again took significant steps forward in terms of House representation during the Clinton years. The Republican Revolution of 1994 had no net effect on New England Democrats in the

---

[9] During the 92nd Congress, the *Biographical Directory* listed 13 Senators due to William Prouty (R-VT) dying while in office; he was replaced by Senator Robert Stafford, also a Republican. Even in the 92nd Congress, 6 of New England's 12 Senate seats were Democratic.

FIGURE 2.1. Democratic Congressional Representation in New England and the South, 1896–2023.

House and cost but one seat in the Senate. Thus, as the GOP was reaping gains in other parts of the country thanks to its anti-government and social conservative messages, New England resisted those appeals as less attuned to their experience and political values. By the end of the twentieth century, New England Democrats controlled half the region's Senate seats and over four-fifths of its House seats. And the twenty-first century has simply improved the Democratic Party's standing in New England congressional delegations with big jumps in the 110th and 111th Congresses (after the 2006 midterms and Barack Obama's first election in 2008) whereby New England Democrats bounced between having 90 and 100 percent of the region's House seats and anywhere from two-thirds to as much as 91.7 percent (eleven out of twelve) of its Senate seats for the last decade and a half.

New England's representational story is quite different from that of other regions. Also depicted in Figure 2.1 is the inverse partisan transformation of the South from 1896 to 2023. The South was between 80 and 100 percent Democratic (in both the House and Senate) for all of the early twentieth century through 1969, but then trended down from the late twentieth century through the twenty-first century. New England became as Democratic a region as the South had been (in terms of congressional delegations, at least), especially after the Obama years (at which point the South was less than 20 percent Democratic in the Senate and less than a third Democratic in the House). Per historical pattern, the rise of New England Democrats and decline of New England Republicans is the mirror image of a decline in Southern Democrats and rise of Southern Republicans.

If the South's Democratic dominance had historically been an outlier compared to party competition in other regions, in the twenty-first century New England emerged as more of an outlier, particularly in regard to Democratic representation in the House of Representatives. Whereas the non-New England Northeast and the West Coast rival New England in terms of Democratic dominance in regard to Senate seats, New England distinguishes itself from the other regions by increasingly eliminating Republican viability in House elections. Whereas New England previously tracked with the other (non-South) regions in terms of the relative balance of House Democrats and Republicans, especially from the New Deal (73rd Congress) through the Great Society (90th Congress) and the Bush years (102nd Congress), after Clinton, New England started to break hard for the Democrats to an extent that no other region does. Overall, with the Interior West and even the Midwest approaching the same levels of Republican dominance as the South during the twenty-first century, it seems fair to conclude that New England is a partisan outlier more than any other region, including even the South.

Breaking out New England from the rest of the Northeast, as is best demonstrated in Figure 2.2, reveals a demonstrable split between those two (otherwise quite alike) regions emerging in the early 1990s. Although the non-New England Northeast was generally *more Democratic* than the New England states from the 1890s to the 1950s, after the 86th Congress (1959–1960) when New England first surpassed the Northeast, the two regions were roughly equal in their proportion of Democratic House members until the 1990s. Indeed, they were nearly identical from the 99th to the 102nd Congresses until a separation took place after 1992, widening thereafter, and with the proportion of House Democrats in New England districts outdistancing those

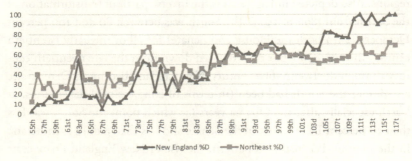

FIGURE 2.2. Democratic Representation in the House in New England and the Northeast, 1896–2023.

from the Northeast in increasing proportions from the Clinton years until now. A full 30 percentage points separated the New England delegations in the 117th Congress (at 100 percent) from the delegations of the rest of the Northeast (69.1 percent of which were Democrats).

The changes at work in New England's congressional delegations—reflecting as they do similar changes in presidential contests—were systemic rather than personal. No extraordinary representative skill or ideological moderation could save Republicans like Connecticut's Christopher Shays from the broader transformations of the party system at work just as few Southern Democrats sustain careers in states and districts increasingly unfavorable to them and their national party's image.

Conclusions

Party leaders and their strategic efforts built partisan coalitions in New England during changing circumstances, often by trying to attract particular demographic groups through outreach, party organization, and issue appeals. Leading up to the New Deal period, Franklin Roosevelt crafted a coalition that included the solid South but also reached out to urban (often immigrant) communities in New England. Seeking to harness that support, party builders like Ed Muskie tried new campaign approaches and built party apparatuses to appeal to groups beyond the party's base; for Muskie in Maine, it was outreach beyond urban areas, mill towns and (typically Catholic) Francos to counter Republican dominance and win the Maine governorship. In being successful while reaching out to different groups Roosevelt and Muskie demonstrate that what is sometimes seen as New England's Yankee heritage is far more complex and diverse. It also reminds us that partisan demographic changes generally must be met by party elites and organizational efforts to reach the potential that demographic changes offer.

Particularly after the Reagan years, Democrats' regional gains in New England intensified. As Reagan grew the GOP coalition in other regions of the country, the rightward Republican shift produced a backlash in New England. According to one analysis, after the 1994 congressional elections, Republican national leadership would become "dominated by Southerners, and the party was facing pressures to pursue the policies of cultural conservatives" costing the GOP support elsewhere as "the Northeast wing was not receptive to this emphasis" (Reiter and Stonecash 2011, 30). But Republican leaders doubled down on their more extreme rhetoric and rightward ideology, responding to dominant regional and ideological constituencies and undermining further its position among other, even erstwhile Republican, regions.

This is as true in New England as anywhere else in the country. Given where the Republican Party has gone since then in pursuing far-right, socially conservative, illiberal forces, and how the Democratic Party defines itself as pro-rights and pro-democracy, it is no surprise that New England has become such a strong part of the Democrats' electoral base. Whether party coalitions can again be disrupted depends on shifting party dynamics in some fundamental way, by some future partisan coalition-builders, in ways that we cannot foresee.

Works Cited

Andersen, Kristi. 1979. *The Creation of a Democratic Majority, 1928–1936*. Chicago: University of Chicago Press.

Applebome, Peter. 2008. "With G.O.P. Congressman's Loss, a Moderate Tradition Ends in New England." *New York Times*, November 5, 2008.

Harold F. Bass, Jr. 1988. "Presidential Party Leadership and Party Reform: Franklin D. Roosevelt and the Abrogation of the Two-Thirds Rule." *Presidential Studies Quarterly* 18, no. 2: 303–317.

Beam, Chris. 1992. "Nicoll, Don Oral History Interview." Edmund S. Muskie Oral History Collection. 424. https://scarab.bates.edu/muskie_oh/424.

Black, Earl, and Merle Black. 2002. *The Rise of Southern Republicans*. Cambridge, MA: Harvard University Press.

Burnham, Walter Dean. 1982. *The Current Crisis in American Politics*. New York: Oxford University Press, 92–117.

Champagne, Anthony, Douglas B. Harris, James W. Riddlesperger, Jr., and Garrison Nelson. 2009. *The Austin-Boston Connection: Five Decades of House Democratic Leadership, 1937–1989*. College Station: Texas A&M Press.

Dunn, Susan. 2010. *Roosevelt's Purge*. Cambridge: Harvard University Press.

Fried, Amy, and Douglas B. Harris. 2020. "In Suspense: Donald Trump's Efforts to Undermine Public Trust in Democracy." *Society* 57, no. 5: 527–533.

Fried, Amy, and Douglas B. Harris. 2021. *At War with Government: How Conservatives Weaponized Distrust from Goldwater to Trump*. New York: Columbia University Press.

Ginsberg, Benjamin, and Martin Shefter. 1988. "The Presidency and the Organization of Interests." In *The Presidency and the Political System* 2nd edition, edited by Michael T. Nelson, 311–330. Washington, DC: CQ Press.

Hopkins, David A. 2017. *Red Fighting Blue: How Geography and Electoral Rules Polarize American Politics*. New York: Cambridge University Press.

Jones, Robert P. 2020. *White Too Long: The Legacy of White Supremacy in American Christianity*. New York: Simon & Schuster.

Key, V. O., Jr. 1955. "A Theory of Critical Elections" *Journal of Politics* 17, no. 1 (February): 3–18.

Kondik, Kyle. 2021. *The Long Red Thread: How Democratic Dominance Gave Way to Republican Advantage in U.S. House Elections*. Athens, OH: Ohio University Press.

Lublin, David. 2021. *The Republican South: Democratization and Partisan Change.* Princeton, NJ: Princeton University Press.

Maiman, Richard J. 2022. *A Man for All Branches: Judge Frank M. Coffin of Maine.* Standish, ME: Tower Publishing.

Maisel, L. Sandy, and Elizabeth J. Ivry. 1997. "If You Don't Like Your Politics, Wait a Minute: Party Politics in Maine at the Century's End." In *Parties & Politics in The New England States, edited by* Jerome M. Mileur, 15–35. Amherst, MA: Polity Press.

Mann, Thomas E., and Norman J. Ornstein. 2012. *It's Even Worse than It Looks: How the American Constitutional System Collided with the New Politics of Extremism.* New York: Basic Books.

Maxwell, Angie, and Todd Shields. 2019. *The Long Southern Strategy: How Chasing White Voters in the South Changed American Politics.* New York: Oxford University Press.

Mileur, Jerome M. 1992. "Dump Dixie—West Is Best: The Geography of a Progressive Democracy." In *The Democrats Must Lead: The Case for a Progressive Democratic Party*, edited by James MacGregor Burns, 97–111. Boulder, CO: Westview Press, 1992.

Mileur, Jerome M. 2005. "The Great Society and the Demise of New Deal Liberalism." In *The Great Society and the High Tide of Liberalism*, edited by Sidney M. Milkis and Jerome M. Mileur, 411–455. Amherst: University of Massachusetts Press.

Nagourney, Adam. 2005. "G.O.P. Right Is Splintered on Schiavo Intervention." *New York Times*, March 23, 2005.

Nelson, Garrison. 2017. *John William McCormack: A Political Biography.* New York: Bloomsbury.

Norman, Jim. 2018. *The Religious Regions of the U.S.* Gallup. https://news.gallup.com/poll/232223/religious-regions.aspx. Retrieved January 23, 2023.

Pew Research Center. 2014. Religious Landscape Study. Available online: https://www.pewresearch.org/religion/religious-landscape-study/. Retrieved February 3, 2023.

Reichley, A. James. 1992. *The Life of the Parties: A History of American Political Parties.* New York: The Free Press.

Reiter, Howard L., and Jeffrey M. Stonecash. 2011. *Counter Realignment: Political Change in the Northeastern United States.* New York: Cambridge University Press.

Rooks, Douglas. 2018. *Rise, Decline and Renewal: The Democratic Party in Maine.* Lanham, MD: Rowman & Littlefield.

Schantz, Harvey L. 1992. "The Erosion of Sectionalism in Presidential Elections." *Polity* 24, no. 3: 355–377.

Schickler, Eric. 2016. *Racial Realignment: The Transformation of American Liberalism, 1932–1965.* Princeton, NJ: Princeton University Press.

Sundquist, James L. 1983. *Dynamics of the Party System* Revised edition. Washington, DC: Brookings.

Tesler, Michael. 2016. *Post-Racial or Most-Racial?: Race and Politics in the Obama Era.* Chicago: University of Chicago Press.

PART II
THE POLITICS OF THE NEW ENGLAND STATES

CHAPTER 3

CONNECTICUT SINGS THE BLUES
Suburbia, Mavericks, and Policy Innovation

Scott L. McLean
Professor of Political Science
Quinnipiac University

This chapter explains how Connecticut became one of the "bluest" Democratic states in the nation. Early in the twentieth century, Connecticut was the prototypical swing state. Between 1928 and 1952, Republicans won four presidential elections, while Democrats won three. Republicans took 6 of the 12 presidential elections between 1956 and 2000, the last being George H.W. Bush in 1988. In 13 Governor's races from 1928 to 1954, 10 were decided by under 5 percent, and Republicans won 7 times, and 6 for the Democrats (State of Connecticut, Office of the Secretary of the State. "Election . . .").

However, as of 2022 only Delaware held a longer Democratic "trifecta"—control of state, executive, and legislative branches (Ballotpedia, n.d., "State Government Trifectas"). While Republicans held the governor's seat between 1993 and 2011, Democrats have held it ever since. Governor Ned Lamont was reelected in 2022 with a 13-point margin. The 2022 state legislative elections resulted in a 98–53 Democratic House majority and a Democratic Senate 24–12 supermajority. Since the defeat of Rep. Chris Shays in 2008, no Connecticut Republican has served in the US House or Senate (Ballotpedia n.d., "Chris Shays").

How did this happen? Other New England states have turned blue, but Connecticut took a peculiar path to "singing the blues." I argue that the state's novel *challenge primary* system was a critical part of the story. The challenge primary allows party leaders at a convention to endorse a nominee for local or state elections, but also allows unendorsed candidates to challenge the endorsed candidate to a primary where the party's registered voters have the final say. Historically, this system institutionalized Connecticut's tradition of the "maverick" politician, holding the parties together by giving upstarts and their group constituents a means of being heard and elected while operating inside the party hierarchy. However, as the state became more suburban after 2000, new voters entered the suburbs and undermined traditional GOP strengths in smaller towns.

As the Republican base became smaller and more conservative, Republican challenge primaries sometimes nominated candidates whose conservatism was out of step with the general election voters in key suburban battlegrounds. At the same time, for both parties, the rise of millionaire maverick candidates able to outspend their opponents further weakened the traditional balance between party leaders and party primary voters. Democratic and Republican party leaders had to bend to the energy of ideological activists using their energy and money in the suburbs to swing the outcome of challenge primaries. In the past decade, Republicans have suffered a loss of state power, while the Democrats' edge in the suburbs relied on unpredictable independents, the existence of a rich progressive maverick governor, and the Republicans' continuing attachment to Donald Trump. As Connecticut suburbs continue to change and politicians leave and enter the scene, both parties will need to address the impact of the challenge primary.

History: Creating the Post-World War II Party-in-Organization

Party competition in the post-World War II era was a product of systemic rural overrepresentation in state government, as established by the 1818 state Constitution, which was not reformed along one-person-one-vote principles until the 1965 Constitution. Rural overrepresentation was a fundamental political fact in Connecticut even in the founding of the colony in 1639 by the Reverend Thomas Hooker. Hooker's Fundamental Orders of 1639 maintained equal representation by town, but not by population, which tended to maintain conservative political elites well into the twentieth century. The 1818 Constitution's formula of two representatives per town, regardless of population, gave rural towns and their leaders outsized influence in state government. For example, in 1900, New Haven, with 108,000 residents, had two representatives, as did Union, a town with 425 residents (Rose 2007, 29). Rural overrepresentation in the General Assembly meant perennial Republican control of the state Senate (from the late 1800s to the early 1930s) and House (from 1858 to 1962).

Connecticut's party organizations in the early twentieth century were unlike those in Massachusetts and Rhode Island, where urban party bosses organized urban immigrant groups to gain power at the state level. In Connecticut, the strongest political machines were rural and Republican, due to the constitutional overrepresentation of small towns. The Republican bosses were the rural inheritors of the Yankee small-town values such as piety, thrift, the work ethic, and business shrewdness. In the twentieth century, the most powerful of these Yankee bosses was J. Henry Roraback. Roraback held virtual control of state government from 1912 until his death in 1937—all without holding a major political office. He rose as a figure in the Republican party from the town of North Canaan to become Republican State Chair in 1912. He then used his positions on corporate boards of rail and utility companies, such as The New Haven Railroad and Connecticut Light and Power, to defend corporations from progressive era regulation and taxation (McKee and Petterson 1997, 117). His reach extended to every piece of legislation in the General Assembly. Every day during General Assembly sessions, Roraback would send messages to Republican leaders and the governor on the wording of every key piece of legislation. He also used his board memberships to recruit successful candidates for governor and General Assembly (McKee and Petterson 1997, 117). Because most Republican legislators owed their continuance in office to the good graces of Roraback, the party adopted a pro-business, anti-regulation stance that has typically characterized Republican policy in Connecticut.

With the Great Depression, Republican power waned. In 1930, Democrats nominated retired Yale University Dean Wilbur Cross for governor. Cross was successful in part because he represented a kind of independent maverick whose progressivism was distanced from party organization leaders. Though Cross was involved with the New Haven Democratic organization, he was a progressive literature professor who called for bipartisan legislative reform. His platform against Lieutenant Governor Ernest Rogers focused on a state civil service merit system, the termination of Prohibition, a progressive tax on the wealthy, and unemployment programs (Cross, 1943). He won by just 1.3 percent and was the only Democrat elected to statewide office in 1930 (State of Connecticut, "Election Results . . ."). Governor Cross was re-elected in 1932 and 1934 by margins under 2 percent. Cross gained popularity by portraying himself as independent, honest, and untouched by the Republican machine. After passing a bipartisan unemployment relief plan, Cross won his third two-year term by a whopping 14 percentage points. Cross finally lost reelection in 1938 by just half a percentage point.

After Cross's time in office, the Republicans still dominated the General Assembly because of constitutional rural overrepresentation. But something had changed. Democratic candidates for statewide office became more capable of winning in the 1940s, and it was partly because of the emerging leadership of John Bailey. Bailey learned the party's ropes in the rough-and-tumble ward politics of Hartford, and in 1932 rose to a position on the state Democratic committee, followed by election as state chair in 1946—a post he held until his death in 1975. Under "Boss Bailey's" chairmanship, Democrats controlled the governor's office between 1955 and 1971, and again for another streak from 1975 to 1991. Bailey hardly fit the description of the typical urban political machine boss, preferring to broker broader coalitions rather than twist arms (Deneen 2005). For instance, when it came to the highest statewide offices of governor and senator, Bailey united liberal Yankees like Chester Bowles with rival Roman Catholic and Jewish candidates such as Thomas Dodd, Abraham Ribicoff, and Ella Grasso (the first female governor in the United States who did not follow her husband into office). Bailey's method of building diverse party tickets and neutralizing potential factional rebellions continues as a Connecticut Democratic strategy even to this day. Eventually, these practices became institutionalized in the challenge primary system.

Connecticut's Novel Challenge Primary System

Perhaps Bailey's most durable legacy in Connecticut's electoral system was his role in shaping Connecticut's unique challenge primary system. The irony is that Bailey had resisted the creation of primaries in Connecticut, and only reluctantly agreed to the challenge primary as a kind of compromise that would retain power for party leaders. By 1955 Connecticut was the last state to adopt legally mandated primaries, and town party leaders, particularly those in the suburbs, were pressuring the General Assembly to require parties to hold primaries. Bailey resisted, but Governor Abraham Ribicoff was sympathetic. Bailey blocked any plan for open primaries in which unaffiliated voters may participate. He was able to persuade the Democratic leaders that primaries would eventually render the old party-committees and nominating convention obsolete. But seeing he could not completely block the introduction of primaries in the state, Bailey encouraged Ribicoff to back a compromise plan. The original 1955 version of the challenge primary retained for party organization the power to endorse party nominees at local and state party conventions. But a candidate winning 20 percent of a convention's vote could petition for a primary, in which only registered party voters would have the right to participate (in 1993 the convention threshold was lowered to 15 percent, which led to more contested primaries) (Janicki 2001). Eventually in 1986 the US Supreme Court ruled that the political parties would be allowed to invite "unaffiliated voters" (i.e., voters not registered with any political party) to participate in a party primary, but neither Democrats nor Republicans have exercised this option yet (Janicki, 2008).

The convention-and-challenge primary system is central to politics in Connecticut because it retains some power for party insiders through the endorsement power but can allow enthusiastic groups of a party's registered voters to potentially override the convention's choices. Certainly, party identification is critical in Connecticut politics, but party affiliation in voter registration is the vital institutional link between party organization and party in the electorate when it comes to candidate recruitment and nomination. As demonstrated next, the regional and ideological base of the registered voter primary electorate in each party, along with their likelihood of voting in the primary, impacts who the nominees are and their competitiveness in the general election. Party registration is not the same as party identification; most unaffiliated voters are split between Democratic and Republican leanings. But before discussing how party identification affects the general election, we must consider each party's base of registered voters eligible to determine the party nominees in a potential challenge primary.

Two critical historical trends in Connecticut politics since the creation of the challenge primary system are illustrated in Figure 3.1. The first is the decline of Republican voter registration and simultaneous rise of Democratic voter registration as a proportion of the electorate. The second is the emergence since the mid-1990s of unaffiliated voters as the largest voting bloc. Democratic and Republican state party registration declined in the 1980s, and by 1995 there were more unaffiliated voters than Democrats or Republicans. Republicans controlled most rural town governments (as is still the case today), but there

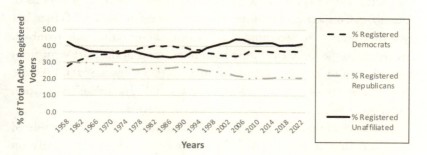

FIGURE 3.1. Connecticut Party Registration Percentages, 1958–2022. Note: Figure shows active registered voters only. Source: Connecticut Office of the Secretary of State https://portal.ct.gov/SOTS/Election-Services/Statistics-and-Data/Statistics-and-Data.

simply are not enough Republicans statewide to win elections without finding more support among unaffiliated voters. Thus the extremely small and increasingly conservative Republican primary electorate risks nominating candidates who are out of step with the rest of the electorate. This gives Democrats some advantages in elections for statewide offices. In addition, since the 1965 Constitution eliminated rural overrepresentation, it has helped tilt the balance in the state's General Assembly toward the Democrats.

Along with the rise of unaffiliated voters has come the slow decline of registered Republicans in the state. As Figure 3.1 shows, Democratic voter registration began to outpace Republicans during the 1960s during Bailey's heyday. By the 1990s, the ranks of unaffiliated voters pulled ahead of Democrats while Republicans remained at the back of the pack. By 2022, the percentage of unaffiliated voters was more than twice the size of registered Republicans. Democrats, too, significantly outpace the GOP in party registration. There are both immediate political factors and underlying socioeconomic factors behind the rise of unaffiliated voters and the decline in Republican registration numbers. Most of them revolve around the major parties' efforts to deal with suburbanization, first in the 1960s and then another burst in the 1990s. The next section considers how suburbanization affected party competition in Connecticut.

How Suburbia Changed the Party Balance

Much of Connecticut's politics revolves around whose voters live where, and as suburbs change, so do the politics. The suburbs and suburban independents shifted from Republican to a Democratic identification edge after 2010. After 1970, Connecticut's suburbs were not only extending out of cities, but even rural areas were becoming more urbanized—or rather, suburbanized. According to the US Census, the rural population of the state went from 22 percent in 1970 to just 12 percent in 2020 (US Census 2022). Likewise (since the census only uses rural-urban categories), the "urban" population shifted from 78 percent in 1970 to 88 percent in 2020.

How much of that urban population in Connecticut should be considered suburban? There is no standard definition, but census figures on population density give a clue. Connecticut is currently ranked as the fourth overall most densely populated US state. Connecticut's 88 percent urban population in 2020 is closer to Massachusetts (92% urban) and Rhode Island (90% urban), than to New Hampshire (60% urban), Vermont (38.9 % urban) or Maine

(38.7% urban). The six most densely populated cities (Bridgeport, Hartford, New Haven, New Britain, West Haven, New London) compose 15.5 percent of Connecticut's population, and so this means that the remaining 72.5 percent of non-urban and non-rural population inhabits areas that could be characterized as suburban (Iowa Community Indicators Program).

It is a jarring juxtaposition that, in 2024, Connecticut is the wealthiest state based on per capita income ($45,668)—just ahead of Massachusetts and it's per capita income of $45,555—yet it also has a 10 percent overall poverty rate and the state contains three of the poorest cities in the United States. Hartford has a 28.4 percent poverty rate—11th highest in the United States—followed by New Haven (24.6% poverty rate, 16th highest poverty rate in the US), and Bridgeport (23% poverty rate) (World Population Review 2024a, 2024b). For decades, observers have thought of the state as "two Connecticuts," where disparities of wealth and educational opportunities intersect with racial differences between cities and suburbs (Powell 2021). Surrounding urban Connecticut are suburban towns with higher economic opportunity, higher costs of living, greater wealth, stronger schools, and fewer minorities. Urban Connecticut faces deindustrialization, troubled schools, high poverty, and is more racially diverse with higher percentages of recent immigrants. Racially exclusionary zoning, higher urban property taxes, and insufficient urban school financing reinforce wealth and opportunity gaps between the cities and suburban areas. Historically, the opportunity gaps in Connecticut have fed into regional party differences. Democrats dominate in the urban areas and suburbs nearest to cities. Republicans remain strong in both the rural northeast "quiet corner" of Windham County, the white working-class areas of the Naugatuck Valley, the northwest corner with Litchfield County, and in the "gold coast" wealthy New York City suburbs of Fairfield County. Additionally, the two Connecticuts are not always regional. Urban-suburban divides often look like a marble cake rather than a layer cake. For example, even the most urbanized and densely populated counties, like Hartford County, New Haven County, and Fairfield County, are patchworks of dense cities, rural areas, and some of the wealthiest suburban neighborhoods in the state.

Connecticut's GOP is further disadvantaged by the fact urban areas have increased their share of the total registration—18.6 percent of the total in 2000 to 24 percent in 2022 (State of Connecticut, *Party Enrollment*). Though Democratic urban registration rates have declined by 2 percentage points between 2000 and 2022, the increased proportion of the population living in urban areas provides Democrats with net electoral gains over that period. Meanwhile urban Republican registration declined from 13.6 percent in 2000 to 9.7 percent in 2022 (State of Connecticut, *Party Enrollment*). The share of unaffiliated voters in cities grew from 29 percent in 2000 to 34.5 percent in 2022 (State of Connecticut, *Party Enrollment*).

The "gold coast" towns of Fairfield County offer an illustrative case study for why Republicans lost much of their grip on the wealthy suburbs. In 2000, voter registration in the Town of Fairfield (population 61,737 in 2021) favored Republicans 33 percent to 25 percent over Democrats. By 2016, Fairfield had become more ethnically diverse and flipped to a slight Democratic advantage—30 percent to 27 percent. In 2022, that grew to a 35 percent to 24 percent voter registration advantage for the Democrats (Barry, 2022). In the Town of Greenwich (population 63,445 in 2021) Republicans held a 45 percent to 20 percent voter registration advantage over Democrats in 2000, which by 2016 slipped to 36 percent to 26 percent (Barry 2022). By 2022, the Democrats achieved a 30 to 28 percent advantage, which led Trump supporters to push traditional Republicans out of the County party committee (Barry 2022).

Though not typical of all Republican suburbs, the Fairfield County story illustrates how the state party struggled to adapt to changes in the national Republican party since the rise of Donald Trump. It became more difficult for moderate or "insider" Republicans to win primaries and harder for primary winners to pivot to the center to win in the general election—all as their advantages in the suburbs wane. In 2016 Hillary Clinton won ultra-wealthy Greenwich easily, 57 percent to 39 percent, as Donald Trump was disliked by the established Republican committee members in the town. After 2016, Trump supporters moved to take control of the Republican town committee and, with mixed success, pushed for more conservative, Trump-friendly candidates. Even though Biden beat Trump with 62 percent to 37 percent in 2020, Fairfield County Republicans doubled down on populism (Barry 2022).

In the 2022 US Senate race, Greenwich Republican Leora Levy benefited among Republicans by embracing Trump's message and by a Trump fundraiser at Mar-a-Lago. Levy lost the state party endorsement to well-known House Republican Leader Themis Klarides, a conservative tax-cutter who nevertheless defended state abortion rights in the wake of the Supreme Court striking down *Roe v. Wade*. Klarides' greater name recognition and popular anti-tax message suggested she would be a strong challenge to Democratic incumbent Senator Richard Blumenthal. Nevertheless, Levy pointed to Klarides' 100 rating from the National Abortion Rights Action League (NARAL) and rallied conservative Republicans to upset Klarides in the GOP challenge primary. Levy ultimately lost to Blumenthal by 15 points statewide, and by 13 points in her hometown of Greenwich (State of Connecticut, "Election Results . . ." 2022).

Party-In Electorate: Unaffiliateds, Independents, and the Battle for Suburbia

Why has there been a decreasing Republican candidate advantage among independent voters? Some reasons include demographics, the rise of conservative activists on town committees, or how the national image of Republicans has changed in the time between the G. W. Bush era to the Trump era. But an underappreciated part of that story is suburban shifts in the demographics of party registration and party identification. In the 1990s, Connecticut and other states saw somewhat of a reversal of the "white flight" from cities that had occurred in the 1960s and 1970s. High-income, high-education white professionals moved into the less-densely populated parts of Connecticut's cities, while at the same time, more educated and professional people of racial and ethnic marginalized groups moved into the suburbs (Lacy 2022). During this era, suburbs nearer to city borders (such as Stamford) became more densely populated, while the major urban centers actually lost population. Hartford, for instance, lost an astonishing 13 percent of its population in the 1990s (Katz 2001). Between the late 2010 and 2020, Connecticut suburbs gradually became more ethnically and racially diverse (Frey 2022).

The most significant political change in Connecticut is the increase in the percentage of self-identified Democrats voters living in the suburbs. Quinnipiac Poll data indicates that, between 2006 and 2022, registered voters identifying or leaning as Republicans held steady at 37 percent, but the percentage of registered voters identifying or leaning as Democrats grew from 46 percent to 53 percent (Quinnipiac University Poll 2022a, 2022b).

How did this change occur? There are three factors. First, there was increased racial-ethnic diversity in the suburbs. Though polls are less precise than census data, the percentage of registered white voters in the state's suburbs declined from 88 percent in 2006 to 74 percent in 2022 (Quinnipiac University Poll 2022a, 2022b).

Second, there was a widening suburban gender gap in party identification favoring Democrats. For decades, more suburban registered women voters in Connecticut identified with Democrats than with Republicans.

The Quinnipiac Poll indicates that neither party held an advantage among registered male voters between 2006 and 2022 (Quinnipiac University Poll 2022a, 2022b). However, Democrats' advantages with women grew between 2006 and 2022 election years. In 2006, 51 percent of registered women voters in the suburbs identified with the Democratic Party. By 2022 the Democratic advantage swelled to 61 percent of suburban women identifying as Democrats (Quinnipiac University Poll 2022a, 2022b).

Third, there was a rise between 2006 and 2022 in Democratic identification among registered college graduates. The percentage of registered college graduates identifying or leaning to Democrats dramatically shifted from 46 percent in 2006 to 57 percent in 2022 (Quinnipiac University Poll 2022a, 2022b). Meanwhile, during the same period, the share of registered college graduates identifying as Republicans declined from 37 percent in 2006 to 33 percent in 2022 (Quinnipiac University Poll 2022a, 2022b).

Still, polling can overlook some of the nuances in these demographic changes. Sociologists can sometimes supplement our view of suburban change. For example, polling does not address the extent to which Republican support faded due to the aging of older suburban Republican-supporting voters, or whether new Democratic-supporting voters moved into suburbia. Sociological analysis suggests that it is mostly explained by new groups moving into Connecticut's suburbs. Sociologist Karyn Lacy (2022) identified three recent factors that contribute to the electoral competitiveness of suburbs: higher percentages of people with below-median incomes, immigrants, and nonwhite middle-class workers (Lacy 2022). As a point of comparison, the towns surrounding metropolitan Hartford now have a higher proportion of non-whites than towns surrounding Boston or Providence (Frey 2022). Less-densely populated towns across Connecticut (such as Hamden, West Hartford, and Stamford), between 2010 and 2020, saw increases in the percentage of African Americans (up 19 percent) and Hispanics (up 58 percent) (CT Data Collaborative 2021). In the suburban regions surrounding that dense urban corridor around Hartford, the percentage of people of color more than tripled, from 9.1 percent in 1990 to 30.5 percent in 2022 (Frey 2022). Since 2010, the large cities (except for Hartford) gained back population (CT Data Collaborative 2021). As suburbs became more densely populated, and more diverse, suburban independents broke more toward Democrats.

Also important was how independent voters have tilted toward Democrats in the past decade. The majority of unaffiliated voters in Connecticut identify as independent, but independent voters usually have a slight preference or leaning toward a political party, and likely vote for candidates of that party across multiple election cycles (Abramowitz 2018, 8). Republicans must gain a large margin among suburban independents to have a realistic chance to win a statewide election. However, as Figure 3.2 indicates, the Democratic Party has gained an edge over Republicans among party identifiers plus party leaners.

Pre-election surveys in the gubernatorial election of 2022 further illustrate this advantage for Democrats. The 2022 NORC/AP VoteCast survey, the most reliable election survey available, shows the Democratic candidate advantages in the suburbs. Governor Ned Lamont came into the 2022 election with a built-in base of 52 percent of the electorate as Democratic party identifiers or Democrat-leaning independents, while 41 percent identify or lean to Republicans (NORC 2022). Quinnipiac Poll data early in the gubernatorial race also show that these party identification levels have been unchanged since at least 2008 (Quinnipiac University Poll 2022a, 2022b). For instance, in pre-election polling for the 2022 governor's race, Bob Stefanowski had a nine-point lead over Governor Ned Lamont among suburban independents (53% to 44%) but was trailing in the suburbs by 14 points and lost the state to Lamont by 13 points (Quinnipiac University Poll 2022a). Lamont had a slight edge with white voters (52% to 48%), a significantly larger lead among whites than national Democrats held in 2022 (NORC 2022). Non-white voters made up 19 percent of Connecticut's 2022 electorate, and Lamont won with a 68 percent to 30 percent edge over Stefanowski. Lamont was favored by 55 percent of voters making over $100,000 per year, compared

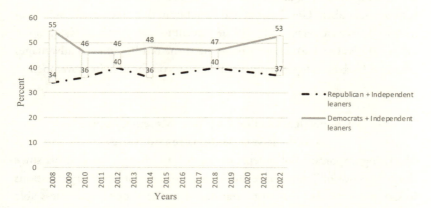

FIGURE 3.2. Suburban Connecticut Voters: Party Identifiers plus Leaners, 2008–2022. Source: Quinnipiac University Poll, Connecticut Polls. (Quinnipiac University Poll 2008b; 2010a; 2014b; 2018b; 2022a).

to 45 percent for Stefanowski. Among voters earning less than $50,000, Lamont's margin was twice that large: 59 percent to 39 percent (NORC 2022). College-educated voters favored Lamont 61 percent to 38 percent for Stefanowski. In the 2022 election, men split their support between Lamont and his opponent Stefanowski, while female voters favored Lamont 60 percent to 38 percent (NORC 2022). Regarding suburban voters, the Quinnipiac Poll found that 61 percent of suburban women identified as Democrats or were Democratic-leaning independents, while suburban men were divided (Quinnipiac Poll 2022a).

Lamont's support among these groups is the result of a decades-long rise of independent voters. Republican strength since 2000 was built on the party's suburban advantage and appeal to anti-tax independents who favored Republican candidates. In 2002 and 2006 gubernatorial races, for example, Quinnipiac Poll's pre-election polling showed independents heavily tilted to Republican candidates. Incumbent Republican Jodi Rell, running for re-election in 2006 against New Haven Democratic Mayor John DeStefano, ended her successful campaign with a 56-point lead among suburban independents (Quinnipiac Poll, 2006c). By 2010, just after the nominations were complete in August in the governor's race, former Stamford Mayor and Democratic nominee Dannel Malloy held an 8-point lead, 40 percent to 32 percent, among suburban independents over Republican Tom Foley (Quinnipiac University Poll 2010b). By May 2014, Republican challenger Tom Foley led incumbent Gov. Malloy 44 percent to 37 percent among suburban independents (Quinnipiac University Poll 2014b). In the 2022 rematch between incumbent Gov. Lamont and Republican Bob Stefanowski, suburban independents were evenly split, with 48 percent to each candidate (Quinnipiac University Poll 2022a). Having neutralized the old Republican advantages among suburban independents, Lamont won comfortably in November.

Connecticut's Political Culture: Maverick Appeal and the Rise of Millionaire Candidates

The rising importance of independents and the changes in suburbia since the emergence of Trump have challenged both major party organizations in Connecticut. As party organizations after the 2000s became less able to control their own nomination processes and more dependent on unaffiliated voters to win elections, it opened new opportunities for maverick politicians within both parties. As mentioned in the discussion of the 1955 establishment of the challenge primary system, even though Connecticut's political culture has strong partisan roots, born in the history of the rural Republican machines and the urban Democratic machines, nevertheless there is a contrary political "maverick" tradition in the state. The maverick tradition finds roots in moralistic reformism and a distrust of insider party leaders. Anti-establishment candidates who challenge the party committees can, at times, rally voters who distrust party insiders or demand political reform, even if they adopt a party label. Connecticut has a long tradition of electing flinty New England maverick politicians who find success challenging their party's orthodoxy. Occasionally a maverick outsider rises in the form of a showman-scoundrel, like when P. T. Barnum, who won a seat in the General Assembly in 1865. More often, though, mavericks were moralistic crusaders combating corruption or calling for reforms, such as Governor Wilbur Cross in the 1930s. Though Cross was not fully a maverick (as he worked through the New Haven Democratic organization), he nevertheless gained popularity by wrapping himself in rhetoric of reformism, high principle, and independent thinking.

The response of party organizations to occasional maverick upstarts in Connecticut have usually followed the John Bailey strategy previously mentioned—pulling them back into the party as allies. For instance, Bailey was always willing to support former opponents like Abraham Ribicoff if it would strengthen the Democratic ticket. Once the challenge primary system was in place, there were opportunities for upstarts within each party to take their case to the party's rank and file.

In the 1970s there arose two classic mavericks worth discussing: Republican Lowell Weicker and Democrat Joseph Lieberman. They were mavericks within their parties and became successful largely due to their relative independence. In this section, I discuss how Weicker and Lieberman stand in contrast to a later kind of party-bucking maverick that emerged in the 2000s: The millionaire maverick candidate. The shift to wealthy outsiders becoming party insiders is an important feature of how Connecticut became so blue.

Lowell Weicker fit a classic mold of the Connecticut maverick. Until Lowell Weicker's election to the US Senate in 1971, the state had not elected a Republican to the Senate since Prescott Bush in 1956. After serving in local and state offices in Greenwich, Weicker won a Senate seat with a narrow plurality against a divided Democratic Party. Why was it divided? Senator Thomas Dodd had been censured by the Senate in 1967 for diverting $116,000 of campaign donations to his personal use. The Democratic vote was split when Dodd refused to resign from the Senate, and ran as an independent against the Democrats' nominee, Joseph Duffey (McLean, 2005). First-term Senator Weicker made a name for himself during the Watergate hearings as a quintessential maverick and a Rockefeller Republican for berating Nixon aides and for being the first Republican to call for Nixon's resignation (Madden 1979; Rose 2007, 60). Weicker embraced the role of maverick, bucking the party with filibusters in favor of civil rights, and a strong pro-choice position on federal funding for abortion for low-income women (Madden 1979; Malone 1981). He took moralistic stances against his own party during the Watergate scandal, and eventually left the party because of the growing support for Reagan-style conservatism in the Connecticut GOP organization.

Weicker's views appealed across party lines, but the Democrats finally found a strong challenger to Weicker in popular State Attorney General Joe Lieberman in 1988. Interestingly, Lieberman was also a maverick. Just as Weicker could win over independents and some Democrats, Lieberman was a centrist Democrat popular with independents and a few Republicans voters. In his 1988 run, Lieberman ran to the left of Weicker on most issues, but he also took positions that were considered "centrist" or even conservative, and Lieberman accepted endorsements from bona fide conservatives including William F. Buckley. Lieberman subsequently defeated Weicker by just 10,000 votes—less than one percent of those votes cast (McKee and Petterson 1997, 126). Once in the Senate, Lieberman allied himself with Senator John McCain, and sided with conservatives in trying to regulate violence in video games. He also condemned his own protege President Bill Clinton from the Senate floor over Clinton's sexual improprieties with an intern and subsequent perjury (though Lieberman still voted not guilty in Clinton's Senate impeachment trial).

Lieberman won landslide re-elections to the Senate in 1994 and 2000 as a Democrat (while also running for US vice president). However, he tested the limits of maverick electability in 2006. By the spring of 2006, Lieberman's opposition to withdrawing from Iraq made him quite unpopular with the left in Connecticut, and newcomer Ned Lamont's star was rising (Quinnipiac University Poll 2006a). At the state convention, most party leaders endorsed Lieberman for the nomination, but Lamont mounted a Democratic primary challenge and defeated Lieberman by three points. Lamont financed his 2006 Senate race out of his own fortune to the tune of $16.8 million and with just $3.5 million in funding generated by internet bloggers (Lightman 2006). He arrived on the scene just as Connecticut was shifting to a public campaign financing system and voluntary spending limits for those using it.

When Lieberman decided to continue his run as an independent, he had nearly 70 percent of Republican likely voters, and nearly 57 percent of independent likely voters by his side (Quinnipiac University Poll 2006b). Lieberman played the moralistic Democratic maverick, blaming his primary loss on party leaders who had lost their way. In the end, Lieberman was elected in a five-way race by 10 points (State of Connecticut, "Election Results . . ."). We can only speculate whether Lieberman would have won if the Republicans had nominated a candidate with the name recognition to bring home Republican votes. The Republicans did not expect Lamont's rise, so they nominated unknown challenger Alan Schlesinger, a Blackjack card-counter found to have huge gambling debts in New Jersey. Schlesinger used the alias "Alan Gold" to register for a gambling card at the Foxwoods casino (Hamilton 2006). Republican Governor Jodi Rell and Republican State Chair George Gallo called on Schlesinger to drop out of the race, to no avail.

Weicker and Lieberman tell us a lot about Connecticut political culture in the early 2000s and independents' willingness to swing across party lines. It also shows how Republican candidates during that time could compete with Democrats for swing voters. In those years, candidates could take stands against their own party on key issues and still find plenty of support among party organization leaders against more ideologically consistent challengers. Lieberman's support from swingable independents in the 2006 Senate election may appear odd today, as we have become accustomed to independents with reliable leanings toward one party.

Perhaps it is just coincidence that millionaire mavericks emerged at about the same time that Connecticut adopted a public campaign financing system. In 2005 the Citizen Election Fund plan was to provide extra grants when self-funders hit certain spending thresholds, but this was struck down by courts in the wake of *Citizens United*. The Citizens Election Program today is widely used to publicly finance candidates for all state offices, save one: governor. Then the 2010 *Citizens United v. F.E.C.* decision opened the door to large-scale Super PAC media purchases in state elections, which increased the incentive for gubernatorial candidates to decline public money and public spending limits in the Citizens Election Program. After Lamont's 2006 Senate primary win, other millionaires in the state turned from fundraising for politicians to financing their own runs for office (De Avila 2014). Republican Linda McMahon, CEO of World Wrestling Entertainment, self-financed

$100 million for two failed US Senate runs in 2010 and 2012 (Applebome 2012). Tom Foley spent $10 million on his way to the 2010 Republican nomination for governor in a losing cause against Democrat Dannel Malloy (Associated Press 2014). Foley opted for public financing in his ultimately unsuccessful rematch with Malloy in 2014, resulting in being outspent. The current maximum public grant is $1.6 million for a gubernatorial primary, and $7.7 million for the general election. To qualify for the grant, a candidate cannot accept individual donations greater than $290. The maximum public financing grant that a candidate for governor could receive is $8 million. To illustrate how insufficient that amount is compared to using self-financing or PAC money, Lamont spent $15.9 million in his 2018 run, and a walloping $25.7 million in 2022, burying in a blizzard of TV and web ads his fellow millionaire, Republican Bob Stefanowski, who spent $6.6 million in 2018 and $14.5 million in 2022 (Pazniokas 2023).

Leaders in both political parties are currently trading proposals to reform the public campaign finance system in ways that may rein in millionaire mavericks. In 2023, the General Assembly began bipartisan discussions on raising the limit on individual donations to gubernatorial candidates from $290 to $1,000. Currently, Republican leaders are proposing to increase the general election grant to governor's candidates from the current $7.7 million to a maximum of $10 million, and Democrats are willing to go even higher, to $15.5 million for the general election and $3.2 million for the primary (Haar 2023). Other proposals have emphasized how long it takes to receive a grant. By the time a candidate receives a public financing grant, a self-funding candidate can have already spent millions. Party leverage over mavericks, therefore, may take new forms in the future. Millionaire mavericks still need the party organization and its ability to turn out base party voters. But at the same time, the party organization is supportive of a candidate paying for advertising and staff to generate support from independents.

Focusing Events, Progressive Policies, and Pressing the Democratic Advantage

With the change from a competitive swing state in the 1950s to the current era of Democratic one-party rule, Connecticut has become a kind of laboratory for progressive ideas, doing what the US Congress cannot do. But the Democrats' policies emerged from several focusing events that shifted public opinion in favor of Democratic issue positions. Focusing events are sudden, attention-grabbing events that trigger opportunities for potential policy change (Birkland 1998). Policy responses to focusing events can mobilize interest groups and public opinion in ways that can produce an electoral advantage for either party. Gradual shifts in urban-suburban-rural demographics gave Democrats an electoral edge, but in the policy realm, several focusing events allowed Democrats to enact progressive policy changes, which in turn tipped the electoral scales their way in the suburbs. The Democratic majority has taken bold initiatives on minimum wage, the environment, ballot access, and more. Greater rights to abortion access, significant gun control (for the United States), an increase in the minimum wage, repeal of the death penalty, drivers' licenses for undocumented immigrants, and mandated paid sick leave were enacted in Connecticut when Congress was too gridlocked to act.

These policies, along with the Trump presidency, have led to intensified ideological cleavages between the parties. Democrats in Connecticut used their advantages in these new divisions with a mixture of progressive idealism and cold electoral calculation. As an illustration, take Connecticut's passage of the nation's toughest gun control laws in the wake of the horrific Sandy Hook school massacre of 2012. On December 14, 2012, a mentally ill twenty-year-old man broke into Sandy Hook Elementary in Newtown, CT and used a semiautomatic rifle to kill 20 first graders and six teachers and staff. It was the worst school shooting in US history at the time (Newman and Hartman 2019, 1528). The horrifying crime set the stage for change in voter bases of the two parties, especially for the Republicans. In 2013, Democratic Governor Malloy and the Democratically controlled General Assembly passed bipartisan restrictions on the state's existing assault rifle ban, to create the most restrictive gun laws in the United States (Associated Press 2013). Yet despite the bipartisanship in the General Assembly, and especially after the laws were upheld in federal court, grassroots gun enthusiasts loudly protested these laws, introducing a new rift in the state's conservative base. Polls in 2013 and 2014 showed that as many as 69 percent of Republican voters in the state opposed the new laws; in rural areas, the Republican opposition was even higher (Quinnipiac University Poll 2014a).

Donald Trump's election in 2016 also proved to be a focusing event in Connecticut. Trump's statements and norm-breaking behavior drew more than just public attention—it brought Connecticut independents closer to Democrats. The crisis of the pandemic allowed progressives to push for health care and electoral reforms. Governor Lamont assumed emergency powers in March of 2020, and the General Assembly extended his powers six times before his powers ended in February 2022. The state suffered 10,000 COVID-related deaths (McQuaid 2022). Although Lamont's actions to protect public health met some resistance, particularly in suburban areas, Connecticut was ranked one of the most effective pandemic responses (Radley et. al. 2022). According to a Quinnipiac Poll taken near the end of his emergency powers, 71 percent of residents approved Lamont's handling of the coronavirus situation (Quinnipiac Poll 2022b).

Democrats in the General Assembly undertook voting reforms in response to the pandemic as well. Even before the pandemic, Connecticut had recently instituted a successful online voter registration system and made allowances for those who could not vote on Election Day because they were sick. During the pandemic, Democrats passed policies so that concern about COVID-19 health risks or the need to stay home to care for an ill family member would meet the "sickness" standard (Dixon 2022). This created a de facto mail-in balloting system. Republicans cried foul, echoing President Trump's rhetoric claiming election theft from mail-in balloting. In the election, Republicans in suburban and rural areas did not make much use of the absentee ballot rules. Meanwhile, Democrats used local party canvassing efforts to encourage voters in suburban and more urbanized towns to apply for absentee ballots. The strategy led to higher-than-expected Democratic voter turnout in 2020 which helped suburban Democrats running for General Assembly. Then in 2022 the General Assembly introduced a ballot measure, which passed with 61 percent support, authorizing in-person early voting in Connecticut (Ballotpedia, "Connecticut 2022 Ballot Measures").

Finally, Democrats quickly defended state reproductive rights even before the Supreme Court in 2022 struck down *Roe v. Wade* in the *Dobbs v. Jackson Women's Health Organization Supreme Court* decision. The General Assembly passed a law on April 22, 2022 to protect out-of-state patients who seek abortion services in Connecticut from legal action taken by states that have outlawed abortion (Haigh 2022). The policy was supported by 67 percent of independents (Quinnipiac University Poll 2022b).

Conclusion

Connecticut's pre-World War II history was dominated by rural Republican machines and urban Democratic machines. Republicans held the upper hand in state government because of a constitutional underrepresentation of cities. In the 1960s with constitutional reform and with urban whites moving to the suburbs, the political and cultural dividing line was between two Connecticuts: Democratic urban Connecticut and the Republican rural-suburban Connecticut. Eventually in the 2010s, Democrats grew stronger in the suburbs, and Republicans now must swing an almost insurmountable number of suburban independents to overcome Democratic advantages in cities.

On January 4, 2023, Connecticut Governor Ned Lamont was inaugurated for his second term. His Republican opponent was Bob Stefanowski, a wealthy self-financing candidate and relatively centrist compared to his primary GOP opponents. Stefanowski only lost to Lamont in 2018 by 3.2 percentage points but lost the 2022 rematch by 13 percent. Although the results of Lamont's emergency COVID-19 powers Connecticut were ranked the third most effective pandemic response, pandemic policies were unpopular in suburban towns (Radley et al. 2022). Lamont had passed a minimum-wage increase, police regulation, and stronger state gun control laws, all of which were less popular in the suburbs than in the cities. In addition, Lamont had generated a large state financing surplus, which he used to give residents a tax cut, thereby blunting Stefanowski's main 2022 campaign issue.

The suburbs inherited something of the old Yankee political culture of individualism and distrust of politicians and party organizations, in the form of independents willing to support mavericks who buck their own party. Suburbs in today's Connecticut are far more complex than the monolithic white suburban enclaves of the 1950s. Immigrants, non-white professionals, and more blue-collar workers increased their suburban presence (Frey 2022; Lacy 2022). Republicans can still win in the suburbs, but it is now a steep uphill climb. For the moment, Democrats dance, while Republicans sing the blues. Still, Democrats would be unwise to overestimate their advantages. This chapter has shown that suburbs have a slight leaning for Democrats, but also that independents are not fully on board (Texiera 2022). Moreover, in 2026 the Democrats cannot count on having a gubernatorial candidate like Ned Lamont who can outspend any Republican. Democratic leaders might take solace in the high price the Republican Party in Connecticut would pay to broaden their appeal. It is unlikely the GOP would exercise their option to allow unaffiliated voters into Republican primaries. It would mean that conservative party activists would have to give up their influence in primaries, which they would not do without a fight. Unless the next millionaire maverick is Republican, Democrats will dance while Republicans keep singing the blues.

Works Cited

Abramowitz, Alan I. 2018. *The Great Alignment: Race, Party Transformation, and the Rise of Donald Trump*. New Haven: Yale University Press.

Applebome, Peter. 2012. "Personal Cost for 2 Senate Bids: $100 Million." *New York Times*. November 3, 2012. https://www.nytimes.com/2012/11/03/nyregion/linda-e-mcmahon-has-spent-nearly-100-million-in-senate-races.html.

Associated Press. 2013. "Connecticut Governor Signs Gun Measures." *New York Times*. April 4, 2013. https://www.nytimes.com/2013/04/05/nyregion/connecticut-lawmakers-pass-gun-limits.html.

Associated Press. 2014. "Foley to Use Public Funding in Connecticut Race." *New Haven Register*. June 3, 2014. https://www.nhregister.com/connecticut/article/Foley-to-use-public-funding-in-Connecticut-race-11385005.php.

Ballotpedia. n.d. "Chris Shays." https://ballotpedia.org/Chris_Shays.

Ballotpedia. n.d. "Connecticut 2022 Ballot Measures." https://ballotpedia.org/Connecticut_2022_ballot_measures.

Ballotpedia. n.d. "State Government Trifectas." https://ballotpedia.org/State_government_trifectas.

Barry, Dan. 2022. "In Rich Suburb, Republicans Vs. 'Trumplicans'." *The New York Times*. November 7, 2022. https://www.nytimes.com/2022/11/06/nyregion/greenwich-connecticut-republicans.html.

Birkland, Thomas A. 1998. "Focusing Events, Mobilization, and Agenda Setting." *Journal of Public Policy* 18, no. 1: 53–74. http://www.jstor.org/stable/4007601.

Cross, Wilbur L. 1943. *Connecticut Yankee: An Autobiography*. New Haven: Yale University Press.

Ilyankou, Ilya. 2021. *"Population Changes in Connecticut, 2010 to 2020." CTdata collaborative*. August 23, 2021. https://www.ctdata.org/blog/population-changes-in-connecticut-2010-to-2020.

De Avila, Joseph. 2014. "Foley to Take Public Money in Connecticut Race." *The Wall Street Journal*. June 4, 2014. https://www.wsj.com/articles/foley-to-take-public-money-in-race-for-connecticut-governor-1401857762.

Deneen, Patrick. 2005. "Bailey, John M." In *The Encyclopedia of New England : The Culture and History of an American Region*, edited by Burt Feintuch and David H. Watters, 1226–1227. New Haven: Yale University Press.

DePietro, Andrew. 2021. "U.S. Poverty Rate by City in 2021." *Forbes*, November 26, 2021. https://www.forbes.com/sites/andrewdepietro/2021/11/26/us-poverty-rate-by-city-in-2021/.

Dixon, Ken. 2022. "Voting by Absentee Ballot in Connecticut Due to COVID to Be Allowable Under Legal Interpretation." *CT Insider*, June 2, 2022. https://www.ctinsider.com/news/article/Voting-by-absentee-ballot-in-Connecticut-due-to-17216164.php.

Frey, William. 2022. *Today's Suburbs are Symbolic of America's Rising Diversity: A 2020 Census Portrait*. Washington, DC: The Brookings Institution. https://www.brookings.edu/research/todays-suburbs-are-symbolic-of-americas-rising-diversity-a-2020-census-portrait/.

Haar, Dan. 2023. "$37M in Public Cash for Governor Race? Could Happen." *CT Insider*. January 20, 2023. https://www.ctinsider.com/politics/article/public-financing-governor-lamont-17730019.php.

Haigh, Susan. 2022. "Connecticut Abortion Law, Tax Changes to Take Effect Friday." *Associated Press*. June 30, 2022. https://apnews.com/article/abortion-health-connecticut-ned-lamont-28b925f3034db1d966b907cc22c17cfd.

Hamilton, Elizabeth. 2006. "A Vow to Stay in the Race." *Hartford Courant*. July 14, 2006. https://www.courant.com/2006/07/14/a-vow-to-stay-in-the-race/.

Janicki, Mary M. 2001. *Legislative History of Challenge Primary Law*. Office of Legislative Research, General Assembly of the State of Connecticut. https://www.cga.ct.gov/2001/rpt/2001-R-0953.htm.

Janicki, Mary M. 2008. *Unaffiliated Voters Allowed to Vote in Primaries*. Office of Legislative Research, General Assembly of the State of Connecticut. https://www.cga.ct.gov/2008/rpt/2008-R-0177.htm.

Katz, Bruce. 2001. "Escape from Connecticut's Cities." Brookings Institute. April 8, 2001. https://www.brookings.edu/opinions/escape-from-connecticuts-cities/.

Lacy, Karyn. 2022. "How Democrats and Republicans Could Be Getting the Suburbs Wrong." NBC News THINK. November 4, 2022. https://www.nbcnews.com/think/opinion/election-2022-democrats-republicans-suburban-voters-wrong-rcna55669.

Lightman, David. 2006. "Senate Rivals Spent Lavishly; $37 Million Breaks Statewide Records." *The Hartford Courant*. December 16, 2006. Section A, Page 2.

Madden, Richard L. 1979. "A Senator and His Party Boss at Loggerheads in Connecticut." *New York Times (1923-)*, February 18, 1979. https://www.nytimes.com/1979/02/18/archives/a-senator-and-his-party-boss-at-loggerheads-in-connecticut.html.

Malone, Julia. 1981. "Senator Weicker: GOP Liberal Who Swims Energetically Against the Tide." *The Christian Science Monitor*, July 2, 1981. https://www.csmonitor.com/1981/0702/070243.html.

McKee, Clyde D. and Petterson, Paul. 1997. "Connecticut: Party Politics as a Steady Habit." In *Parties & Politics in the New England States*, edited by Jerome M. Mileur. Amherst, Mass: Polity Publishing.

McQuaid, Hugh. 2022. "Lamont's Emergency Powers Have Officially Expired." *CTNewsJunkie.com*. February 15, 2022. https://ctnewsjunkie.com/2022/02/15/lamonts-emergency-powers-have-officially-expired/.

Newman, Benjamin J., and Todd K. Hartman. 2019. "Mass Shootings and Public Support for Gun Control." *British Journal of Political Science* 49 (4) (Oct): 1527–1553.

NORC/AP VoteCast Survey. 2022. "Fox News Voter Analysis: Connecticut." https://www.foxnews.com/elections/2022/midterm-results/voter-analysis?year=2022&state=CT. Survey done October 31 to November 8, 2022 with 1873 randomly selected voters. Margin of error +/-2.3%.

Pazniokas, Mark. 2023. "CT Public Financing Faces a Reckoning in Self-Funders Era." *CT Mirror*. January 13, 2023. https://ctmirror.org/2023/01/13/ct-public-financing-campaign-lamont-stefanowski-governors-race/.

Powell, Chris. 2021. "The Sorry State of Two Connecticuts." *The Day*. October 9, 2021. https://www.theday.com/columnists/20211009/the-sorry-state-of-two-connecticuts/.

Quinnipiac University Poll. 2006a. "Lamont Gains on Lieberman Among Connecticut Dems, Quinnipiac University Poll Finds; Rell Rules in Governor's Race." June 8, 2006. https://poll.qu.edu/Poll-Release-Legacy?releaseid=922.

Quinnipiac University Poll. 2006b. "Lieberman Leads Among Likely Connecticut Voters, Quinnipiac University Poll Finds; Strong Democratic Boost Gives Rell 2 -1 Lead." August 17, 2006. https://poll.qu.edu/Poll-Release-Legacy?releaseid=948.

Quinnipiac University Poll. 2006c. "Lieberman Has 12-Point Lead in Connecticut, Quinnipiac University Poll Finds; Rell Is Up By 24 Points with Six Days to Go." November 1, 2006. https://poll.qu.edu/Poll-Release-Legacy?releaseid=978.

Quinnipiac University Poll. 2008a. "Connecticut Voters Are Down, But Still Like Gov. Rell, Quinnipiac University Poll Finds; Mortgage Scandal Takes Small Toll on Sen. Dodd." July 1, 2008. https://poll.qu.edu/Poll-Release-Legacy?releaseid=1189.

Quinnipiac University Poll. 2010b. "McMahon Chops Blumenthal Lead to 10 Pts in Senate Race, Quinnipiac University Connecticut Poll Finds; Simmons Gains Ground on McMahon." August 4, 2010. https://poll.qu.edu/Poll-Release-Legacy?releaseid=1484.

Quinnipiac University Poll. 2014a. "Budget, Taxes Hurt Connecticut Gov, Quinnipiac University Poll Finds; Foley Ties Malloy, Has Big Lead in Republican Field." May 9, 2014 . https://poll.qu.edu/Poll-Release-Legacy?releaseid=2039.

Quinnipiac University Poll. 2014b. "Malloy 47%, Foley 44% in 2-Way Connecticut Gov Race, Quinnipiac University Poll Finds." November 3, 2014. https://poll.qu.edu/Poll-Release-Legacy?releaseid=2108.

Quinnipiac University Poll. 2022a. "Lamont Up By 15 Points in Connecticut Governor's Race, Quinnipiac University Connecticut Poll Finds; Blumenthal Up By 15 Points in Senate Race." October 24, 2022. https://poll.qu.edu/poll-release?releaseid=3860.

Quinnipiac University Poll. 2022b. "Lamont Has 8-Point Lead in Connecticut Governor Race, Quinnipiac University Poll Finds; 58% Say They Are Worse Off Financially Than A Year Quinnipiac Ago." May 26, 2022. https://poll.qu.edu/poll-release?releaseid=3847.

Radley, David C., Jesse Baumgartner, and Sara R. Collins. 2022. "2022 Scorecard on State Health System Performance: How Did States Do During the COVID-19 Pandemic?" Commonwealth Fund. June 16, 2022. https://www.commonwealthfund.org/publications/scorecard/2022/jun/2022-scorecard-state-health-system-performance.

Rose, Gary L. 2007. *Connecticut Government and Politics: An Introduction*. Fairfield, Connecticut: Sacred Heart University Press.

State of Connecticut, Office of the Secretary of the State. "Election Results Archive." https://portal.ct.gov/SOTS/Election-Services/Election-Results/Election-Results-Archive.

State of Connecticut, Office of the Secretary of State. *Party Enrollment in Connecticut*. https://portal.ct.gov/SOTS/Election-Services/Statistics-and-Data/Statistics-and-Data.

Texiera, Ruy. 2022. '*The Democrats' Tenuous Hold on the Suburbs*. American Enterprise Institute. December 9, 2022. https://www.aei.org/op-eds/the-democrats-tenuous-hold-on-the-suburbs/.

U.S. Census. 2022. "QuickFacts Connecticut." https://www.census.gov/quickfacts/CT.

World Population Review. 2024a. "Per Capita Income by State 2024." World Population Review. https://worldpopulationreview.com/state-rankings/per-capita-income-by-state.

World Population Review. 2024b. "Poverty Rate by State 2024." World Population Review. https://worldpopulationreview.com/state-rankings/poverty-rate-by-state.

CHAPTER 4

MAINE

Pushed From Away, The Pine Tree State Sways But Does Not Break

James P. Melcher and Amy Fried
Professor of Political Science | Professor of Political Science
University of Maine Farmington | The University of Maine

Before Mainers voted on expanding background checks for guns in 2016, opponents told them to take a stand against out-of-state proponents. One ad contended, "The New Yorkers are here and they're trying to tell Mainers how to live. NY billionaire Michael Bloomberg is spending $3 million to try and boss Mainers around with Question 3 this election" (National Rifle Association 2016a). And, as a sheriff in another ad put it, the measure was "pushed by a New York billionaire who does not care about Maine" (National Rifle Association 2016b). That message, and others about Maine's low crime rate as well as the initiative's impacts on law-abiding gun owners, prevailed. After spending far more than background check proponents, gun control failed at the polls.

What happened in 2016 reveals much about Maine politics. First, the messaging against the gun measure evoked a cultural tendency, a suspicion toward others "from away"—that is, from anyplace other than Maine.[1] Indeed, whether regarding its political culture or rural heritage, Maine often seems a place apart that wants to stay apart. As we will argue, Maine politics is indeed still different from national politics in its emphasis on independence, civility, and localism, even as it contends with extensive spending from out of state as well as negative politics.

Second, the gun vote demonstrated the state's key regional splits. Background checks were supported in only three of Maine's sixteen counties,

---

[1] While Mainers talk negatively at times in many contexts about people "from away," there is little evidence that Maine voters usually hold this against candidates–though with politicians they had other reasons to dislike, this could be the "cherry on the top" to highlight their dislike (Melcher 2005). Candidates may emphasize their own Maine native bona fides as a contrast to candidates from away, as Susan Collins did in her 2020 campaign against Sarah Gideon (Brewer 2020). According to the 2023 American Community Survey, compared to other states in New England, Maine has the highest percentage of its population born in-state and the highest that are U.S.-born, with the lowest percentage foreign-born.

with the strongest backing—64 percent—in Cumberland County, the location of Portland—Maine's largest city. This illustrated the pattern of urban-rural schisms in the state, which is also reflected in increasing divisions between Maine's two congressional districts.

Third, the state cannot be easily characterized ideologically. During the 2010 Tea Party red wave, Republican Paul LePage won the governorship and his party captured both chambers of the state legislature. In 2014 LePage was re-elected as Mainers voted against rules that would have limited bear hunting. LePage's victories and the state's support for hunting and gun use make Maine look at least potentially conservative. However, when rejecting gun background checks in 2016, Mainers also voted in favor of policies associated with liberalism—marijuana legalization, ranked choice voting, increased funding for education, and a higher minimum wage. Moreover, Democratic presidential candidate Hillary Clinton won statewide, like every Democratic nominee since Bill Clinton's victory in 1992.

Maine was not always this "purple" or unpredictable. Like the other northern New England states, Maine was one of the most solidly Republican states from the Civil War until the mid-twentieth century. From 1856 through 1960, Maine voted for the Democratic candidate only once–in 1912, when William Howard Taft and Theodore Roosevelt split the Republican vote and Woodrow Wilson won with 39 percent of the vote. Republican dominance came into its sharpest relief in 1936, when Maine and Vermont were the only states backing Alf Landon over Franklin Roosevelt. This led to the famous joke by FDR's campaign manager James Farley; playing off the old saying "As Maine goes, so goes the nation," he quipped, "As Maine goes, so goes Vermont" (Hier 2019). Much of the credit of building Maine into a two-party state goes to Democrat Ed Muskie, who helped build party organization and served as governor and US Senator (Rooks 2018).

Maine's demographics have also changed. Maine is, per the 2020 Census, the whitest state, but this situation is not so simple. Maine's population is becoming more diverse (Casey 2021). Immigration to Maine is becoming more common, and while the single largest source of Maine immigrants is still Canada (American Immigration Council 2020), immigrants from Africa and the Middle East have become more significant in the last two decades. Portland has gained a reputation for welcoming immigrants, many from Haiti and Africa, so much so that it is having challenges housing new arrivals (Struck 2022). In Lewiston, the second largest city in Maine, immigrants—many from Somalia and Iraq—now account for 16 percent of the population (Skelton 2021). Their initial arrival sparked both xenophobia and welcome. Yet, by 2022, Maine elected its first two Somali women to the Maine House (one of whom was previously elected mayor of South Portland) (Snider 2022) and elected a Black woman Speaker for the first time (Major 2022).

Not all white people in Maine have always been "Yankees," either. Franco-Americans—many of whom came to Maine in the nineteenth century from Quebec—were not always welcome, with bigotry aimed at their Catholicism and language. The rise of the Ku Klux Klan in Maine in the 1920s was largely a negative response to Franco-American in-migration (Richard 2009). The state enacted the English Education Bill into law in 1919, which barred the use of the French language in Maine schools until its repeal in the 1960s (Smart-Pelletier 2021). In 2010 Paul LePage became the first Franco-American elected governor (LaFlamme 2011).

And of course, long before there were Yankees, there were Native Americans in Maine and many of their descendants still reside in the Pine Tree State. The state has had political tensions with native tribes for decades. Governor Janet Mills earned praise from tribal leaders for signing into law a state ban on school use of Native American mascots and nicknames, renaming Columbus Day "Indigenous Peoples' Day," and giving tribes control over mobile sports betting. But Native American leaders have also been critical of other Mills' policies and that of her predecessors (Acquisto 2019; Russell 2022).

Key Cultural and Institutional Contexts

Maine has long been a paragon of Daniel Elazar's moralistic political culture, which features high civic engagement, low corruption in government, and a premium placed on offering solutions to political problems over partisan politics (Elazar 1984; Palmer et al., 2009, 7–22). Maine's state motto is "Dirigo"— meaning "I lead" or "I direct." As we discuss below, Mainers like to think of their state as showing this trait in national and state politics—particularly in its propensity to value leaders who govern with civility. Mainers show an independent streak, with high rates of ticket-splitting and, as we have already shown, casting votes on initiatives on the same ballot that are not all liberal or conservative. While bristling about outsiders—people from away—trying to change the state and its policies, Mainers participate politically in high numbers, embrace reforms designers say will enhance voter engagement and elected officials' autonomous judgment, and safeguard local control.

CIVILITY, LEADERSHIP, AND INDEPENDENCE

Maine's model for thoughtful, pragmatic leadership is particularly true of its senators, who have garnered favorable reviews nationally for combining competence, pragmatism, and independence. Margaret Chase Smith, Ed Muskie, Bill Cohen, George Mitchell, Olympia Snowe, and Angus King are strong examples; Susan Collins somewhat less so, particularly as she navigated the Trump years. Smith remains revered as a leader who took on Senator Joseph McCarthy. With few exceptions (most notably the confrontational leadership style of Governor Paul LePage), state-level political leadership is also oriented toward governing with civility.

Maine voters are well-known for their high voter turnout. Since adopting same-day voter registration in 1973, Maine has perennially been in the top ten states in the nation in turnout for president, with comparable figures in other elections as well (Maine: An Encyclopedia, n.d.). This is particularly astonishing given that Maine is rarely treated like a battleground state with advertising and massive party-backed get out the vote efforts. In 2020, Maine's turnout rate of 76.3 percent trailed only Minnesota and Colorado (Statista 2020). And in 2022–with no US Senate race on the ballot–Maine's turnout rate of 60.9 percent only trailed Minnesota's 61.6 percent (Meyers 2022).

Maine voters' independence can be seen in their rates of ticket-splitting and in their voter registrations. Since World War II, when Democrats in Maine came back from political oblivion, Mainers are apt to split their ticket. Ticket-splitting "was nowhere, outside the South, higher than in Maine in the decade 1948–58. The most dramatic instance occurred in 1954 when Democrat Edmund Muskie caused a sensation by wresting the governorship from the hitherto dominant Republicans" but Democratic presidential candidate Adlai Stevenson lost the state by forty points (Merwin 1973, 308–9)

Just as high turnout in Maine is supported by laws that make it easy for voters to register and vote, ticket-splitting was accelerated by the repeal of the "big box" ballot, which allowed voters to cast straight tickets by checking a "big box" at the top. Its repeal too encouraged voting for Independent candidates (Caron 2012). It is not a coincidence that Maine elected an Independent candidate for governor, James Longley, in the first election after the big box was eliminated.[2] The next Independent to serve as governor, Angus King,

---

[2] Governor Ken Curtis argued that Republicans worked to eliminate the big box in order to prevent Democrat George Mitchell from being elected Governor in 1974, out of fear that voters would use it to vote straight Democratic in re-electing popular Democratic Senator Ed Muskie. If that was their goal, it worked; while Muskie won, so did Independent Governor candidate James Longley (L'Hommedieu 2010).

enjoyed a long career. He was elected governor in 1994 and re-elected in a landslide in 1998. King won the 2012 election for US Senate and was re-elected in 2018, garnering a large margin.

These are far from the only cases of ticket-splitting in modern Maine politics. In 2020 Republican Susan Collins was the only Senate candidate to carry a state where their party's presidential candidate did not get the most votes (Rakich and Best 2020). Maine voters also did not follow their state's presidential vote in voting for Republicans Olympia Snowe in 2000, Collins in 1996, 2008, and 2020, and Independent King in 2008.

Consider this story about campaign signs as recounted by Shankman in 2020:

> Life-long Republican K.C. Hughes was heading out to the mailbox at his home in Cumberland, Maine, about a week before the election when his neighbor called out a question. Near Hughes' mailbox was a campaign sign for Susan Collins, the Republican U.S. Senate candidate, and another one for Democrat Joe Biden for president. "Who put that sign there?" Hughes said the neighbor asked, gesturing to the Biden sign, as if it had landed on there through some act of subterfuge. "I did!" replied Hughes.

The following week Hughes, and voters statewide, did in fact, select Collins and Biden. But, "[i]n Maine's conservative second district, voters split the ticket a different way, voting to re-elect President Donald Trump and Congressman Jared Golden, a Democrat" (Shankman 2020).

In addition to King and other Independent and third-party candidates who ran in gubernatorial elections over the past quarter century, candidates from outside the two major parties have been elected to lower levels of office. Portland had a significant degree of Green Party organization since the early 2000s, including winning municipal races and electing the second Green in the United States to a state legislature (Quinlan 2016). The Maine Legislature also had multiple Independents of a variety of ideologies over the past twenty-five years—thirty-eight in the House and five in the Senate.

Maine voters' friendliness toward Independents extends to third-party presidential candidates as well. Ross Perot finished second in Maine in 1992—one of only two states where he did so. But Perot was not alone. Third-party candidates John Anderson in 1980, Perot in 1996, Ralph Nader in 2000, and Gary Johnson in 2016 all ran substantially better in Maine than nationally (Leip 2023).

Mainers are politically independent in their own self-declarations as well. Voters who chose not to register with a political party outnumbered Democrats and Republicans from the late 1970s until 2020, when the Democrats barely took the top spot (Thistle 2020). Maisel and Ivry accurately summarize that "Maine stands as a competitive two-party state with what is perhaps the nation's strongest non-major party tradition" (1997, 6).

Maine's political culture of high voter participation and civic engagement is supported by and seen in the processes the state has chosen. Initiatives provide a way to vote on policies. Besides its use of mechanisms that enable high turnout and ticket-splitting, Maine has adopted a slew of reforms that, taken together, set it apart from other states in its willingness to experiment politically with processes that provide new choices for voters and check the power of elected officials. It is to those we turn next.

VOTING ON POLICIES AND CAMPAIGN REFORMS

When it comes to laws affecting elections, Maine is a habitual experimenter. Among Maine's electoral reforms, the state is perhaps best known for its adoption of the district plan for allocating presidential electors—the legislature passed this into law in 1969 without Governor Ken Curtis's signature (who thought the plan was a step in the right direction, but too weak). This plan gives two electoral votes to the winner of the popular vote in the state as a whole and one each to the winners of each congressional district. Only Nebraska has followed Maine's lead in doing so (Melcher 2010).

While Maine's district plan passed as conventional legislation, its election practices and other laws have also been greatly shaped by initiatives. Maine and Massachusetts are the only New England states with statewide initiative votes (NCSL 2022). Initiatives allow voters to put legislation on the ballot to be enacted into law if they get a minimum number of signatures (in Maine, a minimum of 10 percent of the previous vote for governor). As a result of the intensive efforts of newspaper editor and public utilities advocate Roland T. Patten, in 1908 Maine became the first state east of the Mississippi River to establish initiatives (IRI 2022) and is one of only six states east of the Mississippi to have them (Initiative and Referendum Institute, n.d.) Over the past thirty years, Maine voters have had seventy-three chances to vote on initiatives with nearly half (36) coming since 1998 (Maine Legislature 2022).

Initiatives can be mechanisms for grassroots organizations and voters to be the prime movers for policy adoption. On the other hand, deep-pocketed groups can be the major sponsors of initiatives (Duquette and Cunningham 2022); as with the gun background check ballot question discussed at the start of the chapter. This outside funding can spark a backlash, especially in Maine where suspicion of people and groups "from away" runs deep, but it is not inevitable. Consider Maine's adoption of term limits, which were partly spurred by a national movement which had strong support in the early 1990s nationally; twenty-one states enacted term limits between 1990 and 2002 (Stein, Johnson, and Post 2002). Maine's effort was also driven by public reaction toward state legislative leaders, especially the long-serving, powerful House Speaker John Martin, whose power term-limits advocates felt needed to be curbed (Diamon 2018). Like all states except Utah adopting term limits in this era, they were enacted in Maine (in 1993) in an initiative, with backing from the national group U.S. Term Limits (Stein, Johnson and Post 2002; Moen, Palmer and Powell, 2005; Rooks 2014). Maine governors are also term-limited. While there have been legislative efforts to modify or end term limits, these have been unsuccessful. We conjecture this is because Maine voters didn't see the policy as being set "from away" and term limits are viewed as enhancing new streams of leaders from the citizenry. As such, it is consistent with Maine's political culture.

Another election reform passed via initiatives—ranked choice voting (RCV) was in part spurred by a reaction to LePage winning the governorship in 2010 with under 40 percent of the vote, and in part by state and national election reformers, although attempts to adopt it in Maine date back to 2001 (Armstrong 2019). RCV is a system that enables voters to rank their choices; if no candidate wins a majority, a series of tallies will follow that redistribute the choices of the lowest ranked voter choices until one wins a majority. Cities such as San Francisco and Minneapolis use RCV at the local level, but Maine stands out as the first state to enact RCV for statewide elections (Stid, Born and Armstrong 2019). As of 2022, only Alaska has joined them (Radde 2022). Massachusetts rejected this change in 2020 (Clark 2021).

The first RCV initiative passed in 2016. The Maine Supreme Judicial Court then muted its impact, holding that RCV in general elections for governor and state legislature violated the Maine Constitution (Thistle 2017). After the state legislature acted slowly to implement it, advocates qualified another initiative for June 2018 and RCV passed again. RCV applies to races for Congress, state legislative primaries and, beginning in 2020, presidential elections (Sharp 2020) and its use in the 2018 ME-2 election sparked some controversy.[3] These initiatives passed with extensive help from Fair Vote

---

[3] RCV played a critical role in the Second District in 2018 and 2022. In the 2018 race in ME-2, Bruce Poliquin initially had a plurality but lost to Jared Golden after lower place candidates' votes were tallied. Poliquin brought a federal lawsuit but lost. In a sign of how much Maine Republicans strongly disliked ranked choice voting, Gov. LePage wrote "stolen election" on the certification document (Thistle 2018). In 2022, Golden led both in the initial count and after the ranked choice tally. Regarding local implementation, see Anthony, Fried, Glover, and Kimball (2021).

USA, with support from the Maine League of Women Voters and other state groups (Armstrong 2019).

Maine's Clean Elections policy, a public financing scheme adopted in 2000, also reflects Mainers' willingness to enact campaign reforms through initiatives. Candidates for governor and the state legislature have the chance to run for office with public money funded from a tax checkoff program similar to that for presidential elections on federal tax forms. Candidates qualify by raising a set number of $5 donations from the areas they seek to represent and then cannot accept any other campaign donations.

Supporters had high hopes for this initiative: that clean elections would remove candidate dependence on private donations, eliminate the sway of "big money" over candidates, free candidates from fundraising, make elections more competitive, expand the candidate pool to include individuals not connected to big money, and produce more contested races (Campion 1998). But hope is not always rewarded. On the positive side for initiative advocates, 55 percent of all Maine legislative candidates were publicly financed (ran "clean") (Maine Citizens for Clean Elections 2021, 7). But some races still see large amounts of money spent in the form of independent expenditures and leadership PACs.[4]

Mainers are quite concerned about out-of-state support for initiatives, in part because Maine is inexpensive to "play in," meaning that with relatively little money compared to other states, outsiders can have an outsized voice in issue campaigns. However, Mainers push back against external actors. The 2014 initiative to restrict bear hunting is instructive. The idea was opposed by Governor LePage and most of the legislature, but got on the ballot after an estimated 200 signature gatherers hired by a California consulting firm helped meet the signature requirements (Holyoke 2014). Backlash was swift— David Trahan, head of the Maine Sportsmen's Alliance called the practice of groups paying signature gatherers "buying our referendum process" (*Kennebec Journal/Morning Sentinel Editorial Board* 2015). Another dramatic example of out-of-state money connected to this initiative was the distribution of donations to the pro-hunting restrictions campaign. A month before the election Mainers had donated only 1 percent of the funds for hunting limitations

---

[4] Scholars differ on whether publicly financed campaigns garner greater competitiveness, with some arguing they have (Malhotra 2008), or at least have made primaries more competitive (Brogan and Mendilow 2012), and others arguing there is little evidence that they have had much effect on competitiveness (Powell 2012). Clean elections have increased the number of challengers (Mancinelli 2022) and may have a small effect in encouraging more women to run (Wiltse 2018).

initiative proponents Mainers for Fair Bear Hunting, as opposed to 47 percent of funds for the opposition (Fleming 2014). The 2016 background check proposal, and 2021 campaign to block the New England Clean Energy Connect project, also spurred a backlash when Maine voters perceived that people from away—New York and Quebec—used their money to get Maine to do what outsiders wanted. In both cases, the backlash against money "from away" helped lead to these initiatives being defeated.

The "people's veto" is another type of statewide vote on issues. In other states with similar opportunities, it is most commonly called a "veto referendum" (Rogers 2017). Maine's people's veto allows the public to petition to block implementing a new law until a statewide vote is held. If the public votes to veto the new bill, it is rescinded. From 1998 through 2022, Maine had seven people's veto votes. Five of the seven vetoes passed, reversing laws that financed health care with a new tax (2009); enabled gay men and lesbians to marry (2009);[5] lowered income taxes while raising sales taxes (2010); ended same-day voter registration (2011); and delayed the start of RCV (2018). However, 2005 voters decided to keep a law that prohibited discrimination against LGBTQ+ people and, in 2020, retained a law that made it harder for K-12 students to avoid vaccinations (Maine State Legislature Legislative History Collection 2022).

Since 1990, Maine has held more statewide bond referenda than any other state. That is mainly because Maine has the lowest borrowing amount in the nation requiring voter approval. What's more, that low limit has not been raised since 1951. In most cases, these elections do not attract a lot of attention, and there usually is little or no organized opposition to the bonds. In the past twenty-five years, the overwhelming majority of them passed (Melcher 2016, 2019).

As we have shown, Mainers have a variety of mechanisms for adopting or blocking policies at the ballot box. In using them, Maine people have demonstrated active civic participation and an interest in reforms designed to enhance citizen power over elected officials and policy; these fit with and reinforce the state's political culture. When initiatives are seen as largely generated "from away," Mainers tend to reject them. This tendency to support Maine-based autonomy is also seen in the state's emphasis on local control, to which we turn next.

---

[5] In 2012, Mainers adopted same-sex marriage through an initiative, three years before the Supreme Court ruled this was a national right.

LOCAL GOVERNMENT AND LOCAL CONTROL

New England is known for its emphasis on local control dating back to colonial times, and Maine is no exception (Kodrzycki 2013). As of 2020, at least 350 of Maine's 487 municipalities still hold annual town meetings in which all town citizens can vote to enact their budgets and other key issues (Kramlich 2020). Throughout New England, county government is relatively weak compared to other parts of the country (Palmer et al. 2009, 216). At an extreme, Connecticut entirely eliminated county government in 1959 (Watson 1998). And like other New England states, but unlike much of the rest of the nation, Maine does not operate a system of county highways. Nor does it have strong county executive leadership. But Maine counties still do perform some functions, perhaps most notably in law enforcement, corrections and the legal system (Palmer et al. 2009, 217.) One other facet of local government in which Maine is distinctive is that Maine has an enormous area of unorganized territory where there is no government below the county level. It is the only state in New England that has them (Ivy 2022a), and they include only about 9,000 year-round residents—while covering just over half of the land area of the state.

Maine also is the only state remaining with plantations as a form of government, a holdover from Maine's pre-1820 days as a part of Massachusetts. When new settlements began, settlers "planted." Massachusetts established them as plantations, giving plantations limited local government but with less power than a town. The expectation was that plantations would eventually grow enough to be chartered as towns; they did in Massachusetts, but in Maine many did not. Other than Monhegan and Matinicus Islands, plantations were and are rural, generally heavily forested places with a small population and a strong local identity, such as The Forks (Ivy 2022b; Roberts 1979, 20–21).

Maine's reliance on local control reflects a commitment to self-government and representation. The closeness of representatives to those they represent extends to the State House where a few people are represented by each state legislator in Maine. As of 2020, Maine House members represent just over 9,000 constituents, making door-to-door campaigning common (Ballotpedia 2023).

Localism brings with it financial costs due to regional inefficiencies and duplication. These realities complicated Maine's commitment to local control. School districts provide a representative example. Democratic Governor John Baldacci tried to consolidate Maine school districts in hopes of cutting costs.

His Republican successor Paul LePage also made consolidation of school districts a priority, even through his 2022 run for governor (Shepherd 2022). These efforts faced strong resistance though (Goldthwait 2017) as numerous towns have withdrawn from the new consolidated districts in order to return to more local control (Feinberg 2017). This resistance shows that the desire for local control in Maine is still very much alive, and that many towns will push back against efforts to change it.

Thus, while aspects of Maine's political culture—its prizing of autonomy and citizen power—support localist institutional arrangements, other dynamics—including its pragmatism—propel efforts to shift power away from municipalities. Maine's political culture retains its influence over time, but it is not without its contradictions and cross-pressures. We next turn to discussing transformations and continuities in Maine electoral politics and ways in which Maine elected officials embrace or reject Maine's political culture.

Elections and Political Leadership in the Last Quarter Century

One way to understand elections in Maine is simply to look at which party has tended to win. We discuss these partisan trends below and then turn to examining how state-level politics relates to Maine's political culture. In the last quarter century, Maine's voting patterns show its turn away from past Republican dominance, with Democratic monopolies in presidential races statewide. In that time period, Republicans had a majority in the state senate just once. Results for other offices have been more mixed, as seen in Table 4.1.

By 2022, New England's congressional delegation included only one Republican—Sen. Susan Collins. However, from 2000–2022, Collins and her fellow Republican Olympia Snowe won six of Maine's eight US Senate races, with Independent Angus King, who caucuses with Democrats winning the other two. The personal reputations of these Republicans, along with their relative centrism and ability to bring home the bacon, kept them in good stead. Still, both faced some political headwinds. Snowe's decision not to seek re-election in 2012 occurred after numerous Republicans were unhappy with her moderate votes. Collins's general election vote share fell from 68 percent in 2014 to 51 percent in 2020, largely because many of her more liberal and moderate supporters objected to her support for Supreme Court nominee Brett Kavanaugh and other Trump policies and felt that she should have done more to offer resistance to President Trump. Nonetheless,

Table 4.1 Partisan Affiliation of Maine Election Winners, 1998–2022

YEAR	PRESIDENT (STATEWIDE)+	US SENATE	ME-1	ME-2	GOVERNOR	STATE SENATE	STATE HOUSE
1998			Allen (D)	Baldacci (D)	King (I)	Dem	Dem
2000	Gore (D)	Snowe (R)	Allen (D)	Baldacci (D)		Tie++	Dem
2002		Collins (R)	Allen (D)	Michaud (D)	Baldacci (D)	Dem	Dem
2004	Kerry (D)		Allen (D)	Michaud (D)		Dem	Dem
2006		Snowe (R)	Allen (D)	Michaud (D)	Baldacci (D)	Dem	Dem
2008	Obama (D)	Collins (R)	Pingree (D)	Michaud (D)		Dem	Dem
2010			Pingree (D)	Michaud (D)	LePage (R)	GOP	GOP
2012	Obama (D)	King (I)	Pingree (D)	Michaud (D)		Dem	Dem
2014		Collins (R)	Pingree (D)	Poliquin (R)	LePage (R)	GOP	Dem
2016	Clinton (D)		Pingree (D)	Poliquin (R)		GOP	Dem
2018		King (I)	Pingree (D)	Golden (D)	Mills (D)	Dem	Dem
2020	Biden (D)	Collins (R)	Pingree (D)	Golden (D)		Dem	Dem
2022			Pingree (D)	Golden (D)	Mills (D)	Dem	Dem

+ In every year but 2016 and 2020, the statewide presidential winner also won both congressional districts, garnering all four of Maine's electoral votes. In 2016 and 2020, the Democratic candidates, Hillary Clinton and Joe Biden, won statewide as well as the First Congressional District, winning three of the four electoral votes while Republican candidate Donald Trump won one electoral vote because he carried the Second Congressional District.

++ In the 2000 races for the Maine State Senate, Democrats and Republicans won 17 seats each and an Independent won one seat.

Sources: Maine Legislature (Senate and House), Ballotpedia; Other races, Maine Secretary of State.

the ability of both Snowe and Collins to serve so long—and to win consistently as Mainers simultaneously voted Democratic in in presidential contests—shows that moderate Republicans can win statewide, even as the top of their ticket does not.

But some national trends and forces have reached Maine. Out-of-state money puts Maine increasingly under the influence of national money and politics. For example, the notion that such a small state would have the second most expensive US Senate race in 2020 (Miller 2020), funded well over 85 percent by out-of-state donors a month before the election (Piper 2020), would have stunned Margaret Chase Smith. When Smith ran for the Republican nomination for president in 1964, "anyone who sent her money soon received their donation back with a kind note that she simply could not accept it" (Gutgold 2006).[6] Suspicion toward those from away runs deep but today's Maine cannot always prevent their electoral influence.

Maine's US House elections from 1998–2022 reflect the different nature of the two congressional districts. ME-1, which is more urban, educated, and with higher income individuals, voted Democratic every cycle. ME-2 is the largest geographic district east of the Mississippi River and, because rural areas are growing slower than urban areas, has become larger in land area over time. This more rural district, has been more competitive than ME-1, electing moderate Democrats John Baldacci, Mike Michaud, and Jared Golden, as well as establishment Republican Bruce Poliquin. These districts map, largely but imperfectly, onto what Dick Barringer has called the "Two Maines." This is "the divide between the fairly prosperous counties along the southern Maine coast that experience much in-migration from southern New England, and the state's northern and eastern counties that were noticeably less well off" (Mitchell, 2014).

The differences between these congressional districts are real and increasing. Hypothetically these divergences could matter because since 1972, electoral votes can be divided in Maine. But it wasn't until 2016 (and then 2020) that the two districts actually split their presidential vote, with Donald Trump winning ME-2 while losing ME-1 and statewide. Trump thus won one of Maine's four electoral votes in each contest. This geographic schism is also be seen in initiative tallies and people's vetoes—particularly on cultural issues involving hunting, gun rights, and LGBTQ+ rights (Melcher and Fried 2022).

---

[6] Out-of-state money has also been reaching down to state legislative races. One Maine state senate race in 2022 (involving Senate President Troy Jackson) cost over $1 million, attracting much money from away (Molmud 2022).

Besides who wins, another way to think about Maine's choices of elected officials is through the lens of political culture. Maine elected officials have frequently emphasized some key aspects of Maine's political culture, particularly commitments to working with others with civility and toward shared, pragmatic ends.

Consider Maine's governors, a varied ideological bunch. From 1998–2022, there have been seven gubernatorial elections. These involved the 1998 re-election of Independent Angus King with 59 percent of the vote, followed by Democrat John Baldacci and Republican Paul LePage (who both won two terms but never a majority of the vote). LePage's initial election in 2010 coincided with the rise of the Tea Party and national GOP wins. Independent Gov. King and Democrats Baldacci and Mills were center-left, while LePage was a conservative who focused on cutting regulations, social welfare programs and taxes, and raised false claims of election fraud.

Democrat Janet Mills' initial victory in 2018 occurred during a blue wave. She became the first woman governor of Maine and the first governor to win a first term majority of the vote since 1966. Mills won re-election with a 14 point margin in 2022 versus LePage, in an election mostly focused on the economy (particularly inflation) and abortion rights. The 2022 Maine GOP platform was aligned with national Republicanism, opposing same-sex marriage, abortion rights, and teaching about race, sex and gender in schools. In this issue environment, Mills' strong victory over former Governor LePage "included wins in sizable GOP-leaning communities like Brewer, Ellsworth, Gray, Winslow and Hampden. Each has more registered Republicans than Democrats" (Marino 2022).

Despite their truly varied ideological hues, nearly all Maine governors called for working across the aisle and touted Maine as superior at achieving it. In a 2010 radio address, John Baldacci said "As I look to Washington today and around the country to other states, Democrats and Republicans are unable to work together. In Maine, though, it's different" (Baldacci 2010). Commitments to shared governance and mutual respect were also key values expressed by Independent former Governor King and current Democratic Governor Mills. In endorsing Mills' re-election at Moderation Brewing (Bellavance 2022), King lauded Mills for "bipartisan, consensus-driven approach to governing, including her work to bring Democrats, Republicans, and Independents together to solve problems for Maine people," emphasizing that Mills "brings people together to solve problems without drama."

However, the fact that Maine gubernatorial elections commonly have

Independent or third-party candidates splitting the vote can open the door for a candidate who does not embrace Maine's commitments to civility and bipartisanship. Paul LePage provides a colorful example. He was elected twice with but a plurality of the vote by appealing to a loyal base of his party's voters to win. Governor LePage stood out for fighting with legislators of both parties. Known for his intemperate remarks, in 2015 LePage staged an event a reporter compared to "a surrealistic dream." Using props—a pink pig toy and a Christmas tree with pictures of legislators from both parties on it—LePage condemned the budget passed by both chambers. LePage also promised to take much legislative time by line-item vetoing hundreds of items to "show that for five months they wasted our time and this time I'm going to waste a little of their time" (Cousins 2015). Governor LePage vetoed "642 bills— far more than the previous 22 governors *combined*" (Rooks 2021, emphasis added). LePage broke with his own party over his plan to eliminate the state income tax. He also blocked Medicaid expansion, first through multiple vetoes and then by refusing to implement an initiative supported by 59 percent of voters. (Gov. Mills' first action in office was implementing that expansion.)

LePage's actions and statements were inconsistent with Maine's political culture and practices. At the same time, rhetorically embracing shared governance does not mean a lack of conflict between the governor and state legislature. Maine has sometimes experienced prominent intra-partisan tensions. Former Democratic Governor Baldacci and Mills are center-left Democrats who do not always agree with the Democrats controlling the state legislature. For example, in her first term Mills broke with Democrats over the latter's support for a sweeping tribal sovereignty bill. She also vetoed bills backing labor rights for farm workers, curbing prescription drug prices, and protecting employees using paid family leave.

In another pattern of conflictual politics, one chamber of Maine's state legislature was governed by Democrats, Republicans, and an Independent simultaneously. This took place during part of Gov. King's second term. A power-sharing arrangement between state Senate Democrats and Republicans resulted after the 2000 election yielded a partisan tie, along with an Independent, Jill Goldthwait. Instead of caucusing with one party, thus determining which party controlled the body, Goldthwait negotiated a plan with the chamber's leaders—Democrat Mike Michaud and Republican Rick Bennett; both centrists. Michaud and Bennett switched off as Senate President after a year and Goldthwait chaired the powerful Appropriations Committee. Michaud and Bennett "abandoned the traditional pre-session party caucuses, closed-door meetings typically designed to plot procedural and debate strategy. Instead, the two leaders gathered Senate committee leaders in both parties to discuss the day's pending legislative business." (Mistler 2013). However, Governor King, Sen. Goldthwait, and House Democrats were very bothered when the Senate leaders pushed their own budget plan in 2001, ignoring the lower chamber and the governor's work. The promise of shared governance arising from parties working together was not fulfilled.

Moreover, because Maine is one of the few states in the nation with two-year terms for its state Senate instead of four, its governors are more likely to deal with a very different Senate partway through their term. Voters can shift party control during the governor's term and, when it is also time to choose a governor, a swing in the public mood can lead to major turnover in state government. This occurred in the Tea Party election of 2010 when Republicans won what turned out to be a short-lived trifecta.

Clearly, a political culture that stresses civility, independence, and voter control has its limits. This extends to some key offices named in the Maine Constitution. Most states hold statewide elections for attorney general, secretary of state, state auditor, and state treasurer. Maine's Constitution gives this job for each to the state legislature—a key reason why party control of the legislature is so important in Maine. Maine is also one of only five states (including New Hampshire) that has no lieutenant governor. Instead, Maine (like New Hampshire) puts the president of the state Senate first in the line of succession to the governor (NLGA 2023). These arrangements speak to Maine's distinctiveness and its embrace of being a place apart.

Conclusion

Maine is not a monolith, nor is it without its contradictions. As seen in its initiative votes, which often show contrasts between rural and more populated areas, and in its increasing partisan division between its first and second congressional districts in presidential voting, the "two Maines" description is accurate.

Moreover, Maine's geographic divides matter politically. The Republican base is situated in the rural areas of the state; these have lost population relatively or are relatively slow-growing. The increasing share of Mainers living in urban and suburban places makes it harder for GOP candidates and easier for Democratic ones to win statewide. The suburbs—which Republicans Sen.

Susan Collins won in 2020 and former governor and gubernatorial candidate Paul LePage lost in 2022—will continue to be a key political battlefield.

Maine is still different from a lot of national political dynamics. With Mainers' independence in voting, its elections do not always follow national trends. The national trend toward rising straight ticket voting (Abramowitz and Webster 2016; Desilver 2022) has not overtaken Maine, which persists in ticket-splitting and voting for popular incumbents (Shankman 2020; Brewer 2020). While in 2022 Republicans did rather poorly in state races, they can look to voters' tendencies to split their tickets to give them hope for future contests.

However, the state is not unaffected by national political dynamics. The famed civility and pragmatism of Maine politics has declined to some extent. Governor Paul LePage clearly did not fit into that Maine pattern, and more recently some Maine Republicans have embraced the conspiracy theories and florid rhetoric of the party's Trump and post-Trump era. Moreover, Maine Republicans have been embracing right wing culture issues popular nationally, but the state is relatively secular, and the states' voters are pro-choice and back LGBTQ+ rights.

In some ways, Maine remains a place apart in politics. Its localism, small districts, independence, and relatively civil politics endure. But some national trends, such as big election spending from around the country and negative politics, are so powerful that they have challenged Maine's political culture and reached the Pine Tree State.

Works Cited

Abramowitz, Alan I., and Steven Webster. 2016. "The Rise of Negative Partisanship and the Nationalization of U.S. Elections in the 21st century." *Electoral Studies* 41: 12–22.

Acquisto, Alex. 2019. "Mills Signs Bill to Make Maine The First State to Ban Native American School Mascots." *Maine Public*. May 17, 2019. https://www.mainepublic.org/politics/2019-05-17/mills-signs-bill-to-make-maine-the-first-state-to-ban-native-american-school-mascots.

American Immigration Council. 2020. "Fact Sheet: Immigrants in Maine." https://www.americanimmigrationcouncil.org/research/immigrants-in-maine.

Anthony, Joseph, Amy Fried, Robert Glover, and David Kimball. 2021. "Ranked Choice Voting in Maine from the Perspective of Local Election Officials." *Election Law Journal* 20: 254–271.

Armstrong, Katherine J. 2019. "Ranked Choice Voting in Maine." Hewlett Foundation. https://hewlett.org/wp-content/uploads/2019/09/RCV-in-Maine-final-for-web-posting.pdf.

Baldacci, John E. 2010. "Governor John Baldacci's Weekly Radio Address: Bipartisanship and the Budget—Saturday." *Digital Maine*. https://digitalmaine.com/ogvn_audio/201/.

Ballotpedia. 2023. "Population Represented by State Legislators." https://ballotpedia.org/Population_represented_by_state_legislators.

Bellavance, Meaghan. 2022. "Sen. Angus King Endorses Gov. Janet Mills for Re-election." *News Center Maine*. May 17, 2019. https://www.newscentermaine.com/article/news/politics/maine-politics/angus-king-endorses-janet-mills-maine-governor-race/97-eaf06bec-86ec-4e0f-9345-10a7fa69a719.

Brewer, Mark. 2020. "The Political Survival of Susan Collins." Brookings Institution. December 12, 2020. https://www.brookings.edu/blog/fixgov/2020/12/22/the-political-survival-of-susan-collins/.

Brogan, Michael J., and Jonathan Mendilow. 2012. "Public Party Funding and Intraparty Competition: Clean Elections in Maine and Arizona," *International Journal of Humanities and Social Science* 2: 120–132.

Campion, Michael E. 1998. "The Maine Clean Election Act: The Future of Campaign Finance Reform." *Fordham Law Review* 66: 2391–2434.

Caron, Alan. 2012. "Alan Caron: Maine's Independence May Once Again Be a National Topic." *Portland Press Herald*. August 22, 2012. https://www.pressherald.com/2012/08/22/maines-independence-may-once-again-be-a-national-topic_2012-08-23/.

Casey, Michael. 2021. "Maine becomes more diverse but still whitest state in nation." *Associated Press*. August 12, 2021. https://apnews.com/article/maine-census-2020-8d72d29af8c5e528b4197634bbdda8c1.

Clark, Jesse. 2021. "The Effect of Ranked-Choice Voting in Maine." *MIT Election Data and Science Lab*. March 18, 2021. https://electionlab.mit.edu/articles/effect-ranked-choice-voting-maine.

Cousins, Christopher. 2015. "LePage Uses Christmas Tree, Rubber Pigs to Condemn Legislature's Budget." *Bangor Daily News*. June 17, 2015. https://www.bangordailynews.com/2015/06/17/news/lepage-uses-christmas-tree-rubber-pigs-in-latest-condemnation-of-legislatures-budget-bill/.

Desilver, Drew. 2022. "In 2022 Midterms, Nearly All Senate Election Results Again Matched States' Presidential Votes." *Pew Research Center*. December 8, 2022. https://www.pewresearch.org/fact-tank/2022/12/08/in-2022-midterms-nearly-all-senate-election-results-again-matched-states-presidential-votes/.

Diamon, Al. 2018. "Politics and Other Mistakes: It's Time to Term Out Term Limits." *Daily Bulldog*. April 18, 2018. https://dailybulldog.com/opinion/politics-other-mistakes-its-time-to-term-out-term-limits/.

Elazar, Daniel J. 1984. *American Federalism: A View from the States*, Third Edition. New York: Harper Collins.

Feinberg, Robbie. 2017. "10 Years Later, Maine Schools Still Wrestle with District Consolidation." *Maine Public*. September 22, 2017. https://www.mainepublic.org/maine/2017-09-22/10-years-later-maine-schools-still-wrestle-with-district-consolidation#stream/0.

Fleming, Deirdre. 2014. "Bear Debate Marked by Contrast in Funding." *Portland Press Herald*. November 3, 2014. https://www.pressherald.com/2014/10/19/bear-debate-marked-by-contrast-in-funding/.

Goldthwait, Jill. 2017. "LePage in Search of Legacy." *Mount Desert Islander*. April 28, 2017. https://www.mdislander.com/opinion/lepage-in-search-of-legacy/article_2724513b-43d4-5bca-89a3-b3589cbf57c0.html.

Gutgold, Nicola D. 2006. *Paving The Way for Madam President*. Lanham, Maryland: Lexington Books.

Hier, Curtis. 2019. "As Goes Maine, So Goes Vermont—and So Might Your State Go on

Education." *Washington Examiner*. November 7, 2019. https://www.washingtonexaminer.com/opinion/op-eds/as-goes-maine-so-goes-vermont-and-so-might-your-state-go-on-education.

Holyoke, John. 2014. "Signature-Gathering Tactics by Bear-Baiting Opponents Come under Fire." *Lewiston Sun Journal*. January 16, 2014. https://www.sunjournal.com/2014/01/16/signature-gathering-tactics-bear-baiting-opponents-come-fire/.

Initiative and Referendum Institute, University of Southern California (IRI). 2022. "Maine." http://www.iandrinstitute.org/states/state.cfm?id=10.

———. n.d. "Signature, Geographic Distribution and Single Subject (SS) Requirements for Initiative Petitions." http://www.iandrinstitute.org/docs/Almanac-Signature-and-SS-and-GD-Requirements.pdf.

Ivy, Herb ("The Captain"). 2022a. "How Remote Can You Get? Unorganized Territories in Maine." *WBLM-FM*. September 26, 2022. https://wblm.com/all-you-need-to-know-about-maines-remote-and-mysterious-unorganized-territories/.

———. 2022b. "What's The Deal with All The Plantations in Maine?" *WBLM-FM*. April 11, 2022. https://wblm.com/did-you-know-there-are-34-plantations-in-maine-but-its-not-what-you-think/.

Kennebec Journal/Waterville Morning Sentinel Editorial Board. 2015. "Our Opinion: Loophole opens citizen initiatives to outside sway." *Kennebec Journal* and *Waterville Morning Sentinel* (editorial). January 14, 2015. https://www.centralmaine.com/2015/01/14/loophole-opens-citizen-initiatives-to-outside-sway/.

Kodrzycki, Yolanda K. 2013. "The Quest for Cost-Efficient Local Government in New England: What Role for Regional Consolidation?" New England Public Policy Research Center Research Report 13–1. Federal Reserve Bank of Boston. https://www.bostonfed.org/publications/new-england-public-policy-center-research-report/2013/the-quest-for-cost-efficient-local-government-in-new-england-what-role-for-regional-consolidation.aspx.

Kramlich, Will. 2020. "Some Maine Towns Not Holding In-Person Annual Meetings." *Waterville Morning Sentinel*. June 12, 2020. https://www.centralmaine.com/2020/06/11/some-towns-not-holding-in-person-annual-meetings/.

L'Hommedieu, Andrea. 2010. "Interview with Ken Curtis by Andrea L'Hommedieu." George J. Mitchell Oral History Project. Bowdoin College. https://digitalcommons.bowdoin.edu/mitchelloralhistory/158/.

LaFlamme, Mark. 2011. "LePage Wows Franco Crowd in Lewiston." *Lewiston Sun Journal*. March 17, 2011. https://www.sunjournal.com/2011/03/17/lepage-wows-franco-crowd-lewiston/.

Leip, Dave. 2023. US Election Atlas. https://uselectionatlas.org/RESULTS/.

Maine Citizens for Clean Elections. 2021. "Money in Politics Project Report #17: Clean Election Participation Rates and Outcomes." https://www.mainecleanelections.org/sites/default/files/2021_May_Legislative%20Candidate%20MCEA%20Participation%20Analysis_V2.pdf.

Maine Legislature. 2022. "Votes on Maine Initiated Bills, 1911-." https://mainelegislature.org/doc/174.

Maine State Legislature Legislative History Collection. 2022. "Maine Laws Suspended by People's Veto." https://www.maine.gov/legis/lawlib/lldl/peoplesveto/index.html#:~:text=Maine%20Statutes%20on&text=Since%201909%2C%20the%20Maine%20State,%2C%202019%2C%20and%202020.

Maisel, L. Sandy, and Elizabeth J. Ivry. 1997. "If You Don't Like Your Politics, Wait a Minute: Party Politics in Maine at the Century's End." In *Parties & Politics in The New England States,* edited by Jerome M. Mileur, 15–36. Amherst, MA: Polity Press

Major, Derek. 2022. "Maine House of Representatives Elects First Black House Speaker Rachel Talbot Ross." *Black Enterprise*. December 11, 2022. https://www.blackenterprise.com/maine-house-of-representatives-elects-first-black-house-speaker-in-rachel-talbot-ross/.

Malhotra, Neil. 2008. "The Impact of Public Financing on Electoral Competition: Evidence from Arizona and Maine." *State Politics and Policy Quarterly* 8: 263–281.

Mancinelli, Abigail. 2022. "Does Public Financing Motivate Electoral Challengers?" *State Politics and Policy Quarterly* 22: 438–462.

Marino, David, Jr. 2022. "Maine Lawmakers Want Janet Mills to Govern like a Centrist in Her 2nd term." *Bangor Daily News*. December 12, 2022. https://www.bangordailynews.com/2022/12/12/politics/janet-mills-centrism-joam4ozkow/.

Melcher, James P. 2010. "Exploring the Difficulties of Electoral College Reform at the State Level: Maine and Nebraska Lead the Way." In *Electoral Reform: Challenges and Possibilities*, edited by Gary Bugh. Burlington, VT: Ashgate Publishing.

———. 2016. "What Bonds Hold? An Examination of Statewide Bond Referenda in Maine and Other States." *Maine Policy Review* 25: 53–62.

———. 2019. "Maine's 2018 Election: Bonds Continue to Hold." *Maine Policy Review* 28: 74–75.

Melcher, James P., and Amy Fried. "A State Divided: Maine and its Continued Electoral Vote Split." In *Presidential Swing States, Third Edition*, edited by David A. Schultz and Rafael Jacob, 163–192. Lanham, Maryland: Lexington Books, 2022.

Merwin, David. 1973. "Personality and Ticket Splitting in US Federal and Gubernatorial Elections." *Political Studies* 21: 306–310.

Meyers, David. 2022. "Which States Had the Highest Turnout in 2022?" *Fulcrum*. November 14, 2022. https://thefulcrum.us/voter-turnout-by-state-2022.

Miller, Kevin. 2020. "Collins-Gideon Contest Second Most Expensive Senate Race in U.S." *Portland Press Herald*. November 8, 2020. https://www.pressherald.com/2020/11/08/collins-gideon-contest-second-most-expensive-senate-race-in-u-s/.

Mistler, Steve. 2013. "Good Friends, Old Allies, Now Adversaries." *Portland Press Herald*. September 9, 2013. https://www.pressherald.com/2013/09/09/good-friends-old-allies-now-adversaries_2013-09-09/.

Mitchell, Elizabeth. 2014. "Productive Partisanship." In *Politics Then and Now, In Maine and the Nation: Conversations with the Sages*, edited by Richard Barringer and Kenneth Palmer, 60–70. Portland, ME: Muskie School of Public Service and the Osher Lifelong Learning Center, University of Southern Maine. http://muskie.usm.maine.edu/Publications/Politics-Then-and-Now-small.pdf.

Moen, Matthew C., Kenneth T. Palmer, and Richard J. Powell. 2005. *Changing Members: The Maine Legislature in the Era of Term Limits*. Lanham, Maryland: Lexington Books.

Molmud, Jack. 2022. "Consequential Maine Senate Race Flooded with Outsider Money." *News Center Maine*. November 3, 2022. https://www.newscentermaine.com/article/news/politics/consequential-maine-senate-race-flooded-with-outsider-money-politics/97-63e995e1-e0ad-4ee1-a5a9-e43d7f31e793.

National Lieutenant Governors Association (NLGA). 2023. "50-State Data Sheets." https://nlga.us/research/data-on-offc-of-lt-governor/50-state-data-sheets/.

National Rifle Association. 2016a. "Don't Let New Yorkers Control Your Maine Gun Rights." NRA video—YouTube, 0:30. https://www.youtube.com/watch?v=ae2JHLE7Bbk.

———. 2016b. "Sheriffs Oppose Maine Question 3." NRA video—YouTube, 0:30. https://www.youtube.com/watch?v=KHaVko-hrCo.

Palmer, Kenneth T., G. Thomas Taylor, Marcus A. LiBrizzi, and Jean E. Lavigne. 2009. *Maine Politics and Government, Second Edition*. Lincoln: University of Nebraska Press.

Piper, Jessica. 2020. "Out-of-Staters Are Spending Big in Maine's Senate Race." *Bangor Daily News*. October 10, 2020. https://www.bangordailynews.com/2020/08/10/politics/out-of-state-money-plays-outsized-role-in-maines-us-senate-race/.

Powell, Richard J. 2012. "Cleaning House? Assessing the Impact of Maine's Clean Elections Act on Electoral Competitiveness." *Maine Policy Review* 19: 46–54.

Quinlan, Patrick. 2016. "The Rise of the Portland Greens." In *Empowering Progressive Third Parties in the United States: Defeating Duopoly, Advancing Democracy*, edited by Jonathan H. Martin, 31–62. New York: Routledge.

Radde, Kaitlyn. 2022. "The Next Round of Counting Begins in Alaska. Here's How Ranked-Choice Voting Works." *NPR*. November 22, 2022. https://www.npr.org/2022/11/22/1138422560/the-next-round-of-counting-begins-in-alaska-heres-how-ranked-choice-voting-works.

Rakich, Nathaniel, and Ryan Best. 2020. "There Wasn't That Much Split-Ticket Voting in 2020." *FiveThirtyEight*. December 2, 2020. https://fivethirtyeight.com/features/there-wasnt-that-much-split-ticket-voting-in-2020/.

Richard, Mark Paul. 2009. "'This Is Not a Catholic Nation': The Ku Klux Klan Confronts Franco-Americans in Maine." *The New England Quarterly* 82: 285–303.

Roberts, Kenneth L. 1979. *Local Government in Maine*. Augusta, Maine: Maine Municipal Association.

Rogers, Steven. 2017. "Electoral Accountability for State Legislative Roll Calls and Ideological Representation." *American Political Science Review* 111: 555–571.

Rooks, Douglas. 2014. "Term Limits for Legislators Have Been a Bust in Maine." *Portsmouth Herald*. March 2, 2014. https://www.seacoastonline.com/story/news/local/portsmouth-herald/2014/03/02/term-limits-for-legislators-have/38591421007/.

———. 2018. *Rise, Decline and Renewal: The Democratic Party in Maine*. Lanham, Maryland: Hamilton Books.

———. 2021. "Vetoes Spell Potential Trouble for Democrats." *Seacoast Online*. July 11, 2021. https://www.seacoastonline.com/story/opinion/columns/guest/2021/07/11/rooks-vetoes-spell-potential-trouble-democrats/7897649002/.

Russell, Lia. 2022. "Paul LePage Says He Wouldn't Have Negotiated with Tribes Over Sovereignty." *Bangor Daily News*. August 3, 2022. https://www.bangordailynews.com/2022/08/02/politics/lepage-wouldnt-have-negotiated-with-tribes-n6hjn1meon/.

Shankman, Sabrina. 2020. "In Maine, Many Voters Defied the Polls and Split Their Tickets." *Inside Climate News*. November 16, 2020. https://insideclimatenews.org/news/16112020/maine-split-voters-collins-biden/.

Sharp, David. 2020. "Ranked Choice Voting in Maine a go for Presidential Election." *Associated Press*. September 22, 2020. https://apnews.com/article/election-2020-referendums-elections-maine-courts-b5ddd0854037e9687e952cd79e1526df.

Skelton, Katherine. 2021. "Welcome to the Neighborhood: Lewiston Immigrants Help Plan for a Warmer, More Seamless Transition for Refugees." *Lewiston Sun Journal*. May 30, 2021. https://www.sunjournal.com/2021/05/30/welcome-to-the-neighborhood-lewiston-immigrants-help-plan-for-a-warmer-more-seamless-transition-for-refugees/.

Smart-Pelletier, Dylan. "I Will Not Speak French." Franco-Americans of Maine, Then and Now. April 20, 2021. https://francomainestories.net/2021/04/20/i-will-not-speak-french/comment-page-1/.

Snider, Ari. 2022. "Somali-American Statehouse Candidates Make History with One Confirmed Victory and One Apparent Win." *Maine Public*. November 9, 2022. https://www.mainepublic.org/politics/2022-11-09/somali-american-statehouse-candidates-make-history-with-one-confirmed-victory-and-one-apparent-win.

Statista. 2020. "Voter Turnout Rate in the Presidential Election in the United States as of December 7, 2020, by State." https://www.statista.com/statistics/1184621/presidential-election-voter-turnout-rate-state/.
Stein, Robert, Martin Johnson, and Stephanie Shirley Post. 2002. "Public Support for Term Limits: Another Look at Conventional Thinking." *Legislative Studies Quarterly* 27: 459–480.
Stid, Daniel, Kelly Born, and Kathy Armstrong. 2019. "Historical Assessment of the First State-Wide Passage of Ranked Choice Voting in Maine." Hewlett Foundation. September 19, 2019. https://hewlett.org/historical-assessment-of-the-first-state-wide-passage-of-ranked-choice-voting-in-maine/.
Thistle, Scott. 2017. "Maine's Highest Court Rules Ranked-Choice Voting Is Unconstitutional." *Portland Press Herald*. May 24, 2017. https://www.pressherald.com/2017/05/23/maine-high-court-says-ranked-choice-voting-is-unconstitutional/.
———. 2018. "LePage Takes Parting Shot at 'Stolen Election' That Cost Fellow Republican His Seat in Congress." *Portland Press Herald*. December 29, 2018. https://www.pressherald.com/2018/12/28/lepage-leaves-note-of-protest-on-golden-election-certificate/.
———. 2020. "Democrats Take Lead in Voter Registrations in Maine." *Portland Press Herald*. June 28, 2020. https://www.pressherald.com/2020/06/28/democrats-take-lead-in-voter-registrations-in-maine/.
Struck, Doug. 2022. "Maine's Open Door for Refugees Meets a Housing Shortage." *Christian Science Monitor*. July 15, 2022. https://www.csmonitor.com/USA/Society/2022/0715/Maine-s-open-door-for-refugees-meets-a-housing-shortage.
Watson, Judy A. 1998. "County Government Abolishment." Connecticut Office of Legislative Research. January 30, 1998. https://www.cga.ct.gov/PS98/rpt%5Colr%5Chtm/98-R-0086.htm.
Wiltse, David L. 2018. "Subsidizing Equality: Female Candidate Emergence and Clean Elections." *Election Law Journal* 17: 85–99.

CHAPTER 5
POLS, PREACHERS, & PRAGMATISTS
Massachusetts Politics in the Twenty-First Century

Jerold Duquette
Professor of Political Science
Central Connecticut State University

On a bit of a lark, the job search website Zippia recently released its ranking of the country's "snobbiest states," with the "snob-o-meter" determining Massachusetts to be first with Vermont second, Connecticut third, New Hampshire fifth, Rhode Island sixth, and Maine ninth (VerHeist 2021). Though their methodology may warrant a "for entertainment purposes only" warning, the rankings tap into somewhat founded stereotypes about Massachusetts and the New England states. American democracy was born in Massachusetts four centuries ago and many non-New Englanders will tell you Massachusetts won't give it a rest. The oft-noted obnoxiousness of the fans of New England's major professional sports franchises, all located in Massachusetts, may also be worth noting here.

However, when it comes to politics, a key difference between Massachusetts and the rest of New England is the degree of professionalism and job security among elected officials, enabled by mutually reinforcing cultural, institutional, and structural dynamics. Massachusetts is not just the only New England state with any major professional sports franchises but also the sole New England state with a full-time state legislature. At the Massachusetts State House, perched atop Boston's Beacon Hill, state representatives and senators practice their profession year-round, every year.[1]

Not unlike admission to Harvard, the state's (and the nation's) oldest college, the toughest part about going pro in Massachusetts politics may be getting in. Once elected to any state or federal office in the commonwealth, reelection is rarely a nail-biting affair. State legislative elections have ranked at or near the bottom for decades when it comes to competitiveness. The Bay State was ranked 46th in 2022 with 64 percent of state legislators running unopposed for reelection (Lannan 2022a). By comparison, in 2022 New

---

[1] Journalists, commentators, and politicians alike often use *Beacon Hill* as a shorthand way to refer to the state legislature.

Hampshire was ranked second, Maine 15th, Rhode Island 26th, Vermont 29th, and Connecticut 32nd in terms of legislative competitiveness (Ballotpedia 2022). In Massachusetts, no incumbent statewide official has lost a reelection contest since 1982 when former governor Michael Dukakis retook the corner office from Ed King, a fellow Democrat who defeated him in the 1978 Democratic primary.

From the Civil War to 1928, Massachusetts politics remained firmly controlled by descendants of English colonists, Yankee Protestant Republicans. Between 1928 and 1960, the Democratic Party, fueled by waves of Irish Catholic immigrants, took over political control of Massachusetts. Democratic New York Governor Al Smith's run for president in 1928 was "the breakthrough election" for Bay State Democrats, but the 1948 election solidified their burgeoning dominance (Mileur 1997a, 147). In 1948, Democrats discovered the power of ballot measures. Three Republican-backed ballot measures seeking to weaken labor unions and one to liberalize a state law prohibiting doctors from prescribing birth control appeared on the 1948 state ballot. They were unintentionally made-to-order for Democrats trying to coax Irish Catholic workers to the polls. Democratic turnout that year powered Democrat Harry Truman to victory and a better showing in Massachusetts than FDR had managed in any of his White House bids (Mileur 1997b, 83).

The pro-labor, culturally conservative Democrats who emerged in the 1940s and 1950s have remained a significant part of the twenty-first century Democratic coalition in the state. Though many voters now call themselves Independents, they are what political scientists call Democratic *leaners*. Indeed, generally the state's most important electoral conflicts for the past sixty years have been intramural affairs between moralistic progressive Democratic insurgents and individualistic, establishment-friendly Democratic incumbents. This, despite the fact that unenrolled voters in the commonwealth have outnumbered registered Democratic voters every election year since 1990 (O'Brien 2022a).[2]

The defining tensions and cleavages in twenty-first century Massachusetts politics are cultural, with establishment-friendly professional politicians on one side and anti-establishment policy activists and political reformers on the other. They are also institutional, with governors trying to move the state forward during their comparatively brief tenures while state legislative leaders manage that forward movement in ways that preserve their own tenures

---

[2] See "Massachusetts Registered Voter Enrollment: 1948–2022" at https://www.sec.state.ma.us/ele/eleenr/enridx.htm.

long after governors have come and gone. In addition, they are structural in that cultural and institutional tensions play out in the context of single party electoral dominance. Since the 1950s, that single party has been the Democratic Party. Together, these mutually reinforcing cultural, institutional, and structural dynamics fuel the Bay State's particular brand of politics and distinguish it from its New England neighbors.

This chapter additionally views the Bay State's particular politics through the lens of scholar Daniel Elazar's typology of *political culture* in the United States.[3] Elazar classified Massachusetts as an "individualistic" political culture with a "moralistic" streak, providing a useful framework for understanding the assumptions and behavior of both sides in Massachusetts' insider versus outsider politics. The exceptional degree of *legislative supremacy* at the Massachusetts State House, still vital after its extinction in Washington and in state legislatures across America, will also be examined. How does this unusual imbalance of power affect the conduct of politics in the state? Next, what does consistent *one-party rule*, a pattern present to varying degrees in other New England states, tell us about Massachusetts voters? Why do Democrats dominate in a state where independent, or unenrolled, voters outnumber registered Democrats and Republicans combined? And, why are elections for governor virtually always the only high profile races Massachusetts Republicans have been able to win in decades? Finally, the chapter will discuss how and why the political pragmatism of average Bay State voters gives aid and comfort to establishment-friendly professional politicians while frustrating the efforts of anti-establishment activists and reformers, and perpetuating the dominant insider versus outsider (rather than liberal versus conservative or Democratic versus Republican) political cleavage in state politics.

Culture Clash: Pols versus Preachers

Government, New Englanders believed from the beginning, could defend the public good from the selfish machinations of moneyed interests. It could enforce morals through the prohibition or regulation of undesirable activities. It could create a better society through public spending on infrastructure and schools. More than any other group in America, Yankees conceive of government as being run by and for themselves. Everyone is supposed to participate, and there is no greater outrage than to manipulate the political process for private gain. (Woodard 2011, 60).

---

[3] The value in Elazar's typology for the present study is as an analytical framework that provides comparative clarity.

> *There were times when I wanted something. I recall one day when we were in my office and Weld was about to leave. "How about the Metropolitan District Commission?" I asked. "People in your office are still pushing a plan to eliminate it." He stopped in the doorway. "What about it?" "Well, the MDC does valuable work. You know I want it left alone." "You forget," he said, "That I am the governor." "Never mind that stuff," I said. "We're the governor." We both enjoyed a laugh, and then he returned to my desk, leaned toward me and said, "That plan that bothers you—we'll strangle it in its crib" (Bulger 1996, 271).*

The first quotation above describes the political cultural inheritance handed down in all six New England states by the Yankee Protestant descendants of the seventeenth century Pilgrims who settled the region. It reflects the values that led political scientist Daniel Elazar to conclude that, despite its dominant individualistic political culture, Massachusetts has always had a moralistic streak (Elazar 1966). The second quotation is a conversation between state Senate President William Bulger, a hard-nosed Irish Catholic Democrat at the top of his political game in the early 1990s, and then Republican Governor William Weld, a Harvard man who liked "to joke that his ancestors came over on the Mayflower with nothing but the shirts on their backs and a few thousand pounds of gold" (Grunwald 1998). By the time the twenty-first century had dawned, these two professional politicians, both self-conscious echoes of their respective political tribes and traditions, had exited the commonwealth's political stage, but not before demonstrating the triumph of individualistic, transactional, professional politics. Though a proud descendant of moralistic Yankee Protestant forefathers, Governor Weld gamely met state legislative leaders, themselves the proud heirs of individualistic immigrant Catholic forefathers, on their cultural turf. Today, successful politicians of both parties in Massachusetts practice a profession in which expertise in brokering political power, for its own sake and on its own terms, drives electioneering and policymaking. On the other hand, those whose motives and assumptions instead put policy progress in the driver's seat continue to preach and protest and to provide the primary ethos of political insurgency and reform in the commonwealth.

Elazar classified the three southern New England states—Massachusetts, Connecticut, and Rhode Island—as homes to individualistic/moralistic political cultures. New Hampshire was classified as moralistic/individualistic, and Maine and Vermont as straight-up moralistic political cultures. These intra-New England differences in political culture highlight that its degree of political professionalism, not merely its primarily individualistic political culture, distinguish Massachusetts politics from the rest of New England, even its similarly classified southern New England neighbors (Duquette 2002 and 2005).

Moralistic cultures, in Elazar's telling, emphasize the common good in a politics that is centered on issues and policy process and change, not power or personalities. Moralistic cultures, rooted in the Puritans' theological fusion of individual freedom and social conformity to God's Will, are dominated by the belief that *right makes might*. Those who would seek to advance the public interest as public servants owe their allegiance to what is right with the confidence that what is right is also in the public's best interest. From this perspective, what is right is also what the public should want and would in fact, with possession of the whole truth, demand. The political movements and forces pushing against the political establishment in Massachusetts bring this moralistic passion to their efforts to transform the state's politics by expanding popular participation in government and public policy making, and by campaigning, protesting, even suing, for increased government transparency and public accountability. Though their record resembles that of the Washington Generals against the Harlem Globetrotters, the crusaders for moralistic reforms that would upend politics-as-usual on Beacon Hill persist, marking the state's paradoxical brand of politics along the way.

Massachusetts politics is understood by Elazar to be primarily individualistic, which is the opposite of its secondary moralistic cultural streak. Its adherents are self-conscious realists who accept that *might makes right* in politics, like it or not. Individualistic political cultures conjure Madisonian, not Puritan, assumptions and Enlightenment, not Reformation, values. Individualistic political cultures see politics as a marketplace, with political actors competing for the brand and product loyalties of citizen/consumers, all primarily motivated by self-interest. Politics is a competition for market power in which success requires responsiveness to voter demand. For individualistic professional politicians, client-satisfaction, as measured in opinion polls and at the ballot box, unites—by making indistinguishable—the will of the people, the public interest, and their career advancement (Duquette 2005).

The moralistic zeal of Yankee Republicans is no longer associated with the Republican Party of Massachusetts. Its faint echo all but silenced with the effective retirement from politics of Senate President Bulger's respected adversary Governor Bill Weld in 1997. Though positioned most often on the Democratic Party's farthest left reaches, the inheritors of moralistic zeal in contemporary Massachusetts politics are not exactly proud Democrats either. The primary cultural cleavage, and the most salient political one, is between the political establishment and the political anti-establishment, the latter most often over the last half century populated by progressive activists and reformers. With party competition between Democrats and Republicans all but extinct in the state, the only real game in town is between establishment-friendly politicians and anti-establishment insurgents and reformers intent on breaking down the back-room doors behind which career politicians commodify the public interest.

The political journey of the longest serving governor in Massachusetts history, Michael Dukakis, encapsulates the interplay between the two competing cultural approaches to politics in Massachusetts, as well as the lopsided fortunes of each. As a young state legislator in the 1960s Dukakis was the poster boy for Elazar's moralistic streak in Bay State politics. He was a firebrand, anti-establishment, progressive state representative proud of his reputation as a "thorn in the side" of state legislative power brokers with whom he shared Democratic Party membership, but little else (Duquette 2022, 131). In his successful campaign for governor in 1974, Dukakis ran hard against the good old boy, transactional, patronage politics on Beacon Hill, featuring his hopes to bring more progressive and programmatic goals to the policymaking and implementation processes. He was elected with the so-called "Watergate Babies" of 1974, the scores of progressive Democrats voted into Congress on a wave of anti-political corruption sentiment. Dukakis shared the morally-infused confrontational style that attracted millions of voters to these progressive, good government activists in the aftermath of the Watergate scandal (Lawrence 2018). In his first term as governor, however, Dukakis "got a rude awakening." Democratic legislative leaders made it very clear who called the shots at the State House and the Beacon Hill maverick turned governor learned that "right doesn't make might in the Massachusetts State House," even in the governor's office (Duquette 2022, 132).

Having openly refused to develop the kind of friendly legislative and statewide relationships with the key players necessary to ensure his renomination and reelection in 1978, thanks largely to his stubborn insistence on avoiding even the appearance of political patronage or cronyism, Dukakis lost his Democratic renomination fight for a second term. Over the next four years in the Massachusetts political wilderness, Dukakis came to understand that the right makes might, moralistic approach to state legislative politics that had worked for him as a maverick state representative did not translate to success at the top of state government. He came to understand that no matter how right a governor or any other political leader is, nothing meaningful can be accomplished unless enough of the people with the power to prevent change or innovation choose to buy in and do so on their own terms. Dukakis realized how counter-productive it was to reject or condemn the transactional aspects of real-life politics at the State House, and instead came to appreciate the need, even the virtue, of political coalition-building based on overlapping political interests. His making peace with Massachusetts-style transactional politics helped Governor Dukakis win two more terms in the corner office, in 1982 and 1986, and to win the Democratic nomination for president in 1988 (Duquette 2022, 131–34).

The parable of Michael Dukakis' journey from a moralistic progressive ideologue to an individualistic progressive politician who embraced the transactional nature of effective political leadership provided a blueprint for all the Massachusetts governors who have succeeded him. Nonetheless, progressive ideologues and reformers remain prominent, if not powerful, voices in Massachusetts politics today, coming mainly from the back benches in the state legislature and from policy and reform-focused political activists in the state. Information-age politics helped the commonwealth's progressive activists and reformers set up shops, think tanks, and interest groups focused on making Massachusetts more democratic, more transparent, more open to meaningful input and participation from groups and interests long marginalized by the old school, transactional, patronage politics that continues to reign supreme in the commonwealth. Organizations like Progressive Mass and Progressive Democrats of Massachusetts produce studies, op-eds, and reform proposals designed to educate, empower, and expand the electorate by increasing voters' meaningful choices at the ballot box. They endorse and raise money for pro-reform, anti-establishment candidates and ballot measures as well.[4]

The pro politics game at the Massachusetts State House is nevertheless still dominated by power-focused career politicians, a group still disproportionately composed of white men. Even the 2022 election of five women to the state's six statewide constitutional offices, including the first woman and

---

[4] For information on the activities of the group Progressive Mass: https://www.progressivemass.com/. For information on the activities of the group Progressive Democrats of Massachusetts: https://www.progressivedemsofmass.org/.

openly gay governor and the first woman of color as attorney general, has not transformed Massachusetts's when it comes to racial diversity and gender equity in elected office. The Bay State compares well enough nationally on this score, but not nearly as well with its New England neighbors. UMass Boston political scientist Erin O'Brien has convincingly argued that the electoral dominance of the Democratic Party in the commonwealth has contributed to the Bay State's unimpressive record of electing women. Without competition in November elections, Massachusetts Democrats rarely need to recruit and advance new kinds of candidates in order to win or protect state legislative majorities and the mostly white male Democratic career politicians at the state House have every incentive to extend their tenures in office (O'Brien 2022b).

Moralistic activists have tried circumventing State House power brokers by putting their policy proposals directly into voters' hands at the ballot box. High profile ballot measure fights in the state on issues such as campaign finance reform, ranked choice voting, tax cuts, tax increases, charter schools, casino gambling, police reform, and driver's licenses for undocumented immigrants have all produced political clashes between culturally individualistic and culturally moralistic forces in the first two-plus decades of the new century. Far from weakening politics-as-usual in Massachusetts, however, ballot measure fights have actually provided individualistic legislators with a novel sort of political pressure valve. While moralistic reform measures designed to force elected officials to be more responsive and accountable to voters have either failed or been toothless in recent years, Beacon Hill leaders have avoided risky votes by letting issues that pit organized special interests against each other be settled at the ballot box instead of the State House (Duquette and Cunningham 2022). Even the threat of a ballot measure can empower state legislative leaders in brokering compromises between contending special interests behind closed doors in what have come to be known as "grand bargains" (LeBlanc 2018). These grand bargains are struck with the threat of settlement at the ballot box hanging over the heads of the parties concerned. When struck, these bargains often short circuit controversies that would have fueled the campaigns of candidates challenging state legislative incumbents' reelection bids (Duquette and Cunningham 2022). Ballot measure campaigns in recent years aimed at empowering voters, such as the one for ranked choice voting in 2020, generally do not pass muster with voters, and even when such reforms are passed at the ballot box and, as the discussion of clean elections below illustrates, they do not necessarily come to fruition.

Legislative Supremacy and Incumbent Protection at the State House

Public financing of campaigns enjoyed a wave of popularity in New England and Massachusetts was not untouched. However, as with other issues, legislative supremacy in the Bay State determined its fate. In 1996, voters in Maine enacted the Maine Clean Elections Act by ballot initiative which provided some public campaign financing. In 1997, Vermont enacted its own campaign finance law imposing spending limits on campaigns for state office. In 2005, rocked by corruption charges against then Governor John Rowland, Connecticut enacted a public financing program for candidates running for state office. Massachusetts updated its campaign finance laws in 1994. A corruption scandal involving state legislators excepting gifts and junkets, exposed by *The Boston Globe*, sparked reform that increased campaign contribution disclosure requirements and decreased contribution limits. Public campaign financing, however, a reform that would help level the playing field for challengers to incumbent state legislators, was not on the table in Massachusetts until the activists who helped convince Maine voters to pass a clean elections law set up shop in the Bay State. Just two years after their success in Maine, advocates helped convince seven out of ten Massachusetts voters to enact a clean elections law in 1998. As the twenty-first century dawned, it seemed as if the New England states were on the same page regarding campaign finance reform, but unlike in Maine, Vermont, and Connecticut, incumbent politicians at the Massachusetts State House do not have to accept the apparent will of the voters so easily.

Despite 70 percent of Bay State voters supporting the Massachusetts Clean Elections Law at the ballot box in 1998, the public financing system they enacted was never fully implemented. After four and half years of wrangling between the Democratically-controlled state legislature and Republican Governor Mitt Romney, not to mention a state court order to fund it, the legislature simply repealed the law on June 21, 2003 having never appropriated the funds required (New York Times 2003).[5] Clean elections advocates hoped that legislative intransigence would exact a political cost at the ballot box, but in the 2000 elections none of the opponents of clean elections in the state legislature who ran for reelection were defeated (Duquette 2002). The electoral price in the 2004 elections for summarily repealing a law enacted with 70 percent voter approval was again . . . wait for it . . . zero.

---

[5] Laws passed by the voters at the ballot box, once enacted, are no different than any other statutes. While outright repeal of voter-passed laws such as with the Clean Elections Law has been rare in Massachusetts, the legislature regularly modifies voter passed laws in the commonwealth and/or refuses to fully fund them.

Fast forward to 2022. Record high inflation created pressure on state governments across the country to provide tax breaks to residents. Five out of six New England states did just that. One of the 2022 tax breaks enacted in Connecticut, but not Massachusetts, was a suspension of the state's twenty-five cent a gallon gas tax. Inflation at the pump in 2022 was a major Republican Party election year talking point, one that was undoubtedly helpful in convincing Democratic elected officials in many state legislatures and the White House to endorse gas tax holidays. Even the very popular outgoing Republican Governor of Massachusetts Charlie Baker's support for a gas tax holiday was ignored by state legislative leaders on Beacon Hill. Why did a Democratic governor with over-whelming Democratic majorities in the state legislature in Connecticut feel compelled to respond to public and opposition party pressure to suspend the state gas tax, while the Democrats who control the Massachusetts state legislature never gave it serious consideration? A media headline appearing as the state legislature wrapped up its 2022 session tells the tale: "No tax breaks for Massachusetts residents, and few seem to care" (Lannan 2022b). Democratic state legislative incumbents in 2022 had no more to fear from voters in the fall election than did their predecessors in 2000, 2002, and 2004 who ignored and then repealed the voter-passed clean elections law without batting an eye. In the 2022 elections, not a single Democratic incumbent was defeated for reelection.

While US presidents and governors were increasingly becoming the center of government power and purpose during the nineteenth and twentieth centuries, Massachusetts governors remained, in one prominent scholar's estimation, "hamstrung by history" (Schuck 1961). Despite statutory and constitutional amendments that bestowed increased formal powers on Massachusetts governors similar to other governors across the country, the commonwealth's governors have never been able to maintain meaningful or consistent preeminence over public policy making at the Massachusetts State House. Instead, they have been regularly subordinated to the leaders of the state House of Representatives and Senate. The Massachusetts legislature is run by the so-called *big three* (i.e., the House Speaker, Senate President, and the Governor), but it is clear that the House Speaker and Senate President more often support and defend each other's interests and agendas than make common cause with the number three member of the big three, the governor. Governors come and go, after all, but legislative leaders on Beacon Hill . . . not so much (Jenkins 2022; Duquette 2022).

Nonetheless, the first two decades of the twenty-first century have seen

Massachusetts governors ranked by political scientists and pollsters as among the most powerful and popular governors in America. When Democrat Deval Patrick won the governorship in 2006, he was the first Democrat to hold the corner office in sixteen years. When preeminent gubernatorial scholar Thad Beyle published his power rankings of US governors in 2007, Patrick was ranked the most powerful governor in America, a designation based on one key, but ultimately deceptive, criterion. The crucial variable for Beyle was the fact that after sixteen years of Republican governors, Patrick would serve with Democratic super-majorities in both chambers of the state legislature (Prah 2007). From Beyle's perspective, the sky was the limit in Massachusetts with total Democratic control of the State House. Patrick's actual tenure, however, produced no major leftward shifts at the state legislature where Democratic leaders never went along with the most progressive elements of Patrick's and the commonwealth's progressive activists' policy agenda (Duquette 2022, 136–37). Beyle had made the mistake that many scholars, journalists, and political commentators around the country have and still do make when analyzing Massachusetts politics. He assumed that the left versus right partisanship awash everywhere else in American politics then and now, including the Bay State's New England neighbors, would hold sway too at the Massachusetts State House.

Governor Patrick's successor, Republican Charlie Baker, spent all eight years in office ranked no lower than third most popular governor in the United States, according to the *Morning Consult Poll*. His popularity did not translate to preeminence among the big three, however. In his 2014 campaign for governor, Baker conspicuously avoided harsh criticism of Democratic state legislative leaders, despite the opportunity afforded him by the then unfolding Probation Department scandal that laid bare the abuse of patronage hiring by Democratic state legislators. In office, Baker remained careful to avoid stepping too often or too heavily on the toes of Beacon Hill Democratic leaders and chose instead to make a positive working relationship between himself and the House Speaker and Senate President a hallmark of his administration.

Baker accepted the governor's often subordinate role among the so-called big three, understanding that popularity with voters does not translate to legislative power in Massachusetts. He understood this better, in fact, than his Democratic predecessor, Deval Patrick, whose progressive bona fides and shared party membership failed to translate into consistent inter-branch comity at the state House. The term *big three* was coined during the administration of Baker's old boss, Republican Governor Bill Weld, in the 1990s for whom Baker served in key cabinet positions culminating in the job of Secretary of Administration and Finance. Governor Weld had two particularly powerful personalities to contend with in Senate President William Bulger and House Speaker Charles Flaherty each of whom ruled their respective chambers with an iron fist. An important reason legislative supremacy has survived in the Bay State while perishing elsewhere is the ability of legislative leaders to command loyalty and obedience among their chamber's members, a phenomenon that is both cause and effect of the exceptional insulation of state politicians from public opinion in Massachusetts.

Governor Baker's decision not to run for a third term in 2022, despite the fact that he enjoyed a 74 percent approval rating and was even more popular with Independents and Democrats in the state than with Republicans, was seen by many political analysts and commentators as a consequence of his alienation from the Massachusetts Republican Party (Epstein 2021; King and Klein 2021; Kuznitz 2022). Rather than being unlikely to defeat his general election Democratic opponent in the fall, many assumed Baker chose not to run because he feared losing his own party's gubernatorial nod.

In 2019, the Massachusetts Republican State Committee, known as the MassGOP, elected hard-right, pro-Trump and anti-Baker zealot, Jim Lyons as state party chairman. Under Lyons's stewardship the state's Republican Party organization became little more than an outpost of Trump-style culture war conservatism in enemy territory. To his own state party organizational leaders and voter-base then, Baker was a R-I-N-O, (i.e., Republican-In-Name-Only). As such, the Republican primary, not the general election, seemed like Baker's biggest obstacle to reelection in 2022. Less widely appreciated, however, is the reality that no Bay State governor has ever sought a third consecutive four-year term in the corner office, a reality powered by the persistence and maintenance of legislative supremacy at the State House. Behind closed doors, legislative leaders in the Bay State leverage their veto-proof majorities to ensure that governors' policymaking ambitions do not interfere with their power or their members' reelections. This delicate détente is maintained by reciprocal public accommodation and cooperation between governors and legislative leaders. Democratic legislative leaders thus avoid politically dangerous discord with the most visible government official in the state, and the governor gets to share credit for policymaking accomplishments achieved through legislative cooperation. That Massachusetts state legislative elections have long been ranked at or near the bottom of the list in the US for competitiveness suggests this strategy has been quite successful (MassForward 2019, 15).

To this end, Democratic leaders on Beacon Hill have remained conspicuously uncritical of the occupant of the corner office during the reelection campaigns of every Republican governor on the ballot in the last thirty years. Understandably, sustaining an uncritical posture toward Republican incumbent governors running for reelection can be a bit awkward for Democratic legislative leaders' relationships with their party's organizational leaders and progressive activists (Duquette 2022). Having to manage it two reelections in a row may well have been a bridge too far for Democrats in 2022, although Charlie Baker's consistent popularity and high-profile estrangement from the GOP during the Trump presidency, combined with the frequent national media attention he drew for both, made Baker look, for a while at least, like the corner office occupant that might have had the right stuff to win an unprecedented third consecutive four-year term.

In 2022, Democratic Attorney General Maura Healey became the first women and first openly gay person ever elected governor of Massachusetts. She made a name for herself in eight years as the commonwealth's attorney general by aggressively criticizing and repeatedly suing President Trump. Healey enjoyed enough support among the Bay State's progressive activists to be given a virtually free ride to the Democratic nomination. Nonetheless, Healey's campaign for governor was more like a Baker reelection effort than that of a progressive political champion for whom three committed progressive activists had cleared the primary field by effectively ending their gubernatorial bids soon after Healey announced hers.[6] Undisguised admiration for Baker's cooperative approach to governing at the state House and promises to build on his successes, staples of Healey's campaign rhetoric, sent a clear signal to state legislative leaders. Healey had learned the lessons, good and bad, of both fellow Democrat Deval Patrick's and Republican Charlie Baker's tenures in the corner office. For example, progressive activists have been pushing hard in recent years for reforms to make Beacon Hill lawmaking more transparent and more open to the influence of activists and rank-and-file legislators. Their cause got only perfunctory support from Healey on the campaign trail, despite the fact that her election was all but guaranteed by MassGOP's nomination of a Donald Trump acolyte whose only statewide campaign experience was a 20-plus point defeat by Elizabeth Warren in her 2018 reelection to the United States Senate. Healey beat Republican Geoff

---

[6] Harvard professor, Danielle Allen, State Senator Sonia Chang-Diaz, and former state senator Benjamin Downing all ended or suspended their campaigns after Maura Healey entered the race.

Diehl by almost 30 points on Election Day 2022. The sitting attorney general's specifics-light policy promises on the campaign trail included the promise that she would end the practice of interpreting current law as exempting the governor's office from the public records law, but she steered clear of a commitment to impose this view on legislators (Stout and Gross 2022). Then, less than a month after taking office, Healey "clarified" her position on the public records law saying that although she intends to comply with it voluntarily, she will consider public records requests "on a case-by-case basis" and will not file legislation subjecting the governor's office, or anyone else, to the public records law (Herman 2023).

In Washington and in other New England state capitals, the rise of executive supremacy was marked by the increasing capacity of presidents and governors alike to use the bully pulpit to circumvent legislative leaders and build public support directly and thus more efficiently than can legislative leaders, whose members invariably represent multiple and often conflicting political perspectives. Massachusetts, however, has been a clear and notable exception to this historical trend.

The consistent ability of leaders in the Massachusetts state legislature to maintain centralized control over their chambers by commanding the loyalty and deference of their members has helped preserve legislative supremacy at the State House. It has also short-circuited regional political tensions in the state. For example, although people in the western and southeastern parts of the state perennially complain about being ignored by the legislature, these complaints do not produce competitive regional politics. Instead, they give state legislators from these regions a compelling rationale for a transactional approach to their jobs, which is to say, the incentive to campaign on and take credit for getting their districts' fair share from the state legislature. The very small percentages of the state's population from these regions gives state legislative leaders all the leverage they need to keep legislators from outside the Boston metro region in line. The complaints from western and southeastern Massachusetts about not getting their fair shares at the state House reinforce the individualistic cultural orientation that fosters the state's transactional, establishment-friendly politics, and the ability of legislative leaders to maintain top-down control over the legislative process on Beacon Hill.

The prospects for insurgent legislators and good government activists to crack the top-down control of the state legislature by the House Speaker and Senate President may have brightened a bit in the wake of the 2022 state elections due to the efforts of first term state auditor, Diana DiZoglio, to fulfill her campaign promise to force greater transparency on the policymaking operations of the state legislature. Soon after taking office, Auditor DiZoglio, a former state legislator whose progressive policy priorities were often frustrated by Democratic legislative leaders, filed a lawsuit against the state legislature claiming that legislative leaders were illegally obstructing her existing authority to audit the legislature. Simultaneously, DiZoglio endorsed a proposed 2024 ballot initiative that would give the auditor express legal authority to audit the state legislature. If successful, DiZoglio's effort to empower elected state auditors to use their official capacity, authority, and resources, to publicly criticize the state legislature's lack of transparency could potentially make a dent in the powerful incumbency protection capabilities of Democratic legislative leaders long impregnable to the dogged and persistent efforts of anti-establishment, reform-minded legislators and good government reform activists in the state. At the time of this writing, both the merits of the auditor's lawsuit and the fate of the proposed ballot initiative remained undecided.

One-Party Rule Works for Democratic Pols and Pragmatic Voters

The dynamics of Massachusetts politics differ from those of the nation, as there is no pattern of cyclical partisan realignment in the Bay State. The Jacksonian, Civil War, Progressive, New Deal, and other national realignments have left their residues but none has redirected the course of state politics. Rather than periodic ruptures, Massachusetts politics, except for a brief period of two-party competition in the middle decades of the [20th century], has been organized by a succession of one-party regimes that, once in place, have remained in place for an extended period of time (Mileur 1997b, 78).

After 1958 Democrats never surrendered control of either chamber of the state legislature. Since 1991, that control has been preserved and defended by veto-proof legislative majorities. In elections for president and Congress, Republican fortunes lingered, waning over the last two decades of the twentieth and first two decades of the twenty-first centuries. In 1980, Ronald Reagan beat Jimmy Carter in Massachusetts by less than one point. Even so, many so-called Reagan Democrats in the Bay State may have been accounted for by Independent candidate John Anderson's 15 percent showing in the state that year. In 1984, Reagan won Massachusetts by less than three points to Carter vice president Walter Mondale to become the last Republican presidential candidate to win Massachusetts' electoral votes.

Republican US representatives and senators from Massachusetts became endangered species when western Massachusetts Republican Representative Silvio Conte passed away just months after being reelected for the sixteenth time in 1990. The always colorful Conte, much more liberal than his party, was a faint echo of the Yankee Protestant Republicans whose effective surrender in the state coincided with his first election to Congress in 1958. The last Republican US senator elected to a full term by Massachusetts voters was Edward Brooke. Himself one of the last Republican state attorneys-general, Brooke served Massachusetts in the US Senate for two terms, losing his seat in 1978 to Democrat Paul Tsongas.

Only three Republicans have cracked the Democratic monopoly on the commonwealth's Washington delegation in the last thirty years. Massachusetts Republican fortunes in US House elections petered out with Peter Blute and Peter Torkildsen, each managing to win two terms in the US House from 1992 to 1996. Both won in districts outside of the Boston Metro area. Blute's district stretched from central to southeastern Massachusetts and Torkildsen's was in the northeast corner of the state. To the degree that there are areas of Republican strength in the state, they are in low population rural towns outside of the Boston metro area. In 2020, though he was easily beaten by Joe Biden, Donald Trump did win dozens of small rural Massachusetts towns. "Leading the way were several small Western Massachusetts towns, such as Russell, Blandford, Wales, Granville, and Tolland, where Trump received up to 60 percent of local ballots" (DeCosta-Klipa 2020).

In the state's US Senate races, the lone twenty-first century GOP victory came literally over Ted Kennedy's dead body. In 2010 Beacon Hill back bencher Republican State Senator Scott Brown won a special election for Kennedy's seat in the midst of winter and the midst of high partisan drama in Washington over the fate of President Obama's Affordable Care Act (a.k.a. Obamacare). Defeated by Elizabeth Warren less than two years later the story of the very brief Scott Brown era in Massachusetts politics illustrates well both the degree to which Massachusetts politics since the 1990s has been dominated by Democrats and the degree to which electoral competition in the state, with the notable exception of gubernatorial elections, has become an intramural Democratic affair (Duquette 2010, 2013).[7]

Scott Brown's special election in January 2010, was an anomaly owed to the confluence of irregular timing, the huge partisan stakes for the GOP

---

[7] Republican State Treasurer Joe Malone (1991–1998) was the last Republican to hold a statewide constitutional office, other than governor, since 1991.

nationally, and a combination of complacency and dissatisfaction with President Obama and congressional Democrats among the Bay State's progressive activist communities (Duquette 2010, 2013). Brown got lots of media attention circumnavigating the state in a pick-up truck wearing a plaid shirt and playing his guitar in his successful quest to become the GOP's fateful 41st US Senator in the 112th Congress. Senator Kennedy's death had reduced the Democrats' US Senate contingent from a Republican filibuster-killing 60 Democrats to 59, which is why Brown's famous plaid shirt was often accented on the campaign trail by a baseball cap with the number 41 stitched across the front.

GOP desperation to prevent the passage of the Affordable Care Act was enough to make Brown's longshot Senate campaign the only game in town for Republicans across the country. The opportunity to replace the Ted Kennedy, long known as the liberal lion of the Senate and a stalwart fighter for universal healthcare reform, with a filibuster defying 41st Republican was more than enough to inspire an unprecedented Republican national mobilization of money and manpower on behalf of Brown's special election effort during what would otherwise have been the political campaign off season in the fall and winter of 2009.

Scott Brown's 2010 win illustrated the intensity of internal Democratic division between progressive activists and party regulars in Massachusetts, which had been and continues to be the most salient and impactful political divide in the state. It did not, however, illustrate that the MassGOP could win other statewide contests by exploiting the candidate-centric messaging and tactics that make Republicans competitive in gubernatorial contests (Duquette 2013). While Massachusetts voters are not as progressive as progressive activists believe, the most off-putting thing about progressive candidates and campaigns for average Bay State voters is discomfort with the intensity of their anti-establishment and uncompromising rhetoric. Average Massachusetts voters actually trust and generally approve of their elected officials and they do not punish them for political ambition or careerism. They expect their elected officials to be powerful and to leverage that power to advance the interests of their constituents (Duquette and O'Brien 2022). Without all the special, one-time, advantages he had in 2010, Senator Brown's anti-establishment and anti-career politician attacks on Democrat Elizabeth Warren fell on deaf ears at the polls in 2012. Warren beat Brown by eight points on Election Day (Duquette 2013).

Why are gubernatorial elections in Massachusetts the only races that have given Republicans a fighting chance? In 1968, political scientist David

Mayhew argued that Massachusetts voters had produced "split-level bipartyism." Thirty years later, political scientist Jerome Mileur indicated that Mayhew's characterization remained an accurate one, that Bay State voters are open to electing Republicans for high profile statewide offices like US senator and governor, even as they invariably choose Democrats for all the less high-profile offices (Mileur 1997b). When high profile statewide elections are framed as candidate-centered rather than party or policy-centered, party membership becomes less salient. In Massachusetts, elections for governor are most easily framed in candidate-centric ways because the party of the governor is of little practical consequence, thanks to the veto-proof Democratic majorities in the legislature. US Senate races, however, no longer can be effectively framed as candidate-centric affairs, thanks to the now indisputably high partisan stakes of polarized national politics (Duquette 2013).

Another condition has also helped Republican gubernatorial candidates: divisive Democratic gubernatorial primaries. In 2001, Republican Lieutenant Governor Jane Swift became governor when her boss Paul Cellucci resigned to become Ambassador to Canada. Swift was eventually forced out of running in 2002 when Mitt Romney made a Republican bid for the corner office. The Democratic primary that year was a hard-fought contest that saw State Treasurer Shannon O'Brien emerge victorious thanks in part to state Senate President Tom Birmingham and former Clinton labor secretary Robert Reich splitting progressive Democratic primary voters. Republican Mitt Romney was able to exploit the division that left Birmingham's supporters particularly unenthusiastic about O'Brien's general election candidacy (Duquette 2005). In the open seat gubernatorial contest of 2014, Republican Charlie Baker too was able to exploit a divisive Democratic primary in which then state attorney general, Martha Coakley, defeated former state treasurer Steve Grossman. Divisive primaries are particularly problematic in Massachusetts because primaries are held in September, making it difficult to mount an effective effort in general elections just two months later. Maura Healey's 2022 relatively free ride to the Democratic gubernatorial nomination (described prior), also speaks to the point. Democrats had learned their lesson from the 2002 and 2014 open seat races for governor and in 2022 progressive activists effectively stepped aside to avoid intramural Democratic squabbling and insure a Democratic win.

Democrats also benefit from the fact that, unlike its southern New England neighbors Connecticut and Rhode Island, the commonwealth has nonpartisan local elections. Nonpartisan local elections contribute to the state's relatively weak local party organizations.[8] This leaves both Massachusetts parties less able to develop party candidates at the local level, a problem that helps shift party influence to what political scientists call the *party-in-government*. In this case that means elected Democratic state incumbents for whom weak state *party organizations* help prevent strong primary challenges and, by weakening the state's Republican Party's ability to recruit experienced candidates, competitive general election challenges too. Nonpartisan local elections also impact the *party-in-the-electorate*, which is to say partisan voters, by conditioning voters not to think in partisan or ideological terms when choosing elected officials. In this way, nonpartisan local elections may also contribute to the persistent dominance of an insider versus outsider (rather than a liberal versus conservative) political divide in Bay State politics.[9]

Pragmatists Prefer Pros to Preachers

Average Massachusetts voters, despite the near total domination by Democrats at the ballot box and the state House, are not progressive ideologues. They are pragmatists who clearly appreciate, and benefit from, the lack of polarized, culture war politics at the Massachusetts State House. In 2022, sixty percent of registered voters were unenrolled. Twenty-nine percent were Democrats, and just nine percent of the state's registered voters were Republicans. This is the highest ever percentage of Independents and lowest ever percentage of Republican voters in the state.

While only 30 percent of registered voters are Democrats, Democratic candidates in the commonwealth benefit from general congruence between average voters' preference for moderate, nonideological politics and their party's incumbent elected officials' interest in job security (Lehigh 2022). Democrats win elections in the commonwealth by being responsive to voters' material interests, not by running against the government they are seeking to lead. Progressive activists and conservative Republicans, on the other hand, run to varying degrees against the system, the government, and career politicians, a strategy that seems problematic at best in a state where opinion polls show that average voters approve of the job being done by incumbent

---

[8] Though Connecticut and Rhode Island have part-time legislatures, both display some characteristics of professionalized politics and both parties in these states can develop state legislative candidates more effectively, in part, due to partisan local elections.

[9] Political party scholars use the tripartite classification party-in-government, party organizations, and party-in-the electorate to explicate more precisely the causes and effects of political party activity.

elected officials in the state legislature and the governor's office. In fact, polls in recent years have ranked both the Massachusetts governor and state legislature as the most popular respectively in America (Koczela 2021).

Conclusion

The high degree of political professionalism and exceptionally high degree of job security for incumbent elected officials make Bay State politics stand out from its New England neighbors. Mutually reinforcing cultural, institutional, and structural dynamics preserve the commonwealth's establishment-friendly political arena, where political insiders and incumbent office holders are able to insulate themselves exceptionally well from electoral competition and public accountability.

The state's political culture is primarily individualistic. Professional pols compete for the loyalty of voters in the political marketplace. Political outsiders, insurgents, and reformers bring a moralistic cultural orientation to their efforts to challenge the political establishment. They preach about the undemocratic nature of the state's transactional politics practiced by power-hungry politicians who put their career interests above the public interest. These moralistic political challengers and policy activists are perennially frustrated in their efforts to empower the public, particularly marginalized individuals and groups.

The top-down control of the state legislature by the House Speaker and Senate President and the seemingly permanent veto-proof majorities they command, preserve legislative supremacy at the Massachusetts State House making the party affiliation of governors almost irrelevant. In fact, Democratic governors indebted to progressive activists and reformers have had a harder time working with Democratic state legislative leaders than Republican governors. The state legislature is run by the *big three*, the House Speaker, Senate President, and the Governor. Governors, regardless of party, are the junior partners of the big three. Governors protect the speaker and senate president's control over lawmaking and lawmakers by avoiding harsh public criticism of the state legislature. Legislative leaders, in turn, avoid harsh public criticism of cooperative governors. This arrangement allows the big three to produce public policy outcomes that satisfy (or at least do not antagonize) average voters and powerful organized special interests in the state, effectively short-circuiting potential political opposition in the process.

Massachusetts politics has always been dominated by one political party. Since the 1950s that party has been the Democratic Party, which today dominates all partisan elections in the state, with the lone exception of governor. Republican gubernatorial candidates have occasionally been successful in open seat elections by employing candidate-centric campaign narratives. Divisive Democratic primaries in open seat elections combined with the limited time between September primaries and November elections helped elect GOP governors in 2002 and 2014. Ironically perhaps, the state's incumbent-friendly, one-party rule is also aided by nonpartisan local elections. Under-developed local party candidate recruitment operations protect incumbent Democrats from primary and general election challengers and shift partisan influence from Democratic Party organizational leaders and activists to Democratic elected officials.

Finally, career politicians in Massachusetts benefit from a friendly electorate. Bay State voters do not punish politicians for career ambition. They welcome it and expect elected officials to leverage political power to advance their constituents' interests. Anti-establishment challengers, insurgents, and political reformers attack politics-as-usual as undemocratic and corrupt, an approach that attracts high-information progressive voters but alienates average Bay State voters who, according to public opinion polls, give their elected officials and government institutions higher marks than voters of most other states.

Works Cited

Ballotpedia. 2022. "Annual State Legislative Competitiveness Report: Vol. 12, 2022." https://ballotpedia.org/Annual_State_Legislative_Competitiveness_Report:_Vol._12,_2022.

Bulger, William M. 1996. *While the Music Lasts: My Life in Politics*. Boston: Houghton Mifflin Co.

DeCosta-Klipa, Nik. 2020. "Here Are the Massachusetts Communities that Voted for Donald Trump." *Boston.com*. November 4, 2020. https://www.boston.com/news/politics/2020/11/04/massachusetts-trump-towns-2020/.

Duquette, Jerold, and Erin O'Brien. 2022. "Massachusetts Exceptionalism as Identity and Debate." In *The Politics of Massachusetts Exceptionalism: Reputation Meets Reality*, edited by Jerold Duquette and Erin O'Brien, 1–16. Amherst: University of Massachusetts Press.

Duquette, Jerold. 2022. "The Governor of the Commonwealth: A 'Not So' Supreme Executive Magistrate." In *The Politics of Massachusetts Exceptionalism: Reputation Meets Reality*, edited by Jerold Duquette and Erin O'Brien, 116–142. Amherst: University of Massachusetts Press.

Duquette, Jerold, and Maurice Cunningham. 2022. "The Massachusetts Initiative and Referendum Process." In *The Politics of Massachusetts Exceptionalism: Reputation Meets Reality*, edited by Jerold Duquette and Erin O'Brien, 210–230. Amherst: University of Massachusetts Press.

Duquette, Jerold. 2013. "The Scott Brown Era in Massachusetts Politics," *New England Journal of Political Science* 7, no.1: 120–141.

———. 2010. "True Blue Mass" *New England Journal of Political Science* 5, no.1: 155–163.

———. 2005. "Massachusetts Politics in the Twenty-First Century: Recognizing the Impact of Clashing Political Cultures," *New England Journal of Political Science* I, no.1: 1–19.

———. 2002. "Campaign Finance Reform in the Bay State: Is Cleanliness Really Next to Godliness?" In *Money, Politics, and Campaign Finance Reform Laws in the States*, edited by David Schultz. Durham, NC: Carolina Academic Press.

Elazar, Daniel J. 1966. *American Federalism: A View from the States*. New York: Thomas Y. Crowell Company.

Epstein, Reid J. 2021. "Gov. Charlie Baker of Massachusetts Says He Won't Run for Reelection." *New York Times*. December 1, 2021. https://www.nytimes.com/2021/12/01/us/politics/charlie-baker-massachusetts-governor.html.

Grunwald, Michael. 1998. "Weld's Altered Ego." *CommonWealth*, August 1, 1998. https://commonwealthmagazine.org/uncategorized/welds-altered-ego/.

Herman, Colman M. 2023. "Healey Won't File Legislation Subjecting Her Office to Records Law." *CommonWealth*. January 31, 2023. https://commonwealthmagazine.org/politics/public-records/healey-wont-file-legislation-subjecting-her-office-to-records-law/.

Jenkins, Shannon. 2022. "The Massachusetts General Court: Exceptionally Old-School," In *The Politics of Massachusetts Exceptionalism: Reputation Meets Reality*, edited by Jerold Duquette and Erin O'Brien, 95-115. Amherst, MA: University of Massachusetts Press.

King, Alison, and Asher Klein. 2021. "The Complicated GOP Politics Looming Over Baker's Decision Not to Run for Reelection." *NBCBoston.com*. December 1, 2021. https://www.nbcboston.com/news/politics/charlie-baker-massachusetts-republican-party/2580160/.

Kuznitz, Alison. 2022. "Approval Rating: Mass. Gov. Charlie Baker Is Most Popular Governor." *Masslive.com*. October 11, 2022. https://www.masslive.com/politics/2022/10/approval-rating-mass-gov-charlie-baker-is-most-popular-governor.html.

Lannan, Katie. 2022a. "64% of Beacon Hill Lawmakers Face No Reelection Challenge on Nov. 8" *WBGH.org*, September 28, 2022. https://www.wgbh.org/news/politics/2022/09/28/64-of-beacon-hill-lawmakers-face-no-reelection-challenge-nov-8.

———. 2022b. "No Tax Breaks for Massachusetts Residents, and Few Seem to Care." *WGBH.org*, August 4, 2022. https://www.wgbh.org/news/politics/2022/08/04/no-tax-breaks-for-massachusetts-residents-and-few-seem-to-care.

Lawrence, John A. 2018. "How the 'Watergate Babies' Broke American Politics." *Politico*, May 26, 2018. https://www.politico.com/magazine/story/2018/05/26/congress-broke-american-politics-218544/.

LeBlanc, Steve. 2018. "'Grand Bargain' Keeps Voters from Deciding Ballot Questions." *Washington Times*, July 1, 2018. https://www.washingtontimes.com/news/2018/jul/1/grand-bargain-keeps-voters-from-deciding-ballot-qu/?.

Lehigh, Scot. 2022. "Moderate Politics Is the Right Path, Even in Mass." *Boston Globe*, February 3, 2022. https://www.bostonglobe.com/2022/02/03/opinion/moderate-politics-is-right-path-even-mass/?.

New York Times. 2003. *Massachusetts Legislature Repeals Clean Elections Law*. June 21, 2003. https://www.nytimes.com/2003/06/21/us/massachusetts-legislature-repeals-clean-elections-law.html.

MassForward: Advancing Democratic Innovation and Electoral Reform in Massachusetts. 2019. MassInc, November 2019. https://massincmain.wpenginepowered.com/wp-content/uploads/2019/11/MassForward.pdf.

Mileur, Jerome M. 1997a. "Massachusetts," In *State Party Profiles*, edited by Andrew M. Appleton and Daniel S. Ward (Washington, DC: Congressional Quarterly Press), 146–152.

———. 1997b. "Party Politics in the Bay State: The Dominion of Democracy." In *Parties and Politics in the New England States*, edited by Jerome M. Mileur, 77–94. Amherst: Polity Press.

O'Brien, Erin. 2022a. "Voter Access in Massachusetts: From Leader to Laggard," In *The Politics of Massachusetts Exceptionalism: Reputation Meets Reality*, edited by Jerold Duquette and Erin O'Brien, 187–209. Amherst: University of Massachusetts Press.

———. 2022b. "Women, Women of Color in Massachusetts Politics: Not So Exceptional." In *The Politics of Massachusetts Exceptionalism: Reputation Meets Reality*, edited by Jerold Duquette and Erin O'Brien, 254–281. Amherst: University of Massachusetts Press.

Prah, Pamela. 2007. "Massachusetts Gov Rated Most Powerful." *Pew Charitable Trusts: Stateline*, March 9, 2007. http://www.pewtrusts.org/en/research-and-analysis/blogs/stateline/2007/03/09/massachusetts-gov-rated-most-powerful.

Schuck, Victoria. 1961. "The Massachusetts Governorship: Hamstrung by History?" In *State Government and Public Responsibility, 1961: The Role of the Governor in Massachusetts Volume 2*, edited by Robert R. Robbins. Papers of the 1961 Tufts Assembly on Massachusetts Government. Lincoln Filene Center for Citizenship and Public Affairs, Tufts University, Medford, MA.

Stout, Matt and Samantha J. Gross. 2022. "Two Months in, Maura Healey's Pitch for Mass. Governor is Light on the Details." *Boston Globe*. April 9, 2022. https://www.bostonglobe.com/2022/04/09/metro/two-months-maura-healeys-pitch-mass-governor-is-light-details/.

VerHeist, Megan. 2021. "How Snobby Is Your State? A New Ranking Weighs In." *Patch.com*, August 20, 2021. https://patch.com/us/across-america/how-snobby-your-state-new-ranking-weighs.

Woodard, Colin. 2011. *American Nations: A History of the Eleven Rival Regional Cultures of North America*. New York: Penguin Books.

CHAPTER 6

HOW NEW HAMPSHIRE POLITICS TURNED WICKED WEIRD

Christopher J. Galdieri
Professor of Politics
Saint Anselm College

"New Hampshire Is Tiny and Pretty Weird."—Nate Silver, 538 founder

"We're not a red state, we're not a blue state, we're a weird state."—Greg Moore, Republican strategist

Introduction

What makes New Hampshire weird? Let us count some of the ways. While recent decades have seen states shift from red to blue (such as Virginia and Colorado) or blue to red (such as Arkansas and West Virginia), New Hampshire remains doggedly and determinedly purple. In an era of nationwide partisan polarization, it is a state where ticket-splitting is routine: In 2020, New Hampshire voters chose Joe Biden over Donald Trump and re-elected Senator Jeanne Shaheen and the state's two Democratic House members, while at the same time re-electing Republican governor Chris Sununu and giving the GOP control of the state's legislature and executive council. It is one of the least diverse states in the nation, with a population that is almost 93 percent white. Yet in many ways it has been a success story for Democrats in recent decades, in large part because it also has one of the most highly educated populations in the union (Bryant 2022). New Hampshire lacks a major urban center—Manchester, its largest city, had just over 115,000 residents as of 2024—but many residents commute south to Massachusetts to jobs in and around Boston. While it usually goes blue in presidential races, it often does so by narrow enough margins that both major parties view it as a swing state, the only one remaining in New England. New Hampshire Republicans rescued Donald Trump's candidacy in 2016 after he lost the Iowa caucus to Senator Ted Cruz of Texas, but the state voted for Hillary Clinton in the general election and for Joe Biden in 2020. In its January 2024 presidential primary, New Hampshire Republicans went for Trump again—this time beating former South Carolina governor Nikki Haley by eleven percentage points. It is one of the least religious states in America (Newport

2016). Much of its Republican establishment yearns for the glory days when Yankee Republicanism dominated state politics, but newer, coarser voices have pushed the party to the right. In "Live Free or Die" it has the nation's most memorable state motto, but there is widespread disagreement about whether and how that applies to everything from education to abortion to firearms to taxes to even whether New Hampshire should secede from the union.

Weirdness in New Hampshire extends beyond its politics. Despite its small size, it boasts a striking natural diversity, from its short seacoast to its lakes region to its White Mountains. One of those mountains boasted a rock formation dubbed "the Old Man of the Mountain" for its resemblance to a human face in profile, and this rock formation came to represent an idealized vision of a flinty Granite Stater. While the Old Man fell on May 3, 2003, many in the state continue to mourn its passing. It still appears on license plates and on Governor Chris Sununu's campaign signs, and while some (but not all) of his fellow legislators groaned when state representative Tim Cahill of Raymond compared the fall of the Old Man to the 9/11 attacks that took the lives of nearly 3,000 Americans, the legislature nonetheless passed a bill designating May 3 as a day of commemoration and remembrance (NHPR Staff 2023). The state is home to the weather observatory on Mount Washington, which has been described as an ideal zombie redoubt (Quimby 2015). It is one of five states without a sales tax, one of nine without an income tax, one of three that does not require motorcycle drivers to wear helmets, and the only state that does not require car owners to have car insurance or adults to use seatbelts. But the state also has high property taxes, and taxes hotels and restaurant meals and other things that might bring tourists from Massachusetts to New Hampshire. The state bars the operation of private liquor stores, in favor of state-run outlets, and is the only state in New England, as of early 2024, that has not substantially legalized marijuana. Fireworks, however, are spectacularly legal. For all of its libertarianism and puritanism, New Hampshire has long been a state where women succeed in politics to a degree rarely seen elsewhere. After the 2012 election, it became the first state to have not just an all-woman congressional delegation, but also a woman governor. Two women in the history of the United States have been both governor of a state and one of its United States Senators; both are from New Hampshire, and they serve alongside one another today. Its footprint in popular culture is limited but noteworthy. This is the state where *Breaking Bad*'s Walter White went to ground after his drug empire collapsed, and where Vito Spatafore on *The Sopranos* laid low after he was outed. Fictional president Josiah Bartlett from *The West Wing* came from New Hampshire, as did real-life president Franklin Pierce.

To understand the weirdness of modern New Hampshire politics, it is necessary to begin by examining the road the state's politics took to get to their present state.

New Hampshire's Political History

Throughout much of the twentieth century, New Hampshire was a solidly Republican state. The GOP dominated state politics: Republicans held the governorship for all but fifteen years of the century, the state Senate for all but eight, and the state House for all but two. At the federal level, Democrats won only the occasional congressional seat, and the state was reliably Republican, other than in landslides for Franklin Roosevelt and Lyndon Johnson, at the presidential level until 1992. Democratic successes, like a flurry of electoral victories in the 1960s, were minor and left little imprint on the state's politics (Fistek 1997). The state GOP was sufficiently broad and dominant that it could encompass a wide range of viewpoints; in the 1980s, New Hampshire's Republican senators were Gordon Humphrey, a staunch abortion rights opponent, and Warren Rudman, who maneuvered to get David Souter appointed to the Supreme Court in no small part to protect abortion rights (Woodward 2021). The Granite State of the twenty-first century is far more competitive at all levels of government, and a long run of Democratic wins here in presidential elections obscures just how competitive politics in the state has become: New Hampshire is one of the swingiest of swing states, and (alongside its neighbor Maine) one of the few remaining bastions of ticket-splitting in a polarized era.

Several watershed years help explain why New Hampshire is no longer a rock-ribbed Republican state. When Governor Mike Dukakis of Massachusetts began visiting New Hampshire as part of his 1988 presidential campaign, he was struck by how many of the state's voters reminded him of the voters he had met at home during his campaigns for governor. That was in part because many of those voters had moved into the state from Massachusetts as part of a wave of economic growth and an influx of new residents from Massachusetts and other northeastern states. But the recession that the United States experienced in 1991 and 1992 hit New Hampshire particularly hard. New Hampshire's recession started sooner, lasted longer, and hit harder, thanks to a confluence of a collapse in housing prices and the end of the

1980s construction boom, a too-tight labor market, and a downturn in the fortunes of the high-tech industries that had sprung up in the region during the boom years (Berry 1991). Real estate values plummeted, 48,000 jobs vanished between 1988 and the start of the 1992 primary season (Broder 1991), bankruptcy cases doubled between 1990 and 1991 (UPI 1991), and federal regulators shut down seven banks in October of 1991 (Smith 2010). As 1991 ended, 67 percent of Granite Staters reported being dissatisfied with the state of their state, and just 19 percent said they were satisfied with how things were going in the country (Myers 1995). The sour public mood and the presence of new Granite Staters helped Bill Clinton defeat incumbent president George Bush and independent candidate Ross Perot. While some may have been tempted to write this off as a fluke—Clinton received just under 7,000 votes more than Bush, and Perot's presence on the ballot made it easy to argue that he had played spoiler—Clinton carried the state again in 1996, this time beating Bob Dole by nearly 50,000 votes. Also in 1996, the state elected Jeanne Shaheen, who had managed presidential primary campaigns for Jimmy Carter and Gary Hart before winning a seat in the state senate, to the first of her three terms as governor. Shaheen won in part by presenting herself as a pragmatic, moderate, problem-solver; unlike many past Democratic candidates for governor, she pledged to oppose any broad-based state taxes (Toner 1996). Shaheen demonstrated that there was a pathway to victory for Democratic candidates in New Hampshire, if those candidates were careful to distinguish themselves from stereotypes of Democrats as "tax and spend liberals" that were so prevalent in the 1980s and 90s.

The state's Republican Party remained a powerful force during Shaheen's years as governor; it continued to control the state legislature, and New Hampshire returned to the GOP fold for George W. Bush in 2000, in large part thanks to Ralph Nader's candidacy. In 2002, Shaheen ran for the Senate but lost to John E. Sununu, son of the state's former governor, while Craig Benson reclaimed the governorship for Republicans. This proved to be less than the enduring restoration state Republicans thought it would be. In the 2004 presidential contest, New Hampshire went for Democrat John Kerry, becoming the only state to flip from red to blue that year, and Democrat John Lynch defeated Benson in a rare defeat for a first-term New Hampshire governor. In 2006, the backlash to George W. Bush's presidency and the war in Iraq lifted New Hampshire Democrats to heights that would have been unthinkable even ten years prior. John Lynch was re-elected, the state's two Republican congressmen, Jeb Bradley in the first district and

Charlie Bass in the second, lost their seats, and in Concord, Democrats won control of both chambers of the state legislature for the first time since the 1870s, as well as a majority of seats on the state's executive council. This was a seismic enough result that the conservative *Union Leader* newspaper asked whether the Granite State was turning into "New Massahampshire" (Wickham 2007). In 2008, amid the aftermath of the financial collapse that triggered the great recession, Barack Obama easily carried the state against John McCain, Jeanne Shaheen defeated John E. Sununu in a rematch for the US Senate, and Democrats retained control of the state legislature. Some Granite State Democrats began to think that they had turned their state into Blue Hampshire. They did not get to think that for very long, as New Hampshire soon showed that it was more than a new blue state.

Republicans roared back to power in 2010: Republican Kelly Ayotte defeated Paul Hodes for the state's US Senate seat, and Republican Frank Guinta, the mayor of Manchester, defeated Democratic incumbent Carol Shea-Porter in the First Congressional District, while Republican Charlie Bass returned to electoral politics and defeated Ann McLane Kuster in the second district's open-seat race. Republicans also won commanding majorities in the state legislature and swept all five executive council districts. Democrats' only consolation was John Lynch's re-election to a record fourth term as governor, thanks to his personal popularity with voters. In what was becoming a familiar fashion, 2012 saw reversals of many of these outcomes. Barack Obama carried the state despite a strong effort here by part-time Wolfeboro resident Mitt Romney, and Democrat Maggie Hassan was elected to succeed Lynch. Democrats retook the majority in the lower house of the state legislature, while Republicans retained control of the state senate. In both House seats, Democrats defeated in 2010 won rematches with the incumbent Republicans.

Democrats had a reasonably good 2014, at least relative to Democrats in the rest of the country. Jeanne Shaheen won a second term against carpetbagger Scott Brown (Galdieri 2019) and Maggie Hassan won a second term as governor. While Ann Kuster won a second term in the second district, Carol Shea-Porter lost to Frank Guinta for the second time in their third rematch, and Republicans won control of the state House. In 2016, Hillary Clinton barely carried the state against Donald Trump, winning by just 3,000 votes while thousands of voters skipped voting for president at all and thousands of others wrote in people like Bernie Sanders or John Kasich (Cauterucci 2020). Simultaneously, Chris Sununu became the state's first Republican governor in over a decade and Republicans held onto both chambers of the state legislature. Ann Kuster had a close call but held on in the Second Congressional District, while fellow Democrat Carol Shea-Porter defeated Republican Frank Guinta in the First Congressional District even as it went narrowly for Trump. Notably, Democratic Governor Maggie Hassan defeated Senator Kelly Ayotte's bid for a second term in a race that was not called until the morning after the election, while the political world was still reeling from Trump's election. Two years later, Democrats nearly ran the table, winning control of the state legislature and executive council, but falling short of defeating Governor Chris Sununu. In 2020's COVID election, Joe Biden carried the state against Donald Trump by a 60,000-vote, seven-point margin, and Jeanne Shaheen was re-elected to a third term without breaking a sweat. But Governor Sununu won a third term by a two to one margin over his Democratic opponent and his coattails carried Republicans back to power in both houses of the legislature, just in time for another round of the gerrymandering that has helped Republicans hold onto the state senate and executive council in the face of an increasingly mobile and well-educated electorate inclined, all things being equal, to support Democrats.

In the 2022 midterms, Republicans were hopeful that they could capture the state's two House seats and defeat Maggie Hassan in the Senate race. But the GOP party establishment was unable to keep the nominations for these offices from being won by full-throated, election-denying MAGA candidates instead of more mainstream conservatives, and the Democrats won re-election in each race by wider margins than many expected. Chris Sununu won re-election for a fourth term, matching the record set by John Lynch in 2010, but Democrats fought to a near-draw in the state House. The Republicans' 2021 gerrymander did its job and cemented their control of the state senate and executive council for another two years. January 2024's presidential primary results were complicated on the Democratic side by disagreements on where New Hampshire should fall in the primary calendar but, on the Republican side, Donald Trump came on eleven points ahead of his nearness challenger, Nikki Haley—even as MAGA inspired candidates fared poorly in the 2022 midterms.

To the extent that there is a consistent narrative that emerges from recent electoral history in New Hampshire, it is that the Granite State exists in a state of more or less perpetual flux. It is much more than just a blue state. In much of America, political polarization has seen many states firmly drift into one party or the other's column; the term "calcification" has been bandied about quite a lot in the wake of the 2022 midterms. But in New Hampshire, each party is competitive, and each election draws national attention. To paraphrase what has been often said of New England's weather, if you don't like politics in New Hampshire, just wait a little while and it will change. New Hampshire, once a bastion of Yankee Republicanism, has become a weird and purple state in a way that sets it apart from every other state in New England.

Recent Elections

A look at election returns in recent decades makes New Hampshire's shift from a solidly Republican state with occasional, brief successes by individual Democrats to one that is deeply competitive at all levels apparent.

At the presidential level, subsequent elections have demonstrated that New Hampshire's modern foray into the Democratic column in 1992 was no fluke. Other than George W. Bush's win here in 2000, the state has cast its four electoral votes for the Democratic nominee for president in every cycle through 2020. Even in 2016, as Donald Trump was becoming the first Republican in a generation to carry Rust Belt states like Pennsylvania, Michigan, and Wisconsin, Hillary Clinton managed to just barely beat him by about 3,000 votes. This was in part due to a key demographic factor about New Hampshire: Granite Staters' levels of educational attainment are well above the national average, with 55 percent of the state's 2016 voters having a college or postgraduate degree (Galdieri 2020). During the Trump years, educational polarization became a real phenomenon nationwide, and New Hampshire simply didn't have enough potential Trump voters for him to carry the state in his 2016 and 2020 runs. Trump's attention returned to New Hampshire throughout his time in office, and he frequently, and groundlessly, blamed the specter of fraudulent voting for his New Hampshire loss in 2016. But the state is likely to receive attention from both parties in future elections, no matter how blue its track record. 2016 showed that the state can indeed be closely contested, and Granite Staters' willingness to split their tickets makes New Hampshire irresistible to candidates of both parties. And as one of the few swing states remaining on the electoral map, neither party is likely to take its votes for granted.

New Hampshire's elections for the United States Senate during this same period show how the shift in the Granite State's presidential voting preferences took over fifteen years to appear at the federal level. While Bill Clinton was beating Bob Dole in 1996, incumbent Republican Senator Bob Smith

TABLE 6.1: Votes for president in New Hampshire, 1992–2020

YEAR	DEMOCRATIC	VOTE	%	REPUBLICAN	VOTE	%	SELECT THIRD-PARTY*		
1992	**Bill Clinton**	209,040	38.9%	George Bush	202,484	37.7%	Ross Perot (Reform)	121,337	22.6%
1996	**Bill Clinton**	246,214	49.3%	Bob Dole	196,532	39.4%	Ross Perot (Reform)	48,390	9.7%
2000	Al Gore	266,348	46.9%	**George W. Bush**	273,559	48.2%	Ralph Nader (Green)	22,198	3.9%
2004	**John Kerry**	340,511	50.2%	George W. Bush	331,237	48.9%			
2008	**Barack Obama**	384,826	54.4%	John McCain	316,534	44.7%			
2012	**Barack Obama**	369,561	52.0%	Mitt Romney	329,918	46.4%			
2016	**Hillary Clinton**	348,526	47.6%	Donald Trump	345,790	47.2%	Gary Johnson (Libertarian)	30,777	4.2%
2020	**Joe Biden**	424,937	52.9%	Donald Trump	365,660	45.5%			

Only third-party candidates winning a meaningful share of the vote are included.
Sources: New Hampshire Secretary of State's Office; New Hampshire Public Radio Election Database

TABLE 6.2: Votes for US Senate and US House of Representatives

US SENATE

YEAR	DEMOCRATIC	VOTE	%	REPUBLICAN	VOTE	%
1996	Dick Swett	227,397	46.2%	Bob Smith	242,304	49.2%
1998	George Condodemetraky	88,883	28.2%	Judd Gregg	213,477	67.8%
2002	Jeanne Shaheen	207,478	46.4%	John E. Sununu	227,229	50.8%
2004	Doris Granny D. Haddock	221,549	33.7%	Judd Gregg	434,847	66.2%
2008	Jeanne Shaheen	358,438	51.6%	John E. Sununu	314,403	45.3%
2010	Paul Hodes	167,545	36.8%	Kelly Ayotte	273,218	60.0%
2014	Jeanne Shaheen	251,184	51.6%	Scott Brown	235,347	48.4%
2016	Maggie Hassan	354,649	48.0%	Kelly Ayotte	353,632	47.8%
2020	Jeanne Shaheen	450,778	56.6%	Corky Messner	326,229	41.0%
2022	Maggie Hassan	332,193	53.5%	Don Bolduc	275,928	44.4%

DISTRICT 1

YEAR	DEMOCRATIC	VOTE	%	REPUBLICAN	VOTE	%
2002	Martha Fuller Clark	85,426	58.1%	Jeb Bradley	128,993	58.1%
2004	Justin Nadeau	118,226	63.3%	Jeb Bradley	204,836	63.3%
2006	Carol Shea-Porter	100,691	48.6%	Jeb Bradley	95,527	48.6%
2008	Carol Shea-Porter	176,435	45.8%	Jeb Bradley	156,338	45.8%

YEAR	DEMOCRATIC	VOTE	%	REPUBLICAN	VOTE	%
2010	Carol Shea-Porter	95,503	54.0%	Frank Guinta	121,655	54.0%
2012	Carol Shea-Porter	171,650	46.0%	Frank Guinta	158,659	46.0%
2014	Carol Shea-Porter	116,769	51.7%	Frank Guinta	125,508	51.7%
2016	Carol Shea-Porter	162,080	43.0%	Frank Guinta	157,176	43.0%
2018	Chris Pappas	155,884	45.0%	Eddie Edwards	130,996	45.0%
2020	Chris Pappas	205,666	46.2%	Matt Mowers	185,159	46.2%
2022	Chris Pappas	167,391	45.9%	Karoline Leavitt	142,229	45.9%

DISTRICT 2

YEAR	DEMOCRATIC	VOTE	%	REPUBLICAN	VOTE	%
2002	Katrina Swett	90,479	40.8%	Charlie Bass	125,804	56.7%
2004	Paul Hodes	125,280	38.7%	Charlie Bass	191,188	59.1%
2006	Paul Hodes	108,743	55.4%	Charlie Bass	94,088	47.9%
2008	Paul Hodes	188,332	55.2%	Jennifer Horn	138,222	40.5%
2010	Ann McLane Kuster	105,060	46.6%	Charlie Bass	108,610	48.2%
2012	Ann McLane Kuster	169,275	49.1%	Charlie Bass	152,977	44.3%
2014	Ann McLane Kuster	130,700	53.8%	Marilinda Garcia	106,871	44.0%
2016	Ann McLane Kuster	174,371	47.7%	Jim Lawrence	158,825	43.4%
2018	Ann McLane Kuster	155,358	53.4%	Steve Negron	117,990	40.5%
2020	Ann McLane Kuster	208,289	52.0%	Steve Negron	168,886	42.2%
2022	Ann McLane Kuster	171,636	55.4%	Bob Burns	135,579	43.7%

fended off a challenge from former Democratic Congressman Dick Swett in a race so close it was initially called for Swett on Election Night. Two years later, incumbent Republican Judd Gregg was elected to a second term. In 2002, Democrats were hopeful they could win their first Senate race in New Hampshire since 1975 when Governor Jeanne Shaheen ran for the Senate. But several factors led to her loss that year. The first was the post-9/11 political atmosphere, which hampered Democrats' prospects in the 2002 midterms. The second was Congressman John E. Sununu's primary challenge, supported tacitly and not-so-tacitly by many state and national Republican leaders, to incumbent Senator Bob Smith. Smith's erratic behavior in his second term had included a brief presidential run, followed by leaving the GOP and becoming an independent, and then returning to the GOP to claim a committee chairmanship vacated upon the death of Senator John Chaffee of Rhode Island. Sununu, a mainstream conservative and a son of the former governor, had no comparable baggage. And finally, an independent Republican operation hired a telemarketing company to flood Democratic phone banks with incoming calls on Election Day, rendering the Democrats unable, in that land-line era, to make get out the vote calls to voters for much of the day. Democrats blamed this move for Shaheen's defeat and spent years litigating it in the courts (Mark 2007). In 2004, Judd Gregg once again had an easy re-election to his third and final term. One might imagine that around this point, state Republicans breathed a sigh of relief and dared to dream that the state had returned to its natural Republican order.

But it was soon clear that the old order was no more. Democrats' successes in 2006, combined with the public's turn against the war in Iraq and the George W. Bush presidency more generally, along with five years of prosecutions, lawsuits, and headlines regarding the 2002 phone jamming scandal, meant that Sununu began his rematch with Shaheen far behind, and he never made up his lost ground. Shaheen defeated Sununu as part of the blue wave that brought Democrats to the brink of a filibuster-proof Senate majority in 2008. Democrats were hopeful that they could win the state's other Senate seat in 2010, especially after Judd Gregg announced he would not seek another term. But by 2010, the economic collapse that had doomed Republican hopes in 2008 was now under the management of President Barack Obama, and Republican Kelly Ayotte, the state's attorney general, won an easy victory over Congressman Paul Hodes. In 2014, New Hampshire Republicans struggled to find a credible and willing challenger to Jeanne Shaheen, and ultimately settled on Scott Brown, who had lost his bid for a full term in Massachusetts in 2012. Brown relocated to his vacation home in coastal Rye, declared himself a Granite Stater, and gave Shaheen a run for her money despite being a newcomer to the state. Shaheen won re-election with 51.6 percent of the vote, exactly what she had earned in 2008.

In 2016, Democrats recruited Governor Maggie Hassan to run against Kelly Ayotte in her bid for a second term. Ayotte had made a splash during her term in Washington, frequently appearing with fellow Republicans John McCain and Lindsay Graham to discuss national security issues and building a somewhat bipartisan voting record. She had been the subject of vice-presidential buzz in 2012, and many thought she would again be on the short list for the party's 2016 nominee before that nominee turned out to be Donald Trump. But she had also made a number of ham-fisted statements on gun regulation in the wake of the Sandy Hook elementary school massacre. Ayotte was also weighed down by Trump's presence atop the Republican ticket. After months of trying to tap dance around the issue by saying she would support but not endorse Trump, Ayotte announced after the infamous *Access Hollywood* tape that she would write in Mike Pence, Trump's running mate, for president. Hassan, meanwhile, focused on her own record in office and attacked Ayotte for her indecision about Trump. Another factor in the race was the independent candidacy of conservative Aaron Day, who ran to Ayotte's right and attacked her as insufficiently conservative and wobbly in her support of the Second Amendment. Hassan ultimately defeated Ayotte by just 1,017 votes (with Day earning over 17,000) and declared victory the morning after the 2016 election (Lucas, Sisco, and Galdieri 2018).

Few Republicans thought Jeanne Shaheen would be easy to defeat in 2020, particularly after Governor Chris Sununu declined to challenge her. In the absence of a top-tier challenger, the party ultimately nominated Bryant "Corky" Messner, who had practiced law in Colorado before retiring to New Hampshire. The COVID pandemic complicated campaigning for everyone in 2020, but particularly so for Messner, an unknown figure without roots in the state or the state party. While Shaheen was able to use the powers of incumbency to communicate with voters about the pandemic and do things like speak (via Zoom) at Concord High School's outdoors, socially distanced graduation (O'Sullivan 2020), Messner struggled to raise funds and attract attention. Shaheen won a third term with 56.6 percent of the vote.

Two years later, Republicans thought Maggie Hassan would be a ripe target, as a Democrat seeking a second term during the midterm election of an unpopular Democratic president. Republicans once again courted Chris

Sununu to run, but he opted to seek a fourth term as governor instead. Into the breach strode Don Bolduc, a retired brigadier general who had given Corky Messner a run for his money in the 2020 GOP Senate primary. But Bolduc's volatile behavior after his primary loss (including a lengthy and public refusal to endorse Messner), his embrace of Donald Trump's big lie about the 2020 election, and a propensity for wild statements made him unpalatable to mainline Republicans, who searched for an alternative candidate. A series of summits between party power brokers and potential candidates failed to settle on a single alternative, and both Chuck Morse, president of the state Senate, and Kevin Smith, a former state representative who had run for governor in 2010 and then served as town manager of Londonderry, entered the race. Neither was able to establish himself as the better alternative to Bolduc, and a late infusion of independent spending on Morse's behalf was too little, too late to stop Bolduc from winning the nomination. State Republicans gamely closed ranks behind Bolduc, and some polling showed a close race, but on Election Day Hassan won comfortably with 53.5 percent of the vote to Bolduc's 44.4 percent. While Bolduc hoped an emphasis on inflation would carry him to victory, Hassan—always a disciplined campaigner, at times to a fault, at times beyond a fault—focused on Bolduc's shifting positions on the 2020 election and his position on abortion.

A look at elections to New Hampshire's two seats in the House of Representatives since 2002 similarly demonstrates the state's shift to having two competitive parties. In 2002 and 2004, Republicans Jeb Bradley and Charlie Bass easily won their elections; in 2006, when few prognosticators saw either incumbent as endangered, even as the blue backlash to George W. Bush was building throughout the country, both lost their races. In the first district, Carol Shea-Porter, a former local party chair and activist, defeated Bradley, and in the second, attorney Paul Hodes won a rematch with Bass. Shea-Porter and Hodes were easily re-elected to second terms in 2008. 2010 saw Republicans win both seats, as Manchester mayor Frank Guinta defeated Carol Shea-Porter and Charlie Bass beat Ann McLane Kuster in that year's Tea Party wave. Two years later, both of those Democrats came out on top in rematches, buoyed by Barack Obama's strong re-election performance in New Hampshire.

In 2014, the stories of the two districts diverge. In the first district, Republican Frank Guinta returned to defeat Democratic incumbent Carol Shea-Porter in yet another rematch, while Democratic incumbent Ann Kuster held on to her seat against Marilinda Garcia, a former Republican state representative. Kuster has since won re-election every two years, usually by 10-point margins or better; her 2022 victory makes her the first Democrat to win six consecutive terms in Congress in state history. The first district's races have been more competitive and contentious. Carol Shea-Porter returned for one last matchup with Guinta in 2016 and won, even while Donald Trump carried the district. In 2018, Democrat Chris Pappas became New Hampshire's first openly gay federal representative when he defeated Republican Eddie Edwards, and won re-election in 2020 over Matt Mowers, a onetime Chris Christie aide who had moved to New Hampshire to work for the state's Republican Party in advance of Christie's presidential bid and then worked in the Donald Trump administration. Mowers ran again in 2022, but proved insufficiently Trumpish for the primary electorate, and lost the primary to Karoline Leavitt, a 25-year-old who had worked in the Trump White House and ran a hard-right campaign that included a complete denial of the results of the 2020 election and extremist rhetoric against transgender people. This helped her win a crowded primary; it also alienated general election voters, and Pappas won a third term by eight points. In the space of about twenty years, New Hampshire has gone from a state with two reliably Republican seats in the House to a state with one competitive seat in the first district and one that leans blue in the second. Notably, Republicans failed to capitalize on what should have been a favorable environment in 2022 with strong candidates with crossover appeal; instead, two MAGA Republicans proved unable to win votes beyond their base in a general election. In January 2024, however, Republican presidential primary voters gave Donald Trump the nod.

A look at governor's races illustrates several truisms about modern New Hampshire politics: Incumbent governors tend to get re-elected, though that is not an ironclad rule; popular governors can survive the other party's wave elections; and neither party has a permanent hold on the governor's mansion. John Lynch's 2004 defeat of Republican Governor Craig Benson is notable for its rarity, but once ensconced in the governor's office, Lynch won re-election to three more terms. In 2012, Maggie Hassan won an easy victory over Ovide Lamontagne, and a second term despite 2014's red wave nationally. Once Chris Sununu won a tight race in 2016, he did not struggle in any of his re-election bids; his closest race was during 2018's Democratic wave, when he still won a second term without much trouble even as Democrats romped to victory down ballot.

TABLE 6.3 Votes for Governor of New Hampshire, 1996–2022

YEAR	DEMOCRAT	VOTE	%	REPUBLICAN	VOTE	%
1996	Jeanne Shaheen	84,175	57.2%	Ovide Lamontagne	196,321	39.5%
1998	Jeanne Shaheen	210,769	66.1%	Jay Lucas	98,473	30.9%
2000	Jeanne Shaheen	275,038	48.7%	Gordon Humphrey	246,952	43.8%
2002	Mark Fernald	169,277	38.2%	Craig Benson	59,663	58.6%
2004	John Lynch	340,299	51.0%	Craig Benson	325,981	48.9%
2006	John Lynch	298,760	74.0%	Jim Coburn	04,288	25.8%
2008	John Lynch	479,042	70.2%	Joe Kenney	88,555	27.6%
2010	John Lynch	240,346	52.6%	John Stephen	05,616	45.0%
2012	Maggie Hassan	378,934	54.6%	Ovide Lamontagne	95,026	42.5%
2014	Maggie Hassan	54,666	52.4%	Walt Havenstein	30,610	47.4%
2016	Colin Van Ostern	337,589	46.6%	Chris Sununu	54,040	48.8%
2018	Molly Kelly	262,359	45.7%	Chris Sununu	02,764	49.3%
2020	Dan Feltes	264,639	33.4%	Chris Sununu	16,609	65.1%
2022	Tom Sherman	256,766	41.5%	Chris Sununu	52,813	57.0%

The Road Ahead

New Hampshire has become a state where every office is potentially competitive; when elections are not, that is usually because the incumbent has made themselves familiar and useful to Granite State voters. Regardless of party or ideology, incumbents are always careful to talk about bread-and-butter issues and concrete results: The state of the economy, hiring more teachers and nurses, delivering federal dollars to communities where they are needed, and so on. But neither party has laid claim to an enduring majority that allows them to dominate the state as Republicans did for most of the twentieth century. Each party also faces potential divisions or growing pains that could complicate their path forward.

Democrats have established a formula for winning elections in New Hampshire: Run moderate, pragmatic candidates who emphasize their success as problem-solvers and downplay ideology and partisanship. But this approach could lead to headaches in years to come. Nationally, Democrats have become a younger coalition, with increased racial, ethnic, and gender identity diversity (Boak 2022). New Hampshire, by contrast, is one of the whitest states in the union, and the departure of young Granite Staters for Boston and other metropolitan areas after high school and college is a persistent quandary.

It is not hard to imagine tension between New Hampshire Democrats, with an older, whiter constituency, and their national counterparts on issues such as immigration, student loans, foreign policy, and others. At home, the Democrats benefit from the shift in suburban voting patterns that has taken place in New Hampshire, just as it has in the rest of the country, since Donald Trump's 2016 election. Bedford, a Manchester suburb that was a longtime GOP stronghold, voted for Democrat Maggie Hassan by a 4-point margin in 2022; Bow, a suburb of Concord that Hassan lost by 2 percent in 2016, went for her by 20 percent in 2022. But Democrats' successes in suburbs may again make it difficult for Granite State Democrats to stay on the same page as their national party. And as Manchester, once a city full of conservative wards, becomes both more diverse and more liberal, there is a prospect of tension between Democrats from the state's largest city and newly Democratic-friendly voters from the suburbs if and when Democrats ever control the state's government again.

Republicans have headaches of their own. The greatest of these is the sizable MAGA constituency in the party, which is more interested in cultural and grievance politics—and rehashing the 2020 election—than the old Yankee Republicans' focus on low taxes and low levels of regulation on business. This MAGA constituency flexed its muscles in 2022, delivering primary victories to Don Bolduc in the Senate race and to Karoline Leavitt and Bob Burns in the state's House races. But these victories were possible largely due to the atrophy of the state Republican leaders' capacity to influence candidates and would-be candidates. In the Senate race, party leaders failed to coordinate on a mainstream alternative to Bolduc until it was too late. In the Second Congressional District, Governor Chris Sununu endorsed George Hansel, the moderate mayor of Keene, but this was not enough to deliver Hansel a primary win. And in the first, Leavitt won by being the Trumpiest candidate in a field with at least five major candidates. If Republicans are not able to nominate mainstream conservative candidates, they will continue to miss out on opportunities to send Republicans to Congress given the demographic changes in the state.

There are, however, those who have made it difficult for mainstream Republicans to win elections generally. In one of the stranger political sagas in recent American history, New Hampshire has become the site of the so-called Free State Project, a "voluntary resettlement" of libertarian-minded individuals to the Granite State with the goal of turning it into a libertarian paradise (Quimby 2018). In recent years, the group's numbers have achieved a critical enough mass that they have begun to both impact state and local politics, and to provoke backlash and counter-mobilizations. In Croydon, a Free State-affiliated selectman nearly succeeded in an effort to cut the town's school budget by more than half; only a town-wide mobilization was able to reverse the cuts (Barry 2022). In Belknap County, Free Stater state legislators' hard-line stances temporarily shut down the county-owned Gunstock ski resort, which prompted a backlash from both voters, who defeated the legislators in question in the 2022 primary, and Governor Sununu, who said the legislators were "anti-government individuals" and not Republicans (Gokee 2022). But meaningful numbers of Free Staters have won elections to the state legislature as Republicans, and often find allies in the rest of the party. The amateur nature of the state legislature contributes to this; with 400 seats in the lower house and a salary of just $100 per annual session, candidates for the legislature often face little scrutiny, particularly in areas where local media has atrophied.

The issue of abortion is a wild card that could complicate Republicans' future electoral prospects as well. There had long been tension between New Hampshire Republicans and the national party over this issue; while elected Republicans took a wide range of positions on the issue, the party's rank-and-file was more generally supportive of abortion rights. While *Roe v. Wade* was the law of the land, the issue largely abided until after the 2020 election. In 2021, the newly-elected Republican state legislature passed, and Governor Chris Sununu signed, a budget with provisions making it a felony to perform an abortion after twenty-four weeks and requiring an ultrasound for anyone seeking an abortion; the backlash to this was fierce enough that many of these provisions were revised or repealed the following year (Ramer 2021). The Supreme Court's decision in *Dobbs v. Jackson Women's Health Organization* to overturn *Roe v. Wade* in 2022 ensured that the issue dominated many of that year's races, and the decision was particularly unpopular in New Hampshire. A May 2022 poll found that just 15 percent of voters identifying as Republicans thought abortion should be illegal in all circumstances, while 69 percent said it should be legal in limited circumstances and 17 percent said it should always be legal. An election environment in which abortion is both at risk and a salient issue would present tremendous complications for Republican candidates (McKinley, Azem, and Smith 2022).

Adding to the state GOP's headaches is the small but meaningful number of "Never Trump" Republicans who have been vocal critics of Trump and his supporters within the GOP. Some, like former state chair Fergus Cullen, have been critical of Trump but remain part of the state party and have tried to keep it in the political mainstream; others, like former senator Gordon Humphrey, have gone so far as to endorse Trump's opponents and switch their registration to independent (Spodak 2016; DiStaso 2018; Steinhauser 2020).

At the state level, Republicans' current successes are in large part thanks to Governor Chris Sununu's popularity and his ability to appeal to, or at least avoid alienating, the various factions within the state party. Sununu's 2020 landslide re-election delivered the legislature and executive council into Republicans' hands after their 2018 losses; this, in turn, allowed the legislature to draw maps that should ensure the executive council and state senate remain Republican through the next round of redistricting after 2030, barring a blue wave somewhere between the size of a tsunami and a sharknado. With Sununu opting not to seek a record-breaking fifth term in 2024, however, the governor's race and control of the lower house of the legislature are likely to be toss-ups, and that only if the Republicans can avoid nominating a full-throated MAGA candidate for governor.

The structure of New Hampshire's government also complicates matters. The state has abundant opportunities for citizens to run for public office, from the 424-member legislature (which I am obliged to note is the third largest in the English-speaking world, after the United Kingdom's Parliament and the United States Congress) to city and town councils and school boards. Since these positions offer minimal compensation, many of those who run for them are retired, independently wealthy, or have jobs that allow them the flexibility to serve, and most state legislators remain largely anonymous figures beyond their own districts (and sometimes even within those districts). New Hampshire has very few positions that give an ambitious politician the chance to build a statewide electoral reputation before running for governor or Congress, or for a governor to groom a designated successor: The state has no lieutenant governor, the secretary of state and the state treasurer are chosen by the legislature, the attorney general is appointed by the governor. It is not that it is impossible to move from, for instance, the state Senate to a higher office, as Maggie Hassan and Jeanne Shaheen did, or to move from one of these appointed positions to higher office, as Kelly Ayotte did. But candidates from these positions often struggle to introduce themselves to the rest of the state, as seen in the cases of the three sitting for former state senators who have run for governor and lost to Chris Sununu. The executive council can also act as a springboard to higher office, as Chris Sununu and Chris Pappas can attest, but the heavily gerrymandered districts passed in

2010 and 2020 mean it is most likely to be of use to ambitious Republicans through the end of this decade.

New Hampshire has been home to several political dynasties over the years; Chris Sununu is the son of a governor and brother of a former senator; Judd Gregg's father also served as governor; former Congressman Charlie Bass is the son of a congressman and grandson of a governor. But other than Chris Sununu there has been a decided lack of dynastic ambition in the state's recent politics.

That said, it is usually a bad idea to rule anything out when it comes to New Hampshire politics. The 2022 elections provide ample proof of this. While polling suggested that Maggie Hassan and Chris Pappas were locked in tight races, they dispatched their Republican opponents by wide margins. Chris Sununu won another term as governor, but his coattails were not what they had been in 2020, and Republicans barely held their majority in the lower house of the state legislature. Following recounts, the legislature convened on December 7 with a membership consisting of 201 Republicans, 198 Democrats, and one vacant seat. That vacancy was the result of a perfect tie in Rochester and was filled by a special election early in 2023. In such a closely divided chamber, legislating comes down not just to which members are present on a given day—the legislature's part-time status means attendance is often fluid—but which members are having lunch at which restaurant on Concord's Main Street on a given day.

Works Cited

Barry, Dan. 2022. "One Small Step for Democracy in a 'Live Free or Die' Town." *The New York Times*, July 10, 2022, sec. U.S. https://www.nytimes.com/2022/07/10/us/croydon-free-state-politics.html.

Berry, John M. 1991. "Chilly Economic Climate Awaits Candidates in New Hampshire." *Washington Post*, December 28, 1991. https://www.washingtonpost.com/archive/politics/1991/12/28/chilly-economic-climate-awaits-candidates-in-new-hampshire/4dbe4403-0e80-40f4-aab7-8d38cefc5514/.

Boak, Josh. 2022. "Biden Juggling Long List of Issues to Please Dem Coalition." *AP NEWS*. October 22, 2022. https://apnews.com/article/2022-midterm-elections-biden-inflation-prices-congress-35e360e9e59a8890b29c4a16cdf9e3c4.

Broder, David S. 1991. "New Hampshire Recession Is Bad News for Bush." *Tampa Bay Times*. July 24, 1991. https://www.tampabay.com/archive/1991/07/24/new-hampshire-recession-is-bad-news-for-bush/.

Bryant, Jessica. 2022. "The Most Highly Educated States." Best Colleges. May 6, 2022. https://www.bestcolleges.com/news/analysis/2022/01/10/most-highly-educated-states/.

Cauterucci, Christina. 2020. "Is New Hampshire a Swing State Anymore?" *Slate*. November 2, 2020. https://slate.com/news-and-politics/2020/11/new-hampshire-still-swing-state.html.

DiStaso, John. 2018. "NH Primary Source: Former GOP Sen. Humphrey, Now an Independent, Backs Democrat Pappas." *WMUR*. November 3, 2018. https://www.wmur.com/article/nh-primary-source-former-gop-sen-humphrey-now-an-independent-backs-democrat-pappas/24575078.

Fistek, Michelle Anne. 1997. "New Hampshire: Is the Granite Grip of the Republican Party Cracking?" In *Parties & Politics in the New England States*, edited by Jerome M. Mileur, 37–54. Amherst, MA: Polity Publications, Inc.

Galdieri, Christopher J. 2019. *Stranger in a Strange State: The Politics of Carpetbagging from Robert Kennedy to Scott Brown*. Albany: State University of New York Press.

Galdieri, Christopher J. 2020. *Donald Trump and New Hampshire Politics*. Palgrave Studies in US Elections. New York, NY: Palgrave Pivot.

Gokee, Amanda. 2022. "Belknap County Voters Took Anger over Gunstock's Closure to the Polls." *New Hampshire Public Radio*. September 19, 2022. https://www.nhpr.org/nh-news/2022-09-19/belknap-county-voters-took-anger-over-gunstocks-closure-to-the-polls.

Lucas, Jennifer, Tauna S. Sisco, and Christopher J. Galdieri. 2018. "New Hampshire Senate Race: Closest in the Nation." In *The Roads to Congress 2016: American Elections in a Divided Landscape*, edited by Sean D. Foreman and Marcia L. Godwin, 321–37. Cham: Springer International Publishing. https://doi.org/10.1007/978-3-319-58094-4_21.

Mark, David. 2007. "'02 Phone Scandal Still Ringing Dems' Ears." *POLITICO*. August 1, 2007. https://www.politico.com/story/2007/08/02-phone-scandal-still-ringing-dems-ears-005205.

McKinley, Sean P., Zachary S. Azem, and Andrew E. Smith. 2022. "Granite Staters Support Roe, Divided on Support for Ukraine 6/1/2022." The Granite State Poll. University of New Hampshire Survey Center. https://scholars.unh.edu/cgi/viewcontent.cgi?article=1694&context=survey_center_polls.

Myers, R. Kelly. 1995. "New Hampshire Redux." *The Public Perspective* 6, no. 4: 46–48.

Newport, Frank. 2016. "New Hampshire Now Least Religious State in U.S." *Gallup*. February 4, 2016. https://news.gallup.com/poll/189038/new-hampshire-least-religious-state.aspx.

NHPR Staff. 2023. "Push to Honor Old Man of the Mountain Advances in NH State House." New Hampshire Public Radio. March 22, 2023. https://www.nhpr.org/nh-news/2023-03-22/push-to-honor-old-man-of-the-mountain-advances-in-nh-state-house.

O'Sullivan, Tim. 2020. "Concord High Finalizes Plans for Socially Distant June 13 Graduation Ceremony at Memorial Field." *Concord Monitor*. May 21, 2020. https://www.concordmonitor.com/Concord-High-School-socially-distant-graduation-plans-34232833.

Quimby, Taylor. 2015. "Is the Mount Washington Observatory the Ultimate Zombie Fortress?" New Hampshire Public Radio. October 29, 2015. https://www.nhpr.org/word-of-mouth/2015-10-29/is-the-mount-washington-observatory-the-ultimate-zombie-fortress.

Quimby, Taylor. 2018. "You Asked, We Answered: What Is the Free State Project?" *New Hampshire Public Radio*. April 12, 2018. https://www.nhpr.org/nh-news/2018-04-12/you-asked-we-answered-what-is-the-free-state-project.

Ramer, Holly. 2021. "NH Lawmakers OK $13B Budget with School Vouchers, Abortion Limits, 'Divisive Concepts' Ban." *Portsmouth Herald*, June 24, 2021. https://www.seacoastonline.com/story/news/state/2021/06/24/nh-lawmakers-approve-spending-13-5-b-budget-added-items-debated/5335360001/.

Smith, Ashley. 2010. "Recessions' Moments of Chaos." *Nashua Telegraph*, December 27, 2010. https://www.nashuatelegraph.com/news/local-news/2010/12/27/recessions-8217-moments-of-chaos/.

Spodak, Cassie. 2016. "Life as a Republican after #NeverTrump." *CNN Politics* (blog), *CNN*. October 31, 2016. https://www.cnn.com/2016/10/31/politics/gordon-humphrey-presidential-election/index.html.

Steinhauser, Paul. 2020. "On the Trail: Odd Couple Team up Target Common Foe—Trump." *Concord Monitor*. August 28, 2020. https://www.concordmonitor.com/On-the-Trail-by-Paul-Steinhauser-Tump-visits-NH-35962879.

Toner, Robin. 1996. "Political Briefs—The New York Times." *New York Times*, May 2, 1996, sec. B.

UPI. 1991. "Bankruptcy Cases Up In New Hampshire." *Christian Science Monitor*, April 16, 1991. https://www.csmonitor.com/1991/0416/16062.html.

Wickham, Shawne. 2007. "Are We Becoming New Massahampshire?" *New Hampshire Union Leader*, October 5, 2007.

Woodward, Bob. 2021. "Perspective: How Backroom Politics Helped Roe Survive a 1992 Challenge." *Washington Post*. December 3, 2021. https://www.washingtonpost.com/outlook/casey-roe-souter-rudman/2021/12/03/fd28aa40-53c6-11ec-8769-2f4ecdf7a2ad_story.html.

CHAPTER 7

RHODE ISLAND

More Than Yankee, Less Than True Blue

Maureen Moakley
Professor Emerita of Political Science
University of Rhode Island

At the top of the Rhode Island state house is a gold leaf, 11-foot statue called the Independent Man. This curious figure stands above a grandiose building that is the largest and most elaborate of all capitols in New England. Constructed in 1899, when Rhode Island was one of the most prosperous states in the country, it speaks volumes about the history, culture, and politics of the state.

Since its inception, this tiny state was an outlier from traditional notions of Yankee culture with its roots in the Puritan ethic, so much that its New England neighbors disdainfully dubbed the state Rogue Island. Freedom of thought and religion set the colony apart from early norms in New England and flourishing trade and commerce fostered a more individualistic ethic. Smuggling was common under English colonial control and flourishing trade and commerce fostered a more transactional ethic that brought great wealth and prosperity to the state during the eighteenth and nineteenth century (Rutledge 2019). Rhode Island's statue atop its grand capitol suggests that this tiny state, which survived takeover threats from Massachusetts and Connecticut, wanted to convey its dominant position in New England and counter other states' disdain.

Not only has Rhode Island continued to be more than Yankee, but its small size shapes the political culture of the state. Rhode Island, the smallest state in the Union, has a land mass of over 1,300 square miles; north to south the state runs 48 miles, east to west 37 miles. One can drive north up Interstate 95 toward Boston and pass through the state in about an hour. With a population of 1,097,379, it is the second most densely populated state in the country. And with over 400 miles of shoreline, it's called the Ocean State.[1] Providence, the state capitol, sits at the head of Narragansett Bay at the confluence of three rivers. Within a few miles lies the Massachusetts state line.

---

[1] The state's rural area extends to the north and west while the eastern part of the state has dense urban populations and extensive shoreline communities. There are 39 municipal cities and towns.

Within these small geographical bounds there are tight-knit communities and a sense that everyone knows everybody else that breeds closeness and parochialism. Yet there has been significant change. The political proclivities of Rhode Islanders have moved from backing mostly Republicans until the 1920s when the state became dominated by Democrats. In the last 50 years, however, the state is less than true blue in that while elections continue to show Democratic strength, the party machine has unraveled, voters are less inclined to register as partisans, and rural dissension sustains limited GOP electoral support. In the past few decades, however, the ethos of this small state has changed. Women are equal electoral players and greater racial and ethnic diversity is evident. Government has become more open and professionalized, and the state has passed some transformative policies.

To explore these changes, we first look at the historical development of the political culture in Rhode Island and then explore how this has influenced political and economic trends throughout its history. We then consider how recent changes shaped the political life of the state and brought it closer to its New England neighbors.

MORE THAN YANKEE FROM THE START

During the time of Puritan settlements in New England, the colonies created a theocracy in which the church and state set strict adherences for all religious and social norms. Roger Williams rejected these beliefs, was exiled, and then, in 1636, founded the colony of Rhode Island and Providence Plantations. As a colony with no established church and freedom of religion and political thought, it became a refuge for dissidents like Quakers and Jews who settled in the colony and prospered. While community-oriented norms were evident in these tolerant beginnings, strains of individualism emerged early on as trade and commercial endeavors flourished. Historian Gordon Wood notes that in Rhode Island, freedom of religion, trade and commerce created "the most liberal, most entrepreneurial and the most modern of the eighteenth-century colonies" (Wood 1993, 140).

Studies of political culture argue that a state's early founding creates an enduring component of the state's ethos. In a pathbreaking study, Daniel Elazar found that in addition to a common national culture, there are three basic subcultures: moralistic, individualistic, and traditionalistic (Elazar

---

Recent demographic shifts have resulted considerable diversity; the white population is 70.4%, Hispanics are 17.1 percent, Blacks are 8.85 percent, Naïve Americans are 2.1 percent, Asian are 3.7 percent, Native Hawaiian, and Pacific Islanders are 0.2 percent and people of two or more races 3.0 percent (U.S. Census 2020).

1966). New England's early dominant culture was moralistic. It is based on the idea that church and state together were part of a commonwealth of true believers who were bound to participate in politics to promote a good society. In Rhode Island individualistic norms dominated, rooted in freedom of religion and free speech. A form of interest group politics emerged early on, marked by competition and infighting over different religious ideas and political control of settlement turf. This still is evident in the tradition of vocal groups that, in a small state, have access to and influence on the political process. Contemporary studies indicate that current policy and public attitudes reflect a state's founding ethic (Anton 1989).

Rhode Island's eighteenth-century culture allowed for freewheeling trade and commerce, which originally centered around the city of Newport, the commercial center of the colony that included investments in the slave trade which was abolished in 1843. The state continued to prosper as a center of whaling and Narragansett Bay become a base for clipper ships and the China trade. These all brought fabulous wealth to an elite. Rural areas mostly held to Yankee norms of self-sufficiency and thrift, and this is still reflected in the fiscal conservatism and the libertarian bent among Republican officeholders from these areas.

Rhode Island was the birthplace of the Industrial Revolution. It was the first state in the country to establish working industrial mills powered by its rivers. John Brown contracted with Samuel Slater, who brought the English blueprint for these industrial mills to America, and established Slater Mill in 1790 (Valeria Diaz 2018). An industrial boom followed, creating a demand for labor that brought successive waves of European immigrants to work in mills and manufacturing. Hampered by prejudice and ethnic infighting, they struggled to gain access to the social, economic, and political benefits that they were initially denied.

The prosperity of the late nineteenth century continued until the late 1920s when textile mills began to move south for cheaper labor but other manufacturing enterprises like jewelry and machine parts continued to sustain the economy. An increasing military presence in the state up through World War II also boosted the economy; the US Navy become the largest employer in the state until 1972 when the Nixon administration began a pullout of most bases to the South. That, along with the losses in manufacturing, resulted in a long economic decline (Moakley and Cornwell, 2001).

In the early twentieth century, labor organizations were a progressive force and advocated for workers and immigrant groups, fueling industrial growth, and helping to create a rising middle class. While private sector unions remain influential, unions' political power lies with the public service unions to which thousands of state and municipal workers and teachers belong. State pension reform, passed in 2011, curtailed some of the more excessive provisions of union agreements dealing with disability pension contracts and work rules. Yet many municipalities, which were not part of the state system, remain burdened with costly work rules and increasing long-term pension obligations. Providence has an outstanding pension obligation of over one billion dollars with yearly payout costs that continue to escalate. Voters approved a $515 million obligation bond in 2022 to lessen the debt but as interest rates rose, the proposal was halted. (Stevens 2022). Unions are dealing with a strong hand as they assume the state would not allow the capitol city to go bankrupt.

The 2000s have seen an economic rebound as the state reinvents itself in areas of high tech, financial services, medical industries, wind energy and tourism. However, it's still a struggle. An economic report in 2023 acknowledged marked progress, while noting that Rhode Island's economic trajectory continues to lag in New England (Justine 2023).

"LITTLE RHODY," THE SMALLEST STATE

Size shapes the state's political culture. Rhode Island is considered a state where everybody knows everybody else. A *Providence Journal* editor noted that ". . . here in Rhode Island, take six degrees of separation and divide by two" (Ng 2022). This orientation creates many tight-knit communities and lends itself to a cozy interpersonal style, and pride and defensiveness about being a Rhode Islander.

It also sustains a somewhat parochial milieu. Along the highway that runs through the state, as one nears Providence, an enormous blue bug, representing a pest control company, hangs over US Route 95. Costumed on various holidays and events, it has become something of an icon. At Christmas time, it is decked out with lights and local television news stations broadcast the Lighting of the Blue Bug. At the Zoom roll call at the 2020 Democratic National convention, the state party chair relayed the state's vote on a beach holding a plate of calamari. *The Washington Post* commented that it was certainly the 'most irreverent' announcement and the characteristically Rhode Island way to make an appearance on the national stage (Arums and Farzan 2020).

There is an underside to this picture. Among political elites, everybody *does* know everybody else, and this lends itself to an insider advantage and the "I know a guy" syndrome that journalists expose, and reformers decry.

Historian Patrick Conley notes, "There is a unique degree of coziness between political leaders, labor leaders, and social leaders. It's the result of living in a city state." (Gregg 2021)

Rhode Island has a legacy of political corruption. When the Democrats took over government in the 1930s, in addition to significant electoral and administrative reforms, they created a political machine based on patronage and insider deals, administrative bloat, bureaucratic inefficiencies, and their share of political scandals.

Then there was the reign of the Mafia in the post war period. Along with a base in Boston, the Mafia established an operation at Federal Hill, an Italian community in Providence, during the post WWII era. They continued their nefarious activities—including influence in politics—until its decline in the late 1980s when attorney generals and law enforcement convicted and jailed key Mafia operatives. Small scale extortions and bribes occasionally occur, but the mob is no longer a player. Rhode Islanders, however, still have a perverse preoccupation with the Mafia, fueled by continued media focus on the Mafia and its corrupt past, which reinforces dated stereotypes.

The lore of Buddy Cianci, the colorful, corrupt, and charismatic mayor of Providence, adds to this legacy. He was a competent leader and forceful promoter of the Providence Renaissance—a massive infrastructure project that included moving rivers and railroad tracks which brought the city of Providence back from a spiral of decline in the 1980s, creating an urban gem. Cianci was convicted in 2002 of racketeering during his last term in office and sentenced to five years in federal prison. His activities received national attention as books, plays, and a television series that recounted his political life. Other scandals still occur, such as when the Speaker of the House was convicted in 2015 of taking bribes and misusing campaign funds; he too spent time in federal prison. Such instances, however, are less frequent and on a par with many other states.

Data-based rankings show that while Rhode Island is not in the ten least corrupt category but it also not in the most corrupt rankings; the state usually comes up in the middle range (Enten 2015; Dincer and Johnson 2014). But the local media still run old pictures and old stories, and, in some cases, reporters create their own impressionistic rankings that are widely off the mark. These then bubble up on social media platforms and get cited as part of the current milieu.

Rhode Island has a long tradition of citizen participation. The size of the state continues to sustain and empower a tradition of vocal and at times ornery citizen groups with access to and influence on the political process. In recent years demonstrations around racial and economic injustices, funding for public services based on previous support during the COVID pandemic, and higher demands about solving other group interests have emerged. Federal and state mandates that require public input on pending initiatives have also energized citizen groups. People have higher expectations about the government and elected officials are keenly aware of these shifts.

PARTISAN POLITICS—HOW DEMOCRATS CAME TO DOMINANCE.

Until the early 1920s Rhode Island resembled other New England states in that it was solidly Republican; but demographic change began to threaten the dominance of the GOP. Reacting to the threat of a working-class majority of mostly Catholic ethnic groups like the Irish, Republicans were able to sustain their ascendency with broad voting restrictions and severely malapportioned districts that gave outsized representation to Republicans. The strategy was sustained by a compliant court system.

The massive mobilization of Democratic voters came around the presidential candidacy in 1928 of Democrat Al Smith, an Irish Catholic from a working-class background in New York. During that race, the Democratic electorate swelled as other ethnic groups in Rhode Island, who had been wary of Irish domination, joined the party. While Smith was not a particularly strong candidate nationally, Democratic rolls in the state increased by 55 percent (Congressional Quarterly 1994). This trend continued in the election of 1932, when Franklin Roosevelt was elected president and Democratic T.F. Green was reelected governor.

This set the scene for the Bloodless Revolution of 1935. During the 1934 election, with Green as governor, Democrats continued to pick up legislative seats and achieved a majority in the House but were ultimately short two seats in the state Senate. At the annual reorganization meeting on January 1, in a curious machination, the Senate President, Democrat Lieutenant Governor Robert Quinn, was able to invalidate two Republican Senate election totals and swear in waiting two Democratic replacements. Democrats now controlled the governorship, all the five general offices, and the legislature. Existing rules for reorganization allowed the General Assembly to vacate and replace all members of the state Supreme Court to prevent the court from invalidating subsequent policies and reforms on the Democratic Party's agenda. All in one day (DeSimone 2020).

Rhode Island became a solidly blue state. The nexus of Democrats' power was in the urban core in and around the capitol city of Providence. Rural voters, fewer in numbers, remained wary of the Democratic machine and continued to support Republicans for office.

While Democrats continue to win elections, a weaker and hollowed out party system has less influence. The political machine began to unravel in the late 1970s. Expectations changed. Demands for more professional and transparent government followed; reform groups mobilized, lifting the lid on the inefficiency and favoritism of the patronage system. Suburbanization and generational changes loosened partisan ties and the electorate became more independent. Voter dissonance and party upheaval followed, allowing for some GOP victories. Candidate centered campaigns and individual personalities are more the norm. Unaffiliated voters are now the largest contingent of registered voters in the state. As of 2023, registered Republicans are 14 percent of the electorate, Democrats are at 40 percent and unaffiliated voters are 46 percent (Secretary of State 2023).

Elections: Blue with Shadows

Looking at election results since 1998, Table 7.1 shows that since 2000, when Lincoln Chaffee was elected to the US Senate as a Republican, Democrats have controlled the congressional delegation. Republicans won the governorship until 2010 when Lincoln Chafee was elected as an Independent. The Democrats dominated the legislature throughout this period. In 2023, Democrats controlled the federal delegation, the governorship, all general offices, and the state legislature. Local cities and towns, however, present a more nuanced picture.

PRESIDENTIAL VOTE

Presidential elections confirm the strength of the Democrats. Rhode Island voted twice for Eisenhower in 1952 and 1954, for Nixon in 1972 and Reagan in 1984. The state has since supported all Democratic presidential candidates since 1984. Rates of Republican votes took a slight uptick in the 2016 and 2020 elections when Donald Trump was on the ticket. As Figure 7.1 indicates, there is a marked urban—rural divide. Trump carried 14 of 39 municipalities in 2016 and 11 in 2020. His support came mainly from rural parts of the state, who usually support the few Republican legislators in the General Assembly and local Republican officials. But their power is limited as there

TABLE 7.1 Partisan Affiliation of Rhode Island Election Winners, 1998–2022

YEAR	PRESIDENT (STATEWIDE)	US SENATE	RI-1	RI-2	GOVERNOR	STATE SENATE	STATE HOUSE
1998			Kennedy (D)	Weygand (D)	Almond (R)	Dem	Dem
2000	Gore (D)	Chafee (R)	Kennedy (D)	Langevin (D)		Dem	Dem
2002		Reed (D)	Kennedy (D)	Langevin (D)	Carcieri (R)	Dem	Dem
2004	Kerry (D)		Kennedy (D)	Langevin (D)		Dem	Dem
2006		Whitehouse (D)	Kennedy (D)	Langevin (D)*	Carcieri (R)	Dem	Dem
2008	Obama (D)	Reed (D)	Kennedy (D)	Langevin (D)		Dem	Dem
2010			Cicilline (D)	Langevin (D)	Chafee (I)	Dem	Dem
2012	Obama (D)	Whitehouse (D)	Cicilline (D)	Langevin (D)		Dem	Dem
2014		Reed (D)	Cicilline (D)	Langevin (D)	Raimondo (D)	Dem	Dem
2016	Clinton (D)		Cicilline (D)	Langevin (D)		Dem	Dem
2018		Whitehouse (D)	Cicilline (D)	Langevin (D)	Raimondo (D)	Dem	Dem
2020	Biden (D)	Reed (D)	Cicilline (D)**	Langevin (D)		Dem	Dem
2022			Cicilline (D)	Magaziner (D)	McKee (D)	Dem	Dem

* In 2006, no Republican was on the ticket for this election in District 2
** In 2020, no Republican was on the ticket for this election in District 2
Sources: "2006 General Election: Statewide and Federal Races." State of Rhode Island Board of Elections, https://elections.ri.gov/elections/results/2006/generalelection/topticket.php; "Rhode Island's 1st Congressional District Election, 2020." Ballotpedia. https://ballotpedia.org/Rhode_Island%27s_1st_Congressional_District_Election,_2020.

are just under 180,000 voters in GOP towns compared to over 900,000 in Democratic communities (Speakman 2023, 212).

Rural voters tend to reflect a long-standing Yankee ethic about the role of government that includes self-sufficiency and conservatism with a libertarian bent. Sitting GOP legislators express this orientation and tend to oppose policies that smack of the nanny state and some of the large sums of monies earmarked for urban areas. A general complaint is that these communities

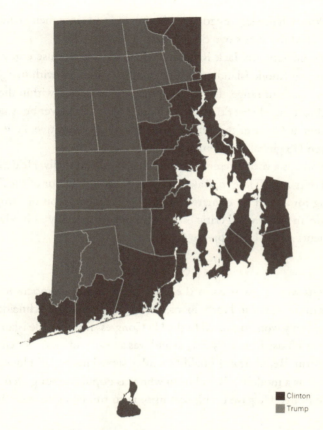

FIGURE 7.1. Presidential Election Results by Municipality, 2016. Source: Eli Sherman, WPRI.com. "Target 12 Report. Here's How RI Cities and Towns Have Voted in Every Presidential Race Since Reagan." October 28, 2020. https://www.wpri.com/target-12/heres-how-ri-cities-and-towns-have-voted-in-every-presidential-race-since-reagan/.

pay their taxes, have functioning municipal governance and schools that are fairly well run. These attitudes are typical of rural constituencies across the country, where resentment appears to be based on perceptions that they ". . . are ignored by policymakers, don't get their fair share of resources, and are disrespected by "city folks" (Krugman 2023).

US SENATE RACES

Republican Lincoln Chafee was elected to the US Senate in 2000 for one term. He had been appointed to the seat in 1999 by Republican Governor Lincoln Chafee upon the death of his father, John Chafee—an icon in Rhode

Island politics. Chafee lost his 2006 re-election bid and since then Democrats have controlled the state's two Senate seats.

Democratic Senators Jack Reed and Sheldon Whitehouse enjoy solid support among Rhode Islanders; both win office handily—with margins in the 60 to 70 percent range. They are popular and respected within the state and prominent members of the Senate. Reed is an inside player but since his appointment as Chair of the Senate Armed Service committee, he is more visible given US global engagements.

Whitehouse is a vocal presence in the Senate and nationally. He delivered a series of over 200 "Time to Wake Up" speeches on the floor of the Senate advocating for action on climate change. He is a champion of campaign finance reform and a vocal critic of dark money—especially as it relates to appointments to the US Supreme Court.

US HOUSE RACES

Republicans won a few seats in the US House during Democratic Party upheavals in the 1980s and early 1990s. Republican Claudine Schneider was the first and only woman elected to the US Congress from Rhode Island. She served in the House from 1983 to 1991 and was an early advocate for environmental reform. Republican Ronald Machtley served in the US House from 1989 to 1995 as a moderate Republican who was popular among Democrats and Republicans. He gave up his seat in 1994 to run unsuccessfully for the US Senate.

Thereafter, Democrats have held Rhode Island's two US House seats, with little competition from the GOP. In addition to weak showings in these elections, in 2006 and 2020 no Republican candidate was on one of the two congressional district tickets.

Patrick Kennedy served in the US House from the First District from 1995 to 2010. He was widely popular, due in part to the Kennedy name and presence in the state. He consistently won with over 70 percent of the vote but retired because of health issues. The seat was taken in 2010 by Democrat David Cicilline, who was a popular incumbent and a prominent member of the House. A gay congressman, he championed LTGBQ+ rights and in 2022 ran for a Democratic House leadership position and lost. In 2023, he resigned to become president and CEO of the state's largest philanthropic organization. In 2023, the District 1 seat was won by Gabe Amo, the first person of color elected to the US House from Rhode Island.

Cicilline had the benefit of having one of the safest seats in the country.

After a middling showing in his first election, he lobbied the 2010 redistricting commission to cede portions of heavily Democratic South Providence to his district, giving his Democratic counterpart in District 2 three heavily Republican towns. While some population distributions were in order, the commission moved thousands more voters into District 1. This created tensions with Representative Jim Langevin as District 2 became more competitive. Since Langevin was a popular incumbent, they resolved the conflict and moved on. Langevin then resigned in 2022.

The issue came home to roost in the 2022 election for the US District 2 race. The GOP fielded Allan Fung, popular former mayor of Cranston, the second largest city in the state. The Democrat candidate Seth Magaziner, a former state treasurer, moved into the district when he ran. In a tough and competitive race, Magaziner prevailed but with just over 50 percent of the vote.

STATE GENERAL OFFICERS

From 1994 to 2006, in tight races, voters elected Republican governors. This was primarily the result of dissonance among Democratic voters and of having a progressive woman on the ticket Democratic ticket in three of these elections. At the time evidently, this was a bridge too far. In 2010, Lincoln Chafee was elected governor for one term as an Independent. The Democrats rebounded when Gina Raimondo won office in 2014 and 2018. When Raimondo resigned in 2020, Democrat Lieutenant Governor Dan McKee moved to that office and appointed a Latina woman, Sabina Matos to the office of Lt. Governor. In 2022, McKee won in the general election and Matos retained the office of Lt. Governor. An overview of the other statewide general offices indicates Democratic dominance and a strong presence of women.

STATE LEGISLATIVE ELECTIONS

The solidly Democratic legislature is ranked as one of the strongest in the country; conversely, the office of the governor is one of the weakest of all fifty states (Hamm and Miller 2018). Thus, the nexus of power often lies in the General Assembly. Heretofore, the legislature, particularly the House, was in the grip of rigid top-down Democratic leadership. Given the weak position of the governor, with no line-item veto and limited appointments, the Speaker of the House can be the most powerful leader in the state.

Up through the early 2020s, the leadership in both houses tended to be more conservative but growing pressure from elected progressives, women and then Governor Raimondo pushed the leadership to accede to more progressive policies. Moreover, a liberal shift in the state empowered progressives (Pew Research Center 2023). This caused interparty strife as progressives challenged the status quo and created divisions within the party. In one notable example, in 2019 pressure to pass the Reproductive Privacy Act, which codified *Roe* into state law, mounted. The Senate President and the Speaker of the House had resisted allowing the bill to come to the floor. Finally, they allowed the bill to come up for a vote; it passed but both leaders voted against it (Kelly 2019).

Then leadership changed. After being challenged in a primary by a progressive in 2020, Senate President Dominick Ruggerio took a liberal turn in the next session, supporting more progressive legislation. The former conservative House speaker in that election was defeated and was replaced, in 2021, by Speaker Joe Shekarchi. Things changed. One member of the legislature noted—"the vibe is different." While keeping a firm grip on power, the speaker opened the system giving individual members and cohorts more independence on committees and on the floor. Shekarchi is more of a moderate. A copy of the Act on Climate hangs on his wall in the speaker's office. This also reflects leadership awareness, especially in the state Senate, that as more women and progressives were elected—in 2022 women reached parity with men in the Senate—support for some progressive policy options was in order.

Legislation is usually negotiated within the context of a moderate-left ideological core. While most state legislatures in the country are becoming more polarized, the Rhode Island General Assembly is one of the least polarized legislatures in the country. (Shor and McCarthy 2011, Hinchliffe and Lee 2016). The research indicates that the average Republican legislator and the average Democrat legislator are less ideologically apart than in other states. Some Republicans are more socially liberal than pro-Catholic conservative Democrats. With Democratic electoral margins in the 80 to 90 percent range, there is little incentive to sharpen partisan differences (Myers 2023). As one liberal but pro-life state senator noted, "Look, basically just about all of us here are various shades—from very pale to dark—of blue." It also suggests why the General Assembly more recently is less prone to sharp intra-party fractionalization between newly elected progressives and a more conservative old guard. More typically, legislators that belong to various caucuses push for their bills but change alliances depending on the issue. Leadership can give some wins to conservatives and accommodate a lot of the progressive agenda, so they chose to operate within the system. In the 2023 leadership elections in the House, while three progressive legislators abstained from re-electing House Speaker Shekarchi, another, David Morales, a member of the Democratic Socialists party, voted to re-elect the speaker. He then lost the Socialist endorsement. He noted in response that he could get more of his agenda realized remaining within the leadership structure (Anderson 2023a).

As a result of these dynamics, this most Catholic state in the Union codified access to abortions into state law (2019), then passed legislation that provides state funds for abortions for Medicaid recipients and state workers (2023). It passed laws that gave drivers licenses (2023), in-state tuition (2021) and child medical care to undocumented immigrants (2022). The legislators also passed the Act on Climate, a sweeping reform with strict monitoring requirements to reduce carbon emissions. (2022). And after an outside evaluation report classified the Providence school system one of the worst in the country, the state took over the system despite strong union objections (2019).

Republican legislators during the initial Trump years were forced to voice muted support for Trump and keep a low profile to satisfy their small electoral constituencies. Generally, they are moderate but in 2023 Republicans held only 14 of the 113 seats in the General Assembly. As a tiny minority, they stay on message and tend to speak with one voice.

In Rhode Island elections, candidates can win with less than 50 percent of the vote. Lincoln Chafee was elected governor in 2010 with 36.1 percent of the vote and Gina Raimondo was elected in 2014 with 40.7 percent of the vote. The Rhode Island constitution allows that a plurality and not a majority is sufficient to win office (Ballotpedia 2023). This presents issues when multiple candidates get into the primary and can skew results away for major party candidates, or elect winners with a low plurality. In the 2023 special primary election for an open seat for a US House seat, 11 Democratic candidates were on the primary ballot. There have been calls to change the Constitution to require a majority instead of a plurality to be elected which would require voter approval. There is also a movement to change the primary system through legislation to rank choice or top two nonpartisan primaries (Gregg 2023).

There is no voter referendum in Rhode Island; voters can only vote on bond issues and proposed constitutional amendments. The constitution mandates that every ten years voters are asked if they want a constitutional convention to change the rules. Each decade the question gets slipped onto the ballot with as little fanfare as possible. The state leadership is firmly against it and with general concern about dark money, it gives legislative leadership cover with change unlikely.

WOMEN AND POLITICS

Women had been making slow progress during the 1980s and 1990s, gaining office in some municipal and legislative races. Republican women were able to win statewide and made congressional breakthroughs, given Democratic Party upheavals. Republican Claudine Schneider served in the US House from 1983 through 1991 as the first and only woman elected to the US Congress from Rhode Island. Several repeated wins for statewide general offices were made by GOP women as secretary of state, attorney general, and state treasurer. Their tenure was generally well received, so women were in the game for higher office.

Except for governor. Myrth York, an accomplished, progressive woman received the Democratic nomination in 1994, 1998 and 2002 and lost each time in the general election. During that period, there was a national reluctance to elect women as chief executive (Crampton, 2021). Democrat Gina Raimondo broke through in 2012, but in a three-way race with less than 50 percent of the vote. That year, there were only nine women governors in the country. Her tenure, however, dispelled the notion that a woman couldn't be an effective chief executive.

Raimondo came from the Italian middle class and achieved notable academic success as a Harvard and Yale Law graduate and Rhodes Scholar. Elected as General Treasurer in 2011, she voiced concerns about the solvency of the underfunded state pension system. Most pols obliquely acknowledged the problem, but the accepted remedy was to amortize the debt, incurring larger payout obligations down the road. The idea of revamping the system that would create stricter work rules and cuts for state union workers was considered a nonstarter. Raimondo also raised concerns about the solvency of municipal pension systems which were not under her purview.

In 2011, the city of Central Falls was forced to declare bankruptcy. Everything changed. Leaders in the state legislature along with Governor Lincoln Chafee and then Treasurer Raimondo, pushed to pass legislation in 2012 that completely revamped the state pension system. There was fierce pushback from the unions, but the law withstood court challenges and the reform is considered a national model (Dickerson 2013).

As governor, Raimondo's ratings during her first term were tepid and showed a significant gender gap with women being more supportive than men (Moakley 2019). While many did not support some of her policies, she found her footing with the legislature and was reelected in 2016. Her standing increased due to innovative initiatives that she championed and her handling of the COVID pandemic. In 2020, she resigned as governor to take a position in the Biden administration as US Secretary of Commerce. Democratic Lieutenant Governor Dan McKee became governor, and he appointed Sabina Matos, a Latina, as lieutenant governor.

The elections of 2022 made it clear that women had arrived. In the Democratic primary for governor, two of the top four candidates were women, who together received 57.1 percent of the vote to sitting Governor Dan McKee's 32.8 percent. In the Republican contest, the only credible candidate was a woman who ran and lost in the general election.

Women continued to make their mark in the statewide races for general offices. The state ranks twelfth in the nation in the number of elected women in executive offices in the country (Center for American Women and Politics 2023). In the state judiciary, as of 2022, 38 percent of all judicial officers are women, women are chief judges in three of the five state court systems, and they are now a majority on the state supreme court.

Similar patterns appear for state legislative offices. In 2003, the legislature was downsized from 50 to 35 in the Senate, and 100 to 75 in the House. At that point, women were less than 20 percent of the General Assembly. By 2022, 44 percent of the body were women and the state ranked fourth highest for women legislators in the country (Center for American Women and Politics 2023). The changes were influenced by progressive groups like the Rhode Island Political Cooperative that trained and fielded many first-time women candidates that went on to win. Legislative success encouraged other women, new to electoral politics, to run. Another force was the Working Families Party (WFP), a progressive party group that focused on the minimum wage and other progressive economic issues; they also supported and endorsed progressive candidates, many of whom were women.

What explains this marked success? A general overview suggests several reinforcing factors. The success of Raimondo, especially her leadership in reforming the pension system, changed perceptions about the capacity of women to govern. The recent liberal shift in the state opened more possibilities for women (Pew Research Center 2023). The energy and competence women displayed in leadership positions in the public and private mattered; in a small state, you get noticed. Particularly notable was the energy of minority women—especially Latinas—in organizing their constituencies and winning office. One Latino operative noted that although they are considered a patriarchal society, women do the work and win (Rodriguez 2022).

Politics and Shifting Demographics

Rhode Island has a long and colorful history of various ethnic groups that settled in the state. Initially drawn from European countries, these groups endured prejudice and discrimination, settled in communities with their compatriots, and eventually broke into politics. Given ethnic rivalries and enduring prejudices, such integration could take several generations. This was not the case for Latinos.

The Immigration Act of 1965 lifted race-based restrictions allowing more Asians, Latin Americans, and Africans into the country. These groups had a less burdensome experience than earlier immigrants in that Civil Rights legislation in the 1960s mitigated some overt prejudices and federal policies like food stamps, Medicaid, public housing, and other forms of public assistance helped immigrant populations integrate into the community and eventually access political influence.

Rhode Island had small pockets of Mexicans, Puerto Ricans and Cubans that settled in the state in the post WWII period but the surge in the Latino population came in the late 1980 through the early 2000s. Some early émigrés came from urban areas in New York City to the environs of Rhode Island where lass harsh and more open possibilities existed. In New York, ethnic rivalries among Puerto Ricans and Dominicans blunted Latino power.

In the compact setting of Rhode Island, a few of these émigré leaders devised a strategy to create a cohesive Latino political force. "We didn't want to be like New York or Boston where ethnic rivalries among Latinos stalled progress" noted one political operative (Rodriguez 2022). They organized outreach efforts to different Latino communities to encourage voter turnout and created a PAC fund to support and train Latino candidates to run for office. In addition, to prevent entrenched leadership, they established a Latino Leadership Institute that mandated rotating leadership from various communities; it also promoted the history, culture, and successes of the Latino community in the state (Martinez, 2014). The strategy was notably successful in incorporating Latinos into the economic, social, and political life of Rhode Island.

This translated into remarkable electoral success at all levels of government; Latinos serve as city councilors and mayors, in the legislature and as statewide elected officers. Latino mayors were elected in the capitol city of Providence from 2011 to 2023. In 2022, a Latina Secretary of State swore in a Latina Lieutenant governor, and as of 2023 two of the five General Officers—General Treasurer and Lieutenant Governor—are held by Latinos.

In tandem with this, waves of immigrants largely from El Salvador, Honduras, Nicaragua, Guatemala, and Columbia migrated to the state; between 2000 and 2010 the Latino population grew by over 40 percent. Some were undocumented. Estimates put the undocumented population at about 30,000 which is about 14 percent of the total immigrant population. These estimates include all immigrants, but a significant portion appear to be Latino (American Immigration Council 2020).

The state is relatively supportive of the undocumented population. The General Assembly passed legislation giving drivers licenses and child health care to this population and allowing undocumented students to qualify for in-state tuition at state colleges. Formerly undocumented state legislators and council members have acknowledged their former status and are respected and effective members of the political elite.

Projections leading up to the 2020 census indicated that there was an undercount in 2010 particularly in poorer urban areas, where many undocumented people live. Community activists organized a campaign to get an accurate count and added about 38,000 people to the rolls. Earlier estimates suggested that in 2022 the state would lose one of its two US House seats. The additional numbers saved the delegation from being cut. Evidently, the effort was too robust as later census estimates list Rhode Island with an overcount of just over 5 percent. The state, however, was able to retain its two-seat delegation (Sapolsky 2022).

Asians, Native Hawaiians, and Pacific Islanders, with a population of just under 4 percent, have also emerged on the political scene. They achieved local, legislative, and mayoral success and are leaders in business, nonprofit and state administrative positions. During the Vietnam War immigrants from Asian countries settled in the state and tended to keep their heads down. Successive generations and new arrivals have taken a more active role. In 2023 the legislative Black-Latino legislative caucus renamed itself the Black, Latino, Indigenous, Asian American and Pacific Islander caucus to reflect ethnic additions to the legislature.

Although the Black population in the state has declined, it has become an influential voice in the public square. Groups like Black Lives Matter had a notable impact on public perceptions of the Black community. Political action committees have been successful in promoting a progressive agenda and recruiting Black people to run for office and to seek influential public and private administrative posts. Voters have supported them in elections, and the state administration, nonprofits and private enterprises have provided opportunities for employment. A thoughtful committee report to consider reparations for Black Rhode Islanders was undertaken looking primarily at housing and educational opportunities for this community (Russo 2022). Disparities continue but these changes suggest significant progress. In a 2023, in special Democratic primary election in US District 2, a moderate-left African American Gabe Amo won handily carrying all but three of the municipalities in the district.

For Native Americans most of the tribal land was taken by force or deceit, impoverishing, and marginalizing the remaining Narragansetts for generations. They are now just over 1 percent of the population—a meager constituency. Their plight has been acknowledged and programs and policies to support the Native Americans were implemented. Scholarship funds have been established, small portions of tribal land have been ceded back to the Narragansetts, tribal museums have been expanded and universities and other public entities acknowledge their presence on former tribal lands and offer programs that pay tribute to their history and culture. The center of the Narragansetts community is their life on their remaining tribal lands. But municipalities near the reservations have employed legal consultants to block any building development or business enterprises on their reservations unless they sign away their sovereign immunity (Nunes 2023).

Minorities in the state have been empowered to advance their status as leaders. Public interest groups and foundations invest in research projects, influence, and money to create leadership opportunities for minorities. The Rhode Island Foundation, the state's largest philanthropic organization, initiated an Equity Leadership program to "build a pipeline of future leaders in established positions of leadership throughout the state" (Rhode Island Foundation 2023). Each year they support about 30 promising minorities for leadership positions in educational, administrative, and board positions throughout the state. Again, in a small state, these initiatives have an impact. Minorities hold positions in these sectors and are emerging as respected new leaders in Rhode Island.

Into the Future: What's in a Name?

Rhode Island and the Providence Plantations had been the state's name since its inception. The name reflected the fact that the prominent trading center of Newport, on Aquidneck Island, was named Rhode Island by early explorers and became the site of commerce and trade during colonial times.

The Providence Plantations referred to the farming lands in and around Providence, where Roger Williams settled; it was then a backwater in the colony.

As public awareness of injustices toward Blacks and Native Americans emerged, a movement to omit Providence Plantations from the state's name gained support. The question was put on the ballot in the form of a constitutional amendment in 2010; it was roundly defeated by 78 percent of the voters. In Rhode Island, recognition and pride in the state's founder, Roger Williams, runs deep. During the next decade, unrest related to George Floyd's murder, awareness of and support for policies to ameliorate historical and current injustices mounted and the liberal shift in attitudes occurred. A second amendment was put on the ballot in 2020 and passed with 53 percent of the vote; a small majority but a remarkable change in voters' attitudes in one decade (Mooney 2020).

The name change underscores how the politics in Rhode Island has shifted. In a few decades voters have become more liberal and have supported progressives, women, and minorities in public office. Lawmakers and state officials in turn, have responded with more progressive policies. Pension reform broke encrusted assumptions about what policy changes were possible. Rhode Island has adopted innovative laws on climate change and sweeping "out of the box" initiatives that would make Rhode Island the first statewide public developer of affordable housing (Farzan 2023). Support for educational programs, poverty and social service assistance, minimum wage increases, and opportunities for minority advancement, while still up for debate, are now embedded in the policy agenda.

To be sure, beyond more lofty initiatives there are plenty of insider deals, and accommodation to favored interests that ply legislators with contributions and push polities that fall far short of the public interest. Interest group politics is alive and well in Rhode Island. And critical issues remain unresolved. Educational reform is vital to the state's economic and social progress but competing interests continue to stall reform. Debates and pushbacks on tax policy, budget allocations, social reforms and the size and efficiency of government will continue as different groups voice their expectations and concerns about the future of the state.

In 2023, the Independent Man was taken down from the capitol dome for reconstruction. (Anderson 2023b.) After some showings around the state, the restored version will then be placed back atop the statehouse still looking out over New England. The original name considered for the statue was

Hope—the motto of Rhode Island, displayed on its flag. Perhaps this new iteration of the statue will reflect hope as part of the state's contemporary ethos as it moves it closer to its New England neighbors.

Works Cited

American Immigration Council. 2020. "Immigrants in Rhode Island." August 6, 2020. https://www.americanimmigrationcouncil.org/research/immigrants-in-rhode-island#:~:text=More%20than%2018%2C000%20U.S.%20citizens,total%20state%20population%20in%202016.

Anderson, Patrick. 2023a. "After Voting for Shekarchi for Speaker, Rep. Morales Loses Democratic Socialists Endorsement." *The Providence Journal*, February 7, 2023.

Anderson, Patrick. 2023b. "The Iconic Independent Man Statue on RI State House Is Coming Down for Restoration." *Providence Journal*, October 10, 2023. https://www.providencejournal.com/story/news/politics/state/2023/10/10/independent-man-statue-may-come-down-off-ri-state-house-before-thanksgiving/71129352007/.

Anton, Thomas J. 1989. *American Federalism and Public Policy: How the System Works*. New York: Random House.

Arums, Teo, and Antonia Noori Farzan. 2020. "Calamari, Rhode Island's Controversial State Appetizer, Becomes an Unexpected Star of Democratic Convention." *The Washington Post*, August 19, 2020. https://www.washingtonpost.com/nation/2020/08/19/calamari-rhode-island-comeback-dnc/.

Ballotpedia. 2023. "Rhode Island's 1st Congressional District special election, 2023." https://ballotpedia.org/Rhode_Island%27s_1st_Congressional_District_special_election,_2023.

Congressional Quarterly. 1994. "Guide to U.S. Elections." 3rd Edition. Washington DC.

Center for American Women and Politics. 2023. "Rhode Island State Facts." Eagleton Institute of Politics. https://cawp.rutgers.edu/facts/state-state-information/rhode-island.

Crampton, Liz. 2021. "There Are Just 9 Female Governors. Both Parties Want Change." *Politico*, September 2021. https://www.politico.com/news/2021/09/29/the-fifty-women-governors-499533.

DeSimone, Russell. 2020. *Fighting Bob Quinn: Political Reformer and People's Advocate*. Providence: The Rhode Island Publications Society.

Dickerson, John G. 2013. "Gina Raimondo's Shining Example—Pension Reform In Rhode Island." *California Policy Center*, January 28, 2013. https://californiapolicycenter.org/gina-raimondos-shining-example-pension-reform-in-rhode-island/.

Dincer, Oruzgan, and Michael Johnston. 2014. "Measuring Illegal and Legal Corruption in American States: Some Results from the Corruption in American Survey." *Harvard University. Edmond & Lily Safar Center for Ethics*, December 1, 2014. https://ethics.harvard.edu/blog/measuring-illegal-and-legal-corruption-american-states-some-results-safra.

Elazar, Daniel J. 1966. *American Federalism: A View from the States*. New York: Thomas Crowell.

Enten, Harry. 2015. "Ranking the States from Most to Least Corrupt." *FiveThirtyEight*, January 23, 2015. https://fivethirtyeight.com/features/ranking-the-states-from-most-to-least-corrupt/.

Farzan, Antonia Noori. 2023. "Bill Would Create $50 Million Revolving Fund to Develop Public Housing." *The Providence Journal*, March 21, 2023. https://www.providencejournal.com/story/news/politics/2023/03/21/will-the-public-sector-have-to-build-the-housing-ri-needs/70021000007/.

Gregg, Katherine. 2021. "Political Scene: 3 Tales from RI 'Where Everybody Knows Everybody Else.'" *The Providence Journal*, March 14, 2021. https://www.providencejournal.com/story/news/politics/2021/03/14/political-scene-3-tales-ri-where-everybody-knows-everybody-else/4601847001/.

Gregg, Katherine. 2023. "Should RI Scrap Separate Republican, Democratic Primaries? This Group Says Yes." *The Providence Journal*, February 8, 2023. https://www.providencejournal.com/story/news/politics/2023/02/08/nonpartisan-primaries-in-ri-should-be-considered-group-says-in-report/69880722007/.

Hamm, Keith E. and Nancy Miller. (2018), "Legislative Politics in the States." In *Politics in the American States: A Comparative Analysis* 11th edition, edited by Virginian Grey, Russell L. Hanson, and Thad Kauser, 187–234. Thousand Oaks, CA: CQ Press.

Kelly, Caroline. 2019. "Rhode Island Governor Signs Abortion Protection Bill." *CNN Politics*. https://www.cnn.com/2019/06/20/politics/rhode-island-governor-signs-abortion-protection-bill/index.html.

Justine, Oliva. 2023. "KPI Briefing: Rhode Island Economic Growth Stalls in Q4, Continues to Lag Region and Nation." *RIPEC. Rhode Island Public Expenditure Council*, January 30, 2023. https://ripec.org/2022-q4-kpi-briefing/.

Krugman, Paul. 2023. "Can Anything Be Done to Assuage Rural Rage?" *The New York Times*. January 26, 2023. https://www.nytimes.com/2023/01/26/opinion/rural-voters-economy.html.

Martinez, Maria. 2014. *Latino History in Rhode Island Nuestras Racie*. Rhode Island: The History Press.

Moakley, Maureen. 2019. "A Gender Gap Against Raimondo." *Providence Journal*, November 13, 2019. https://www.provgardener.com/news-item/my-turn-maureen-moakley-gender-gap-against-raimondo.

Moakley, Maureen, and Elmer Cornwell. 2001. "Epilogue." *Rhode Island Politics and Government*. Lincoln and London: University of Nebraska Press.

Mooney, Tom. 2020. "We're Just Rhode Island Now: Voters Decide to Drop 'Plantations' from State Name." *The Providence Journal*, November 5, 2020. https://www.providencejournal.com/story/news/local/2020/11/04/close-vote-ri-does-away-plantations-state-name/6159803002/.

Myers, Adam. 2023."The General Assembly" in *The State of Rhode Island: Government and Politics*. Providence Rhode Island: Rhode Island Publications Society.

Ng, David. 2022. "Opinion/Ng: For a RI Doctor and Me, It's Only Three Degrees of Separation Instead of Six." *The Providence Journal*. January 16, 2022. https://www.providencejournal.com/story/news/columns/2022/01/16/providence-journal-editor-david-ng-shares-nyc-childhood-connection-miriam-hospital-doctor/9103245002/.

Nunes, Alex. 2023. "In Charlestown, Critics Say Special Solicitor Position Is 'Discriminating against One Group of People'." *The Public's Radio*. January 25, 2023. https://thepublicsradio.org/article/in-charlestown-critics-say-special-solicitor-position-is-discriminating-against-one-group-of-people.

Pew Research Center. 2023. "Religious Landscape Study: Political Ideology by State." https://www.pewresearch.org/religion/religious-landscape-study/compare/political-ideology/by/state/.

Rodriguez, Pablo. Interview with the author. June 8, 2022.

The Rhode Island Foundation. 2023. "Equity Leadership Initiative." Providence Rhode Island. https://rifoundation.org/community-investments/equity-leadership-initiative.

Russo, Amy. 2022. "New Providence Board Weighs How to Offer Reparations, from Housing to Education." *The Providence Journal*, April 19, 2022. https://www.providencejournal.com/story/news/local/2022/04/19/providence-weighs-reparations-payments-housing-education/7356501001.

Rutledge, Andrew. "Rogue Island." *The Rhode Island Historical Society*. February 1, 2019. https://www.rihs.org/rogueisland2/#:~:text=Smugglin%20was%20a%20cornerstone%20%20of,"Rogue%20Island%20"%20by%20officials.

Sapolsky, Hans. 2022. "Census Bureau Admits Overcounting 7 Blue States, Just 1 Red State." *The Heritage Foundation*. August 22, 2022. https://www.heritage.org/election-integrity/commentary/census-bureau-admits-overcounting-7-blue-states-just-1-red-state#:~:text=After%20each%20census%2C%20the%20bureau,%2C%20Rhode%20Island%2C%20and%20Utah.

Secretary of State. 2023. Rhode Island Voter Registration. https://datahub.sos.ri.gov/RegisteredVoter.aspx.

Shor, Boris and McCarthy, Nolan. 2011. "The Ideological Mapping of American Legislatures," *American Political Science Review* 105: 530–551.

Speakman, June. 2023. "Local Government." *The State of Rhode Island: Government and Politics*. Providence Rhode Island: The Rhode Island Publications Society.

Stevens, Matthew. 2020. "Providence Voters Vote In Favor of a $515 M Pension Bond. *Rhode Island News*, ABC 6 https://www.abc6.com/providence-voters-vote-in-favor-of-515-million-pension-bond/.

U.S. Census Bureau. 2020. "QuickFacts." *U.S. Census Bureau*. https://www.census.gov/quickfacts/fact/table/US/PST045221.

Valeria Diaz, Maria. 2018. "Old Slater Mill." *Atlas Obscura*. November 19, 2018. https://www.atlasobscura.com/places/old-slater-mill-historic-site.

Wood, Gordon. 1991. The *Radicalism of the American Revolution*. New York; Vintage Books.

CHAPTER 8

VERMONT POLITICS IN THE MODERN AGE
From Red to Blue

Paul Petterson
Professor of Political Science
Central Connecticut State University

If you want to understand the changes and continuities in Vermont politics since 1945, two of its most visible US Senators over that period are a good place to start. Republican George Aiken—who served in the US Senate from 1940 to 1974—was as Republican and Yankee as they come, describing himself as a "New England hill farmer" in 1938 and even when he was governor of the state. Yet he argued to the Republican National Committee in December 1937 that the Republican Party had to face "the necessity of reorganizing" and be "responsive to the enlightened opinion of the voters whom you profess to serve" if it wished to return to being a national majority party (Aiken 1938, 216). By his last years in the Senate, he had maintained the mixture of a beloved political figure who only had to spend $17.09 in his 1968 reelection campaign and an independent-minded leader who called for rethinking efforts to reform Vietnam by brute military force in 1966, a policy against the views in the Republican Party (Associated Press 1968, Bushnell 2020). Aiken showed a willingness to champion progressive reforms not favored by his party in the small-state politics of Vermont.

On the surface, there could be no more profound political contrast to Aiken, no one less "Yankee" and more "blue," than the current senior US Senator from Vermont, Bernie Sanders. Sanders was born in Brooklyn, NY, and was part of a wave of migration to Vermont in the 1960s. Inspired by the back to the land movement and initially working as a carpenter and freelance journalist, Sanders was a proud democratic socialist (McNamee 2023) who kept his strong Brooklyn accent. By the early 1970s, Sanders started to pursue elective office, joining the radical Liberty Union Party and receiving only 1,571 votes in his initial run for the US Senate in 1972 (Sherman 1991, 98). But Sanders persisted and used door-to-door grassroots politicking to unseat the Democratic mayor in Burlington in March 1981, winning by just ten votes (Sherman 1991, 175). His eight-year administration was a "more than blue" combination of local and international progressive activism (including support for the Sandinistas in Nicaragua that led his supporters to be nicknamed Sandernistas) and working both against and with the local police and business community to improve daily life for the residents of Burlington (Sanders and Gutman 1997, 45–76; Ward 1984). Sanders then went to Congress, first in the House and then the Senate, serving as an Independent who caucused with Democrats while retaining an ornery, unfailing tendency to criticize both parties when he thought warranted. The working class coalition that Sanders built in Burlington, and his atypical position on gun rights, may also help to explain the higher support for Democrats among non-college educated white voters in Vermont, compared to other New England states.

Despite their differences, Sanders's and Aiken's willingness to go against the grain of the moment in both policy and party politics, their stubborn independence, ever rewarded by Vermonters at the ballot box, fit the state's political culture. However, the shift from Aiken to Sanders reflected changes in the state's population and politics. Outsiders moved in, making the state less Yankee, shifting from solidly Republican to favoring Democrats.

Vermont's geography and demography influenced its economic and political development. Vermont formed out of land disputed by New Hampshire and New York, and its rocky, mountainous geology in much of the state made it a difficult area for widespread farming, so it experienced large out-migration when the Midwest and West opened up through the nineteenth century (Meeks 1986, 47–86, 89). The significant in-migration since the 1960s, which has contributed mightily to the state's transition from red to blue, has nonetheless left Vermont both the smallest New England state by population, with only 647,000 residents, and the whitest New England state. Vermont is 94 percent white, making it one of the least diverse states in the nation (US Census 2022).

This combination of small size and racial homogeneity has given Vermont its particularly local and personal political culture, persisting even in the globalized internet age. Solving the puzzle of how this rural white state became a bastion of political progressivism requires examination of the Green Mountain State's post World War Two political development.

From the 1850s to the 1950s Vermont was home to an unrivaled Republican Party political machine. According to political scientist Garrison Nelson, "Because the GOPs control of the state was so total, the offices in the state belonged to the party and not to the incumbent." So secure was the GOPs control that the party was able to keep peace between Republicans in eastern and western Vermont by alternating the governorship between the two regions, which were separated by the Green Mountains (Nelson 1997). Enforcement of what was called the "Mountain Rule" required considerable coordination and planning of a sort only possible in a solidly one-party state, especially since gubernatorial aspirants in Vermont were required to advance up the political ladder before running for the top job. In open seat elections, the Republican loyalist from the region currently not holding the governorship, and highest on the office ladder stretching from a seat in the state legislature to the governor's chair, would be the GOP nominee, and as such, the clear choice of the voters (Nelson 1997).

Over the nearly eight decades since the end of World War II, a combination of forces transformed the partisan complexion of the state. But even in the late 1950s, political scientist Duane Lockard identified Vermont as a "political paradox," as conservative but with "a liberal strain" suggesting there were already currents flowing within Vermont that would lead it to becoming a reliably Democratic state (Lockard 1959, 8).

Tensions in the Postwar Republican Party

As Vermont approached the 1946 election, one root of its future political evolution was already evident. The conservative Proctor family organization, which ran a successful marble mining company, had dominated the state Republican Party for decades but was challenged in 1936 by a dissident, more liberal Republican group in the candidacy of George Aiken, who beat the Proctor candidate for governor in 1936 and 1938. In 1940, Aiken then ran successfully for an open US Senate seat, beating the Proctor-affiliated candidate, Ralph Flanders, in the Republican primary (Lockard 1959, 15–18). As we will see, Aiken was but the first (and most durable) representative of an increasingly influential liberal wing within the Republican Party.

In the 1946 election, Vermont not only reelected Aiken to the Senate, but it elected a Republican political challenger, war hero Ernest W. Gibson, as governor, replacing the incumbent governor Mortimer Proctor (one of a number of Proctors to hold the governorship).

While Gibson left the governor's office for a federal judgeship in 1950, he left a legacy of liberal reforms in taxation and social welfare benefits codified in state law (Lockard 1959, 18–20). The success of Aiken and Gibson was indicative of an ideological split within the Republican Party of the time, a divide that demonstrated the existence of an opening for a more liberally oriented, yet still Republican dominated, politics in the state.

In 1950, Governor Gibson was replaced by Governors Harold Arthur (1950–51) and Lee Emerson (1951–55), both from the conservative wing of the state Republican Party. Vermont's 1950 population of 378,000 had grown only slightly since 1910 (Morton 1970, 35), and continued to be predominantly rural. Had these patterns persisted in the decades that followed, perhaps Vermont might have remained reliably Republican and conservative. But political and demographic currents, regional and national, were beginning to impact Vermont politics.

Democrats Emerge Amid Economic and Demographic Changes

In 1958, Democrats saw their first clear political breakthrough when candidate William Meyer narrowly won the US House race against former governor Harold Arthur; it was a temporary gain, as Meyer lost his reelection bid in 1960 to Governor Robert Stafford (VT Secretary of State, n.d.). The 1958 Democratic candidate for governor, Bernard Leddy, also lost so narrowly that a recount was requested, an almost unheard of event at the time (Bryan 1974, 105). As Vermont scholar Frank Bryan notes, this victory and near victory were hinted at by Democratic results in the 1952 election. The seeds of party change were thus planted in Vermont before its transformation by the flood of new Vermonters in the 1960s who, like Bernie Sanders, saw something in the Green Mountain State that they were not getting in their home states (Bryan 1974, 99–105).

Progressives like Sanders brought both romantic notions of returning to nature and higher quality of life standards in Vermont. They also brought higher expectations of government's role in society that required modernization of the state's infrastructure and economy. The coming of the Interstate Highway System gradually upgraded the state's infrastructure, connecting Vermont more easily to the population centers of the Northeast, boosting tourism, and signaling the state's journey from a conservative political backwater to progressive social, cultural, and political trend setter. The significance of the changes that would come to Vermont on the interstate were poignantly reflected in 1961 by Senator George Aiken who, while speaking at the dedication of a new section of interstate 91, said "We're on the verge of the greatest development Vermont has ever seen." What his audience may not have realized was that Aiken was celebrating the completion of a stretch of highway that had "buried his boyhood home" (Mansfield 2013).

The economic progress aided by the interstate is evidenced by the rapid growth of IBM's Essex Junction plant (from 445 employees in 1957 to 2,500 in 1965). This factory brought high technology and industry to Vermont, reshaping its economy and thereby its workforce and towns, particularly in the state's most populous county, Chittenden County (Sherman 1991, 55).

In 1962, amid the economic and demographic changes discussed above, Vermont's Democrats saw their first major electoral success in more than a century with the election of Governor Philip Hoff. While Hoff narrowly won (50.6 percent) against incumbent Governor F. Ray Keyser in 1962, he was reelected with 64.9 percent of the vote in 1964 and 57.7 percent of the vote in 1966, demonstrating that Democratic electoral strength was growing and not transient (Thurber 1968, 72). Combined with a Democratic sweep of other statewide non-congressional offices in 1962, Democrats had decisively established a two-party political dynamic in the state (Thurber 1968, 75). But as Thurber notes, it was at that point a bifurcated dynamic; Republicans still dominated congressional and presidential contests (excepting Lyndon Johnson's unusual victory in Vermont in 1964).

The Democratic political gains of 1962 combined with the changing economy and demographics of the state gave momentum to Democrats, but the fallout from a US Supreme Court decision handed down in the spring of 1962 would prove to be crucial in the Democratic takeover of Vermont. In *Baker v. Carr*, the Court mandated that legislative districts be based on "one man, one vote." In other words, legislative districts must include relatively equal numbers of voters in them. Because representation in the Vermont legislature was then by town, regardless of population, the Court's ruling required the redistricting of the Vermont legislature. The House was reduced from 246 representatives, one for each town in the state, to 150 representatives apportioned by population (Sherman 1991, 59). In a single decisive constitutional blow, the Court shifted the balance of political and policy influence in Vermont from over-represented voters living in small towns to voters in the state's larger cities and towns, which were themselves growing due to the recent influx of out of state immigrants. In practical terms, the voice of more urban and suburban Vermonters, often seeking more liberal policy changes, took on their accurate demographic weight in the legislature for the first time.

Two-Party Competition and the Rise of the Sanders Progressives

In 1968, Governor Hoff decided not to seek reelection, and the Republicans regained control of the governorship with Deane Davis, who won 56 percent of the vote, and was reelected in 1970 with 58 percent of the vote (Bryan 1974,

117). While this may have at the time have looked like the return of normal Republican dominance, it was not. By 1972, a Democrat, Thomas Salmon, soundly defeated Republican Luther Hackett for the governorship, after a divisive Republican primary that echoed the earlier 1940s split in the party (Bryan 1974, 117). From this point onward, Vermont has witnessed a kind of "gubernatorial power sharing" between the Republican and Democratic parties, with each party controlling the governorship for four to eight years before losing to the opposing party (Governor Howard Dean being the outlier with eleven years in office). The pattern can be seen in the list of governors below:

Thomas Salmon (D): 1973–77
Richard Snelling (R): 1977–85
Madeline Kunin (D): 1985–91
Richard Snelling (R): 1991 (died in office)
Howard Dean (D): 1991–2003
James Douglas (R): 2003–11
Peter Shumlin (D): 2011–17
Phil Scott (R): 2017–present
(VT Secretary of State, n.d.).

The first six of the governors listed above, from Salmon through Douglas, were all migrants to the state. Shumlin and Scott are the only Vermont natives elected governor in the last fifty years. Though Vermonters have often reveled in their penchant to alternate between Democratic and Republican governors, it bears noting that no incumbent governor running for reelection during this period has ever been turned out by the voters. Instead, Vermonters opt to wait for open seat elections to give the other party a shot at leading the state. Vermont has not turned out a sitting governor seeking reelection since the 1962 Hoff/Keyser race, a pattern which will also be seen (to a greater or lesser degree) in modern US House and US Senate races in Vermont.

In congressional elections in Vermont, the picture was one of a gradual partisan shift from the 1970s to the 1990s, rather than the alternating pattern of partisan control seen in the contests for governor. This evolution occurred both between the two parties, and within the Republican Party itself. In many ways, it began with an unexpected death.

On September 10, 1971, US Senator Winston Prouty (who had been reelected in 1970) died in office. Vermont's US House member, Robert

Stafford (R), was appointed to fill the vacancy, but only after pressure by President Nixon on Governor Davis. Stafford, who was closer to the Aiken and moderate wing of the Republican Party, then won a special election for the full term in 1972 (Hand 2002, 285). In his subsequent sixteen years in the Senate (before retiring in 1988), Stafford would see the national Republican Party shift increasingly away from his moderate and pro-environmental policy positions.

Stafford's 1972 election was also notable as one of Bernie Sanders's earliest efforts to run for public office, when he ran on the third-party Liberty Union ticket and won 2.2 percent of the vote (VT Secretary of State, n.d.). Vermont politics would evolve substantially in the interim between 1972 and his next run in 2006.

Two years later, 1974 witnessed the next Democratic breakthrough in the state, one that was highly unexpected. It was precipitated by US Senator George Aiken's decision to retire after thirty-four years in the Senate. Once Aiken announced his retirement, Vermont's US House Representative, Richard Mallary, announced his candidacy for the Aiken's Senate seat, and was the expected front runner. Though the Republican Party ladder/pathway to higher office had ceased to function predictably, it still had done so for US Senate seats prior to the 1974 contest. Mallary's Democratic opponent, Patrick Leahy, won the seat by just under 4,000 votes despite being a newcomer to statewide electoral politics. Two factors stand out in explaining the outcome. First, Mallary, despite being an incumbent congressman, was out of step with some Republicans in the state. Second, Leahy benefited from the same widespread anti-Republican sentiment that helped send scores of Democrats to Washington in the year of the Watergate scandal and President Nixon's resignation (Hand 2002, 292).

With Rep. Mallary contesting the US Senate seat in 1974, Vermont's US House seat was again open, and the race once again demonstrated Vermont's willingness to vote across party lines. After a bitter primary, former State Attorney General James Jeffords (who had lost the 1972 GOP gubernatorial primary) won the election drawing bipartisan support in spite of the aforementioned anti-Republican sentiment awash in the country in 1974 (Hand 2022, 292). By 1988, Jeffords would win the US Senate seat made available by Robert Stafford's retirement (VT Secretary of State, n.d.), continuing the tradition of New England moderate Republicanism that was becoming increasingly endangered in post-Watergate national politics. He would be succeeded in the House by Republican Peter Smith, who won the seat with only 41 percent of the vote in a three-way race that presaged the next Vermont political transformation in 1990 (VT Secretary of State, n.d.).

By the early 1980s, Vermont's congressional political landscape had cemented its developing moderate-to-left-of-center bipartisanship. Patrick Leahy was narrowly reelected to the Senate in 1980, and Jim Jeffords found himself at variance with the new Reagan administration on tax and budget votes, while Robert Stafford's work on education policy put him in conflict with Reagan administration priorities on education (Jeffords 2003, 174–180; Walker 1988). But at a local level, another tectonic political event occurred in, of all things, a local mayoral race.

In March of 1981, Bernie Sanders shocked the Democratic establishment of Burlington, Vermont, by winning the mayoral election as a Progressive by ten votes. After running for state offices for years as a long shot Liberty Union candidate, Sanders won this local race through heavy neighborhood organizing. Sanders won reelection as mayor in 1983, 1985, and 1987, building a progressive political organization and continuing to contest statewide races (including the US House race in 1988) (Sanders 1997, 45–81). By 1990, he was running again for the US House seat against the then-incumbent Rep. Peter Smith. It was a history-making contest.

With a Democratic candidate, Dolores Sandoval, who received little party support, Sanders was able to effectively challenge the Republican incumbent, Smith, in a one-on-one contest. Sanders won the race with 60 percent of the vote, ironically helped by his then supportive stance on gun rights, which led some gun rights advocates to support Sanders over Smith who had voted for an assault weapons ban. On election night, Smith said: "It wasn't my night. This was Bernie's night" (Sanders 1997, 85–88). With Sanders's reelection in 1992, two-thirds of Vermont's delegation in Washington was firmly Democratic or Independent, a transformation that would continue in the decades to follow (VT Secretary of State, n.d.).

Another important milestone in this period was the 1984 election of Madeline Kunin as Vermont's first woman governor. Kunin, who worked her way up the political ladder through leadership service in the legislature and as lieutenant governor under Richard Snelling, was instrumental in opening many doors of political advancement to women during her three terms as governor (1985–1991). Many of Vermont's current female politicians and political leaders were either mentored or inspired by Kunin's example (Kunin 1994). She would help usher in the increasing liberalization of the state's policies and politics by the 1990s. Vermont was becoming increasingly "more than Yankee" and increasingly blue.

Vermont as Nationally Deep Blue, 1992–2023

There was one last statewide mountain for Vermont Democrats to climb by 1992: carrying Vermont for the Democratic presidential candidate, previously achieved only in 1964. Thanks in part to the three-way race between incumbent Republican President George Bush, Democratic nominee Bill Clinton, and Independent Ross Perot, Clinton was able to win Vermont, and the Democratic Party nominee has carried Vermont in every subsequent election through 2020 by generally increasing percentages, as indicated below:

1992—Bill Clinton—46%
1996—Bill Clinton—53%
2000—Al Gore—51%
2004—John Kerry—59%
2008—Barack Obama—67%
2012—Barack Obama—67%
2016—Hillary Clinton—57%
2020—Joseph Biden—66%
(VT Secretary of State, n.d.).

This string of results has decisively put Vermont in the "deep blue" category for presidential election results; only the District of Columbia and Hawaii typically turn in higher percentages for the Democratic nominee. This dramatic reversal from historic patterns is perhaps the strongest indicator of the partisan and ideological shift in the balance of the Vermont electorate, making it certainly more than its historic Republican Yankee. But its bipartisan rotation of the governor's office since 1962 also shows that it remains "more than blue" in its political behavior.

Vermont has also had a higher profile in twenty-first century presidential politics thanks to the colorful, though unsuccessful, candidacies of Howard Dean and Bernie Sanders. Unlike Vermont's two actual US presidents, Chester Arthur and Calvin Coolidge, who were born in Vermont but made their political careers elsewhere, Sanders and Dean were both born in New York but built their political careers in Vermont. The two highest profile

Vermont politicians over the first two decades of the twenty-first century embody the political transformation brought to Vermont by non-native Vermonters.

In 1990, Democrat Howard Dean was elected lieutenant governor to serve under the elected Republican governor, Richard Snelling (himself returning to the governor's office after an earlier 1977–1985 service as governor) (VT Secretary of State, n.d.). This outcome reflects Vermont's practice of conducting separate votes for governor and lieutenant governor, which normally would just be a symbolic power sharing outcome.[1] Then fate intervened: on August 13, 1991, Governor Snelling died of a heart attack (Hevesi 1991). As lieutenant governor, Dean succeeded him—and proceeded to a decade of successful races for the governorship (VT Secretary of State, n.d.).

After building a ten-year policy record, Dean decided to contest for higher ground. Not seeking reelection for governor in 2002, he began to pursue the presidency the next year, and emerged as a surprisingly strong candidate for the 2004 Democratic nomination thanks in part to his early adoption of the Meetup platform then coming into use. Meetup.com was a website well-suited to sensibilities of Vermont politicians because it was a high-tech way to leverage the power of retail politics. Though initially a heavy favorite in the Iowa caucuses, Dean lost to Massachusetts Senator John Kerry and then fatally damaged his further prospects for the nomination with what came to be known as the "scream heard round the world," a boisterous shout in a post-Iowa caucus speech (Tan 2016). Dean ultimately became the Chairperson of the Democratic National Committee in 2005, using that role to promote a "fifty state" Democratic strategy that helped elect Barack Obama in 2008 (Dean 2008).

By 2015, it fell to US Senator Bernie Sanders to put Vermont back in the presidential spotlight. Declaring his presidential candidacy at Waterfront Park in Burlington on May 26, 2015, Sanders surprised some pundits by demonstrating a major national following in the months that followed. He and Hillary Clinton contested through almost the entire Democratic primary season, until Clinton finally gained enough delegates to secure the nomination. The disaffection of some Sanders voters is thought by some to have helped Donald Trump beat Clinton in the 2016 general election. Sanders's 2016 run gave him national stature, and he contested the 2020 Democratic nomination race against Joe Biden and other candidates. Sanders again lost

---

[1] Vermont is one of 18 states that elects its lieutenant governors separately from governors.

but again was the runner-up to the nominee. Between Sanders and Dean then, Vermont officeholders have played a notable role in national Democratic politics, punching well above their weight from one of the smallest states in the country.

The shift in presidential voting has been largely paralleled in voting for other statewide offices, excepting the gubernatorial voting dynamic discussed earlier. In US Senate elections, the "Aiken seat" (held by George Aiken 1940–1974) was continuously held by Democrat Patrick Leahy from 1974–2022. After his close election victory in 1974, Leahy narrowly won reelection in 1980 over Stewart Ledbetter, convincingly beat former Governor Richard Snelling in 1986, and cruised to clear majority victories in the five elections that followed. With Democrat Peter Welch easily winning the seat in 2022, the "Aiken seat" has now remained in Democratic hands for more than half a century (VT Secretary of State, n.d.).

Senator Leahy's reelection campaign in 1998 featured one of the most quintessential episodes in Vermont politics: the candidacy of farmer Fred Tuttle. In 1998, a well-to-do Massachusetts businessman, Jack McMullen, declared his intentions to run for the Republican Senate nomination in Vermont (McMullen owned a home in Vermont). While there was negative reaction from some quarters at this possibility, a challenge to McMullen's candidacy came from an unexpected source. A locally made movie in 1996, *Man with A Plan*, had portrayed a real-life Vermont farmer (Fred Tuttle) who runs for, and wins, a seat in the US House from Vermont. The movie's director, John O'Brien, put Fred Tuttle's name forward to run against McMullen as a way to promote the film. It became more than he and Fred imagined (Baruth 2016).

Fred Tuttle's candidacy caught the public's imagination. Tuttle's simple and genuine Vermont ways were a clear contrast to McMullen's perceived efforts to use his personal wealth to fund and win a Senate race. Tuttle was well-treated by the media, and his personality captured the public's imagination. Vermont's open primary system, and the lack of a primary against Leahy, also led to crossover voting, which gave Fred Tuttle a convincing primary victory. Once he was the nominee, Tuttle made it clear he was going to vote for Leahy (Baruth 2016). This "only in Vermont" episode symbolizes the mix of the local and personal political culture of an older Vermont, and more modern liberal politics, that continues to make Vermont a political paradox of tradition and liberalism, both "more than Yankee" and "more than blue."

The recent history of Vermont's other Senate seat, the "Stafford seat," also reflects Vermont's continuing "blue" shift. James Jeffords, first elected to the seat in 1988, found his moderate liberalism progressively isolated in the increasingly conservative Republican politics of Washington, even as he was reelected in 1994 and 2000 by comfortable margins. This isolation culminated in May of 2001, when Jeffords decided that education funding promises made by newly elected President George W. Bush were not being honored. This policy difference pushed Jeffords to leave the Republican Party and become an Independent, tipping the power balance in the US Senate to the Democratic Party (thus making his action a personal one with national implications) (Jeffords 2003, 253–283). Jeffords's action was widely supported back in Vermont, and he served as an Independent until his retirement in 2006. This marked the first time that no Republican represented Vermont in the Senate since the 1850s, and this continued when Independent Bernie Sanders won the Senate seat in 2006. Notably, while Sanders won only 2.2 percent of the vote in his 1972 third-party run for this seat, he won the seat in 2006 by a 2–1 margin (66% of the vote). Sanders has been easily reelected in 2012 and 2018, maintaining the seat as an Independent even as he ran for president as a Democrat in 2016 and 2020 (VT Secretary of State, n.d.).

Vermont's US House seat has also been in consistently Independent or Democratic hands since 1990. After his initial victory in 1990, Bernie Sanders won reelection in every House race until he ran for the Senate in 2006, and Democrat Peter Welch succeeded him. Welch too won every one of his reelection campaigns before he successfully ran for Leahy's Senate seat in 2022. Vermont's current representative, Democrat Becca Balint, made history in her own race by being the first woman sent to Congress from Vermont in 2022, and the first openly LGBTQ+ representative from Vermont (VT Secretary of State, n.d.). Rep. Balint's election also reveals another facet of the Vermont paradox: while Vermont has become increasingly liberal, it was also the last of the fifty states to send a woman to Congress, likely due in large part to Vermonters rarely (or in the US Senate case, never) voting out a congressional incumbent, an institutionally conservative tradition. Again, Vermont displays elements that are both "more than Yankee" and "more than blue."

In terms of institutional rules, Vermont has a number of practices that give its politics more of a (small d) democratic and nonpartisan character. Vermont continues to elect its governors for a two-year term, rare nationally (only neighboring New Hampshire follows this practice). While some critics might suggest this provides for too little time to govern without the next election on the horizon, Vermont voters in practice have addressed this, by giving Vermont governors at least three terms in office since 1976, and not voting out an incumbent Governor running for reelection since 1962 (VT Secretary of State, n.d.).

In addition to frequent gubernatorial elections, Vermont has also maintained the rules of open primaries and no officially required party registration. Thus, despite Vermont's surface political history as dominated first by Republicans and then by Democrats, that has never been the whole story. Vermont's nonpartisan system has allowed the local and personal character of the state's politics to persist into the modern age, where who you are and what you do often matters more to Vermonters then the party label you happen to wear. Very Yankee. Voters can vote in a Republican primary in one election, and in a Democratic primary in the next. This helps to explain outcomes such as the 2022 election, where Democrat Peter Welch (US Senate) and Republican Phil Scott (Governor) both won election with more than 60 percent of the vote (VT Secretary of State, n.d.). It also explains the electoral persistence of Republican Representative and Senator James Jeffords, who continued to win nomination and election as a Republican even as some self-identified Republicans became hostile to him over his divergences from the Reagan administration in the 1980s. For the majority of Vermonters, that did not matter.

One other phenomenon denotes Vermont's twenty-first century "liberally oriented bipartisanship": the relationship of Republican Governors James Douglas and Phil Scott to the presidents in Washington (particularly Barack Obama and Joseph Biden). In his fourth and final term as governor, Douglas was one of the few elected Republicans to publicly support President Obama's health care reform efforts, against the prevailing tone of the national Republican Party. In the same vein, Governor Scott carved out his own relationship to Washington politics, making it public that he did not vote for Donald Trump in either 2016 or 2020, making Vermont an early leader in active efforts to fight COVID-19 (despite national Republican skepticism), and supporting President Biden on key policy initiatives. Party labels do not tightly control or define Vermont elected officials. In addition to the electoral realm, Vermont has demonstrated its increasingly liberal character in a number of policy areas, as well as demographic shifts and divides.

Policy and Demographic Developments in Vermont

Vermont's development contributes to its distinct politics. Vermont has preserved the character and architecture of many of its small towns and has consciously limited the impact of industrialization. By the time modern technological industries came to Vermont, the state had already established an environmental protection policy mindset and agenda, and an appreciation of the need to preserve Vermont's historic character and unspoiled nature in order to grow and protect the state's thriving tourism industry. In environmental policy, Vermont was an early leader in banning the use of highway billboards in 1967, which still gives the state a distinct appearance compared to its neighbors (Resmer 2021). Vermont also passed a landmark land use law, Act 250, in 1970, which has substantially (if imperfectly) guided development within the state (Sherman 1991, 99–110). These dynamics help Vermont maintain a set of political priorities that give equal weight to economic progress and to environmental and historic preservation, a combination of both liberal and conservative elements of politics.

A policy that gained Vermont national attention was the approval of civil unions for gay and lesbian couples in 1999 and 2000. Propelled initially by a 1999 Vermont Supreme Court ruling in favor of civil unions (the precursor to later marriage equality rulings and laws), the Vermont legislature passed a bill legalizing civil unions. This was a significant political contest in Vermont, with competing slogans of "Take Back Vermont" and "Take Vermont Forward" distributed on signs and bumper stickers around the state. Nine Vermont state legislators who supported civil unions were successfully targeted for defeat in 2000 by conservative groups, including five Republicans. The civil unions fight was an indicator of Vermont's continuing political divides at the local and regional level (Moats 2004), but the outcome is indicative of Vermont's long-standing openness to welcoming new people and ideas into its political communities.

Indeed, demographically, Vermont has changed. Vermont grew substantially from the 1950s, going from 390,000 residents in 1960 to 647,248 in 2024 (World Population Review 2024). While small in absolute terms, for Vermont this has been transformative. Many of the migrants during this period tended to be liberal, and over time, more racially diverse (although Vermont remains one of the whitest states in the nation). Vermont now has a small but significant refugee population from the Middle East and Africa, particularly in Chittenden County, its largest center of population. As with other states, refugees in Vermont have also been resettled in smaller cities and similarly met mixed reactions (Bose 2018).

This in-migration, combined with the aging of Vermont's native born population over the same time span, has led to a distinctly different political atmosphere than in 1960, when the pre-redistricting legislature had one House representative for each of Vermont's 246 towns. It is also noteworthy that Vermont's current congressional delegation is the first in Vermont history to not include any native-born Vermonter. Vermont politics now speaks with a more equal, diverse, and urban and suburban tone, but has not lost its small town neighborly inflection, since even statewide politicians are expected to personally connect with a populace that is still the third smallest in the nation.

Conclusion: Vermont as a Distinctive Yankee Blue State

Vermont continues to be paradoxical in its politics, as Duane Lockard had perceived in 1959. Despite its progressive politics, Vermont is not a fully "one-party state." Pat Leahy and Bernie Sanders won reelection in years when Republicans Richard Snelling, James Douglas, and Phil Scott won election or reelection to the Governor's office. Since the 1960s, Vermont voters have regularly given the Governor's office to both parties on a revolving basis, an expression of ongoing bipartisan political attitudes.

Moreover, Vermont voters are generally satisfied with those it elects to the most prominent statewide offices. No incumbent US Senator has ever lost a bid for reelection. In US House elections since 1962, only Peter Smith (1990) lost a bid for reelection, and even his 1990 loss is less of a change than it appears—Smith won the seat in 1988 with 41 percent of the vote in a three-way race with Independent Bernie Sanders and Democrat Paul Poirier; when facing solely Sanders in 1990, he received 40 percent of the vote, a virtually identical total. As noted earlier, no incumbent governor has lost a bid for reelection since F. Ray Keyser in 1962 (VT Secretary of State, n.d.). Vermonters have tended to overwhelmingly stay with those they choose.

After experiencing an influx of migrants that helped move the state left and recently becoming less white as new immigrants settle in the state, Vermont is uniquely positioned for the political future, open to change but determined to see that such change is not at the expense of the state, its traditions, culture, or political sensibilities. It will continue to be simultaneously "more than Yankee" and "more than blue."

Works Cited

Aiken, George. 1938. *Speaking From Vermont*. New York: Frederick A. Stokes Company.
Associated Press. 1968. "Aiken's Costs Up—to $17." *New York Times*. September 13, 1968. https://timesmachine.nytimes.com/timesmachine/1968/09/13/76933329.html?pageNumber=93.
Baruth, Phil. 2016. "The Political Art behind Fred Tuttle, the Man with a Plan." *VTDigger*, November 27, 2016. https://vtdigger.org/2016/11/27/baruth-political-art-behind-fred-tuttle-man-plan/.

Bose, Pablo S. 2018. "Welcome and Hope, and Fear, and Loathing: The Politics of Refugee Resettlement in Vermont." *Peace and Conflict: Journal of Peace Psychology* 24, no. 3, 320–329.

Bryan, Frank. 1974. *Yankee Politics in Rural Vermont.* Hanover, NH: University Press of New England.

Bushnell, Mark. 2020. "Then Again: The Real Story of George Aiken's Oft-Quoted Advice on Vietnam." *VTDigger.* August 16, 2020. https://vtdigger.org/2020/08/16/then-again-the-real-story-of-george-aikens-oft-quoted-advice-on-vietnam/.

Dean, Howard. 2008. "Dean Explains The Democrats' '50 State Strategy'." *NPR's Talk Of The Nation.* November 13, 2008. https://www.npr.org/2008/11/13/96956854/dean-explains-the-democrats-50-state-strategy.

Hand, Samuel B. 2002. *The Star That Set: The Vermont Republican Party, 1854–1974.* Lanham, MD: Lexington Books.

Hevesi, Dennis. 1991. "Richard A. Snelling, 64, Is Dead: Governor of Vermont for 9 Years." *New York Times.* August 15, 1991. https://www.nytimes.com/1991/08/15/us/richard-a-snelling-64-is-dead-governor-of-vermont-for-9-years.html.

Jeffords, James. 2003. *An Independent Man: Adventures of a Public Servant.* New York: Simon and Schuster.

Kunin, Madeleine M. 1994. *Living a Political Life.* New York: Vintage Books.

Lockard, Duane. 1959. *New England State Politics.* Princeton, NJ: Princeton University Press.

Mansfield, Howard. 2013. "I Will Not Leave: Romaine Tenney Loved His Vermont Farm To Death." *New England.com.* March 31, 2013. https://newengland.com/yankee/eminent-domain-romaine-tenney-farm/.

Moats, David. 2004. *Civil Wars: A Battle for Gay Marriage.* New York: Harcourt, Inc.

McNamee, Gregory Lewis. "Bernie Sanders." Encyclopedia Britannica. https://www.britannica.com/biography/Bernie-Sanders.

Morton, Rogers C.B. 1975. *Historical Statistics of the United States: Colonial Times To 1970, Part 1.* Washington, D.C.: U.S. Bureau of Census.

Nelson, Garrison. 1997. "Vermont Politics Transformed: How Come It Got Fixed When It Warn't Broke?" In *Parties and Politics in the New England States*, edited by Jerome M. Mileur. Amherst, MA: Polity Press.

Resmer, Cathy. 2021. "Good Citizen Stories: Passing Vermont's Billboard Ban." *Seven Days.* January 27, 2021. https://www.sevendaysvt.com/vermont/good-citizen-stories-passing-vermonts-billboard-ban/Content?oid=32191996.

Sanders, Bernie, and Huck Gutman. 1997. *Outsider In The House.* New York: Verso.

Sherman, Joe. 1991. *Fast Lane On A Dirt Road: Vermont Transformed 1945–1990.* Woodstock, VT: The Countryman Press.

Tan, Avianne. 2016. *"The Dean Scream": Remembering the Infamous Iowa Caucus Speech . ABC News*, February 4, 2016. https://abcnews.go.com/Politics/dean-scream-remembering-infamous-iowa-caucus-speech/story?id=36711830.

Thurber, Harris E. 1968. "Vermont: The Stirrings of Change." In *Party Politics in The New England States, edited by George Goodwin Jr and Victoria Schuck, 71-78.* Durham, NH: The New England Center for Continuing Education.

U.S. Census. 2022. "U.S. Census Bureau Quick Facts Vermont." https://www.census.gov/quickfacts/fact/table/VT/PST045221.

Vermont Secretary of State. N.d. Election Results Archive—Elections Division. https://electionarchive.vermont.gov/elections/search/year_from:1958/year_to:1962/office_id:5.

———. n.d. Election Results Archive—Elections Division. https://electionarchive.vermont.gov/elections/search/year_from:1972/year_to:2022/office_id:3/stage:General.

Walker, Reagan. 1988. "Stafford: Republican Rebel During Reagan's Revolution." *Education Week*. November 02, 1988. https://www.edweek.org/education/stafford-republican-rebel-during-reagans-revolution/1988/11.

Ward, Stephen. "Sandanista's Sister Sanderistas." *Vanguard Press*. June 24, 1984. https://www.scribd.com/doc/239120139/Sandinistas-Sister-Sanderistas-Vanguard-Press-June-24-1984#.

World Population Review. "Vermont Population 2024." January 17, 2024. https://worldpopulationreview.com/states/vermont-population.

PART III
ISSUES IN NEW ENGLAND POLITICS

CHAPTER 9

CIVIC PARTICIPATION IN NEW ENGLAND

Rachael Cobb
Associate Professor of Political Science
Suffolk University

New Englanders describe themselves as a participatory bunch. The long tradition of town meetings that purportedly made direct democracy a reality in small towns across the region, and celebrated by nineteenth century New England philosophers, put New England on the map as a region dedicated to "small d" democracy, infused with a participatory spirit. Today, if one were to describe the health of democracy in the fifty states of the United States, a casual observer of the New England region would likely characterize its states as dedicated to expanding voter access and marching toward a fully participatory democracy. Likely notable too is that New England appears to be moving in an altogether opposite direction from those states passing laws to restrict voter access, suppress the vote, and make the act of voting more costly and more difficult.

The decentralized nature of American government has produced multiple electoral policy shifts in the states over the course of the twenty-first century. Some of these reforms explicitly focused on expanding voter access, with the goal of making voting more convenient and accessible. Examples include establishing a longer time horizon in which to vote beyond Election Day, i.e., early voting, vote-by-mail, and the creation of voting "centers," which enable voters to not only vote early but also to solve registration issues on site, get replacement ballots, and often avoid election-day lines. Other alterations take the opposite approach, instead focusing on protecting the system against alleged fraud and abuse. Examples include reducing the early voting period, enacting tougher requirements for acceptable forms of voter identification, or prohibiting prepaid postage when voting my mail. Such protective measures are distinctly restrictive in nature. The rate of such measures heated up in recent few years—2021 and 2022 were blockbuster years for states seeking to pass restrictive voting laws. Since 2021, state legislatures across the United States, enacted forty-two restrictive voting laws in twenty-one states, far more than in any year since the Brennan Center began tracking voter access legislation in the states in 2011.

During this period of extraordinary efforts to limit voting, only one New England state passed restrictive voting laws: New Hampshire. New Hampshire's Senate Bill 418 and House Bill 523 made same-day registration more cumbersome. SB 418 requires unregistered voters who do not have proper documentation to cast an "affidavit ballot" stating that photocopies would be sent to the Secretary of State's office within seven days; if the documents do not arrive to the Secretary of State's office on time, the Secretary of State must notify the town who then must remove the voter's ballot and hold a recount of the votes. HB 523 requires a person who registers to vote without identification to have their photo taken before their registration is complete.

During that same period, Massachusetts passed a voting measure designed to make permanent many pandemic measures increasing access to the ballot including establishing no-excuse mail voting, expanding early voting, and requiring the Secretary of State's office to send mail-in ballot applications to registered voters before each presidential primary, state primary, and biennial state election. In June 2022, Governor Charlie Baker, a Republican, signed the VOTES act into law.

All six New England states proposed legislation designed to expand access. Maine expanded access via the initiative process, seeing ranked-choice voting, term-limits, and a "Clean Elections" measure pass via citizen vote (Melcher and Fried, this volume). Despite New Hampshire's restrictions, it continues to have same-day registration (as it has since 1994), one of the most expansive voting reforms that eliminates the hurdles of advance voter registration, permitting people to register and then vote on Election Day itself.

The remainder of this chapter unpacks the health of civic participation in New England, investigating the success of the Town Meeting model along with the New England states' achievements (or lack thereof) vis-à-vis modernizing their election administration systems and voter turnout in general. It examines the degree to which the New England states have succeeded in making elections responsive and fair by reviewing a set of broad voter access and election modernization initiatives, including issues around voter registration (voter registration deadlines, online voter registration, and automatic voter registration) as well as early voting rules, vote-by-mail requirements, and voter identification processes. The chapter then turns to another key component of civic life—how, if at all, civics are taught in schools.

What emerges from this holistic investigation is that the New England region is neither a panacea of voter access nor a harsh environment of highly restrictive measures.[1] The idealized vision of New England as a place filled with engaged, town-hall attending super voter citizens and politicians dedicated to expanding democracy is not the reality. Politicians in New England behave as politicians often do: protect their own self-interest and their re-election opportunities. And citizens in New England behave as citizens often do: engage in elections when the stakes are meaningful and the costs of participation are relatively low.

Participating in Local Government: The New England Town Meeting
The ability of citizens to impact their daily lives through the democratic process is most powerful at the local level. It is at the local level that citizens can meet directly with local officials and vote on matters of maintaining public safety, managing public transportation, maintaining public infrastructure, and providing essential services such as schools and hospitals. Additionally, local governments regulate land use and zoning, and can play key roles in economic development and environmental protection.

The town meeting is a distinguishing and iconic feature of the New England region, viewed by some as a fundamental expression of American democracy (Bryan 2010; Robinson 2011; Zimmerman 1999). In its purest form, its design permits every citizen the opportunity to represent him or herself on issues of concern to the community and to vote directly in his or her own interest. Thomas Jefferson, Alex de Tocqueville, Henry David Thoreau, and Ralph Waldo Emerson praised the town meeting design for its involvement of ordinary citizens in "real democracy." The town meeting, a legislature of citizens, is intended to be the true expression of direct democracy. Citizens come together and make real laws. It is not a public meeting; it is not a forum. It is a citizen legislature. Town meetings are settings in which registered voters "attend public meetings to debate and vote on a variety of policy, administrative and budgetary issues" (DeSantis and Hill 2004, 166)—including levying taxes. A variation of town meeting developed more recently, beginning in 1915 in Brookline, Massachusetts: the representative

---

[1] *Election Law Journal* ranked New Hampshire as the worst state in the entire United States on its "cost of voting" index which rates states along voter expansion laws. States with measures such as same-day registration, early voting, and vote by mail rank highly. States with restrictive laws such as voter ID requirements rank lower. New Hampshire does have same-day registration, one of the most expansive voter access laws; at the same time, New Hampshire does not have early voting or vote-by-mail. It also has newer, more restrictive ID requirements (Schraufnagel, Pomante, and Li 2022).

town meeting. All New England states, save Rhode Island, have adopted this form (Jenkins, Broges, and Roscoe 2016) which enables town voters to select people to represent and vote for them at town meeting. In Massachusetts, three-fourths of the 351 cities and towns employ the town meeting as the *primary* form of municipal government (Townsend and Reiss 2022).

Scholars investigate town meetings, in part, to ascertain if their lofty participatory promises are consistent with the on-the-ground reality. Joseph Zimmerman (1999) examined town meetings in all the New England states; he argues they remain a vital source of grassroots democracy, despite low attendance. Frank Bryan's study of Vermont town meetings acknowledges that town meetings fall short in integrating historically marginalized groups, but points out that the broader electoral system has not done so too. The net positives, he argues, including teaching civic skills and values, procedural rules, and public conduct are worthy and important traditions to maintain. Finally, Donald Robinson (2011) performs a deep dive, examining participatory democracy in the Berkshire town of Ashfield, Massachusetts. His case study focuses on democratic self-governance within town meetings and how citizens shape government actions. While not all participate, he argues, decisions made in these meetings bind all town residents. Robinson concludes that while town meeting democracy provides deep satisfaction to participants, like all governance methods, it has its inherent limitations. Zimmerman stresses their resilience against interest group influence, Bryan underscores their educational value despite limitations, and Robinson's study showcases democratic self-governance in action within these gatherings.

If the goal of town meeting is to bring people together to engage in "small d" democracy—a set of norms, values and practices focusing on mutual respect, tolerance of vigorous political dissent, and full participation of a populace dedicated to governing its own affairs—the town meeting model has failed to bring such a vision to fruition. Perhaps that vision never existed. A 2019 special issue of the *Journal of Deliberative Democracy* dedicated itself to the New England town meeting, titling the issue "A Founding Myth of American Democracy." Michael Zuckerman's essay, *The Mirage of Democracy: The Town Meeting in America*, notes that colonial town meetings were not democratic in any sense of the word. Forbidding dissent, rejecting majority rule, and disdaining conflict, the New England town meeting began, he argues, as a place that required conformity. "Town meetings," he writes, "were a means to muster . . . common assent," (Zuckerman 2019, 16). Today's town meetings are characterized by low participation and even lower representation.

A 1996 study of turnout at annual town meetings in Massachusetts communities found average turnout to be 7.6 percent of registered voters (DeSantis and Renner 1997), lower than even the low turnout that characterizes most municipal elections held in off-years (Marschall and Lappie 2018). Field (2019, 14) asserts that "landownership is almost a de facto prerequisite for participating in a town meeting" and points out that the town meeting form of government only works when the population density is relatively low. In 2016, a local government coordinating body in Massachusetts undertook a review of the governance structure and civic participation levels in nine communities. They asked community members about the efficacy and efficiency of the town meeting form of government. Fewer than half of respondents reported finding the town meeting effective. Seventy-seven percent found the town meeting to be inefficient; and 36 percent reported attending regularly. Moreover, only 11 percent of respondents said they were very satisfied with how their town meeting operated.

Thus, in actuality, and despite its idealization, there is little love for the town meeting form of government, and low levels of participation define it. New England is not just "more than Yankee" in this regard; it appears "beyond Yankee."

Voter Turnout

New England is known for its unique system of local governance, where cities and towns maintain a significant level of autonomy in managing their affairs, including the scheduling of local elections. Low participation also characterizes local elections in the New England region. Turnout in most local elections, especially when they are off-year with state and national races, is low. And "off-year" is even confusing to voters as off-year local elections in New England are not held on a consistent date. Some towns hold local elections in April; others in June. The form of voting differs from city-to-city and town-to-town.

One way to counter low turnout is to have competitive local elections. Marschall and Lappie found that in a sample of recent elections in ten of the nation's largest thirty cities, turnout averaged only 15 percent of the citizen voting-age population (Marschall and Lappie, 2018, 221). But when local elections actually had contestation (as opposed to uncontested races), turnout increased. Electoral competitiveness and contestation are thus key factors that promote turnout, participation, and engagement.

Data measuring the competitiveness of local elections is hard to come by. At the state legislative level, however, states are ranked. Massachusetts ranks at the bottom for electoral competitiveness in state legislatures. According to *Ballotpedia's 2022 Annual State Legislative Competitiveness Report* which analyzes all state legislative seats across the United States, only 30 percent of Massachusetts's 200 legislative seats up for election were contested by both parties. By contrast, New Hampshire, the least professionalized state legislature in the country, ranked second for the most competitive state legislative races, with 91 percent of the 424 seats up for election contested by both parties. Maine ranks fifteenth for most competitive. The remaining New England states are in the middle of the pack with Rhode Island ranking 26, Vermont ranking 29, and Connecticut ranking 31 (Ballotpedia 2022). New England states thus represent the full range of competitiveness in legislative seats. Part of legislative seat competitiveness can be explained by legislative professionalism—professional legislatures have perquisites that help them maintain their incumbency status, including robust constituency service (Berry, Berkman, and Schneiderman 2000; Carey, Niemi, and Powell 2000; Hogan, 2004).

While turnout and competitiveness in local elections is low, participation in state and national elections for the New England states is fairly high. The New England states consistently rank above the national average in presidential elections and midterm elections, except for Rhode Island. In 2004, 2012, and 2020, Rhode Island ranked just below the national average for turnout.[2] Since 1996, Maine has ranked first or second for turnout (trading places with Minnesota) except in 2012 when it dipped to fifth. Maine is neither a swing state nor does it hold gubernatorial elections in presidential election years; it does, however, have a district plan for elector allocation giving two electoral votes to the state's popular vote winner and one electoral vote to the popular vote winner in each congressional district.

What propels such high participation for Maine? Palmer (2010) asserts a cultural argument, arguing that Maine's "devotion to participatory culture" drives its high turnout, noting that unlike other high-turnout states that have "above-average levels of income and education," (27) Maine's turnout remains high despite Maine ranking in the middle of states for median household income (Statista 2022) and education (Statista 2021). Two key

---

[2] In 1998, New Hampshire was the only New England state to dip below the national average of 39.3 percent, with a turnout rate of 37.6 percent. In 2018, Rhode Island also dipped below the national average of 50 percent, with a turnout rate of 47.5 percent. https://www.electproject.org/election-data/voter-turnout-data.

additional variables are likely the Pine Tree state's same-day voter registration law and their overall propensity to successfully put "clean" election reforms and expanded voter access to the voters (Melcher and Fried, this volume).

Overall, the focus on national politics and the high turnout in national elections is part of a broader trend in American politics. Issues and campaigns focused on the national-level capture the attention of a wider range of people and inspire many to get involved. On the negative side, however, nationalization can lead to a lack of attention and resources for state and local issues. It can also lead to greater polarization of political views, lack of compromise and the undermining of electoral accountability (Hopkins 2018).

Voting Rights in the New England States

Policies that promote access to voting are well known by scholars but differentially utilized by the six New England states. Convenience voting refers to methods of voting that make it easier for citizens to cast their ballots, such as early voting, vote-by-mail, and automatic voter registration and online voter registration. Laws such as early voting and vote-by-mail have become increasingly popular in the United States in recent years, as they allow voters to participate in elections without having to take time off work or travel to polling places on Election Day.

Implementation of convenience measures varies across New England. Only New Hampshire does not have early voting; Connecticut passed a ballot referendum in November 2022 permitting an amendment to the state constitution which required in-person voting on Election Day (Edison 2022). The other four have some type, but the number of days varies among the states. New Hampshire is the only New England state without automatic voter registration; Rhode Island and Massachusetts are the only New England states that do not have same-day registration. These convenience measures such as early voting are not used in all elections (i.e., municipal elections). Just as the form of convenience measures varies across states, so too does their use vary by election type. Overall, convenience voting is aimed at increasing voter turnout and making the voting process more accessible to all eligible citizens.

REGISTRATION DEADLINES AND SAME-DAY REGISTRATION

Voter registration deadlines place a significant cost on potential voters. Citizens must know a deadline exists; they must proactively register by a proscribed deadline which differs between states; and they must provide appropriate documentation at the time of registration which also differs among states. Registration deadlines are especially burdensome to people who move frequently and who infrequently use government offices, including young people who have not yet formed a habit of voting, minorities, and people with low-incomes (Gerber, Green, and Shachar 2003).

Same-day registration (also called Election Day registration) is a reform that enables voters to register to vote on the same day they cast a ballot. Voting rights advocates view same-day registration as a critical policy that has a positive impact for increasing voter turnout. Scholarship conducted in the late 1990s through the early 2000s found that same-day registration boosted turnout anywhere between 3 percent to 9 percent (Highton and Wolfinger 1998) and cut into the social-class bias in American elections (Rigby and Springer 2011).

Two New England states have had same-day voter registration for decades. Maine enacted same-day registration in 1973 in a bill sponsored by Republicans and supported by Republicans and Democrats. According to a *Bangor Daily News* article describing the passage of the 1973 legislation, "[d]ebate on the House floor was dry and tame with no hint of partisan differences in the Republican-controlled Legislature" (*Bangor Daily News*). New Hampshire enacted same-day voter registration in 1996 under a Republican governor and legislature as an alternative to the National Voter Registration Act of 1993, also known as "Motor Voter."

In 2011, Maine's Republican governor and Republican-controlled legislature removed same-day registration prompting Democrats to launch a "people's veto campaign." The measure to restore same-day registration passed, 59.9 percent to 39.2 percent (Ballotpedia n.d.).

In 2000, Connecticut, Massachusetts, Rhode Island, and Vermont all had voter registration deadlines. By 2022, only Massachusetts and Rhode Island remained as the two New England states with such deadlines though Massachusetts reduced the deadline from twenty to ten days in 2021. Rhode Island, along with eight other states (Arkansas, Alaska, Louisiana, Missouri, Ohio, South Carolina, Tennessee and Texas), have the longest registration deadline in the country: thirty days. Table 9.1 shows the number of days prior to election day a voter must register to vote by state, between 1996 and 2022. The trend shows gradual convergence, though not complete, toward eliminating voter registration ahead of Election Day.

TABLE 9.1 Days Prior to Election Voter Must Register by New England State

	1996	2000	2004	2008	2012	2016	2020	2022
CT	14	14	14	14	0	0	0	0
ME	0	0	0	0	0	0	0	0
MA	20	20	20	20	20	20	20	10
NH	0	0	0	0	0	0	0	0
RI	30	30	30	30	30	30	30	30
VT	17	17	17	8	8	6	0	0

Source: https://costofvotingindex.com/

FELON VOTING RIGHTS

In the United States, six million people, or one in every forty US adults, are legally ineligible to vote because of felony disenfranchisement. These laws restrict voting rights for those convicted of a felony-level crime. One in thirteen voting-age African Americans are ineligible to vote because of felony disenfranchisement (Uggen, Larson, and Shannon 2016). This is on top of the fact that people who have had any carceral contact vote less often, though the causal mechanisms are unclear (White 2019). Spending even a few days or weeks in jail impacts whether people will vote in the future (White 2019). The New England states stand out as having among the least restrictive laws in the country and among the lowest level of disenfranchisement rates in the United States (Uggen et al. 2022). In the United States, only two states and the District of Columbia ensure that no one ever loses the right to vote, including when they are incarcerated. Both states are New England states—Maine and Vermont. The remaining four New England states restrict felons from voting while incarcerated but permit automatic restoration of voting rights upon release. In 2021, Connecticut passed SB 1202 and joined Massachusetts, New Hampshire, and Rhode Island in permitting the automatic restoration of voting rights regardless of parole status (NCSL 2022a).

The Sentencing Project examined level disenfranchisement rates (the disenfranchised population with felony convictions as a percentage of the adult voting eligible population in each state) and found that the New England states had among the lowest disenfranchisement rates in the country. Maine and Vermont had zero percent disenfranchised individuals. New Hampshire had the highest percentage among the New England states with .50 percent followed by .26 percent in Connecticut, .2 percent Rhode Island and .15 percent in Massachusetts. By contrast, Mississippi had just over 10 percent of disenfranchised individuals with felony convictions (the highest in the country) followed by Tennessee with 9 percent (Uggen et al. 2022). The national average was 2 percent (Uggen et al. 2022). On this metric, New England adheres to its participatory ideal.

ONLINE VOTER REGISTRATION

Over the past twenty-five years as states have modernized their election systems, some states have provided multiple modalities for citizens to register to vote, including being able to register online. Online voter registration (OVR) allows citizens to register to vote online (not cast their ballots online). First adopted by Arizona in 2002, forty states allowed citizens to register through a secure, online portal by 2022. Beyond providing a convenient method to register, OVR lowers costs and decreases data errors. Connecticut was the first New England state to adopt OVR in 2012, followed by Massachusetts in 2014, Vermont in 2015, Rhode Island in 2016, and Maine in 2021. Only New Hampshire does not provide online voter registration, though, as noted, it does provide same-day registration.

AUTOMATIC VOTER REGISTRATION

Over "half of all countries and territories have compulsory voter registration" (Schumacher and Connaughton 2020). Citizens often need not fill out any forms, nor stand in lines—they simply receive a unique identifier, like a Social Security number—their voting number—that follows them for life. Automatic Voter Registration (AVR) takes an "opt-out" approach whereby eligible citizens who interact with state agencies such as the Registry of Motor Vehicles or are automatically registered to vote unless they explicitly request to be removed from the voter list. Oregon was the first state to implement an AVR system in 2016. Since then, twenty-one other states have followed suit including five of the six New England states (Connecticut in 2016, Rhode Island and Vermont in 2017, Massachusetts in 2018, and Maine in 2019). New Hampshire is the only New England state not to have AVR.

EARLY VOTING AND VOTE-BY-MAIL

Prior to the 1970s, elections were almost exclusively place and time-bound. Voters could cast their ballot at their polling place on Election Day. While absentee voting became temporarily widespread as a result of voting during the Civil War, it was not until early part of the twentieth century states codified laws and procedures permitting citizens to vote absentee. Absentee voting, however, placed strict limits around what constituted an appropriate "excuse" to vote in this manner: absence from the jurisdiction on Election Day, sickness, or military service oversees. In the 1970s, California introduced "no-excuse" absentee balloting. In the late 1980s, Texas adopted a form of early voting, followed by Tennessee (Testimony, John C. Fortier, 2014). Convenience voting measures—vote-by-mail, early in-person voting, and even electronic voting—have become commonplace across the United States in the last twenty years. Today, forty-six states have some form of early in-person voting; thirty-five states and Washington DC have no-excuse absentee voting, of which eight automatically mail a ballot to every eligible voter (National Conference of State Legislatures [NCSL] 2023).

New Hampshire and Connecticut are two of only four states in the United States that do not have any form of early voting. Massachusetts residents may vote seventeen days before election for state elections during regular business hours and on weekends. Vermont offers citizens vote-by-mail beginning forty-five days before election day. Maine and Rhode Island both have in-person absentee voting which the National Conference of State Legislatures (NCSL 2023) defines as "when a voter requests, completes and signs an absentee ballot in a polling place." Maine enables citizens to vote in-person absentee 20–45 days before Election Day while Rhode Island permits citizens to vote in-person absentee twenty days before Election Day. As of 2022, Vermont became the eighth state to conduct elections entirely by mail, though only for general elections.

VOTER IDENTIFICATION REQUIREMENTS

Since the 2000 election, states across the United States have adopted voter identification requirements. In 2000, fourteen states required voters present some form of identification. By 2022, thirty-five states required it. Among the New England states, Connecticut adopted a voter identification requirement in 1993, Rhode Island adopted it in 2011, and New Hampshire adopted it in 2012. Massachusetts, Maine and Vermont do not require that voters bring identification or any documentation with them to vote. While no two states have identical laws establishing what form of ID is acceptable, there are broad classification schemes, ranging from the most restrictive (requiring a particular photo identification), to requiring a non-photo document such as a utility bill or bank statement, to less restrictive forms in which an ID is requested but not required. Rhode Island has the most restrictive law of the New England states, which requires voters to present a valid document showing a photo; otherwise the person can only vote provisionally. The NCSL, however, characterizes Rhode Island as a non-strict photo-ID state, meaning that "at least some voters without acceptable identification have an option to cast a ballot that will be counted without further action on the part of the voter" (NCSL 2022b). New Hampshire requests that voters show an identification document with a photo on it, such as a driver's license, passport, or other valid IDs issued by the government. Connecticut also requests an identification that has the potential voter's address, signature, or photograph. In both states, voters without any of these forms of ID may sign an affidavit in lieu of presenting an ID. Thus, the NCSL characterizes New Hampshire and Connecticut as non-strict non-photo ID states.

Political scientists studying voter identification requirement passage find that partisan competition plays a key role in determining adoption of voter identification requirements, with the Republican Party playing a central role in pushing for such measures, especially in competitive states, in pushing for policy adoption (Bentele and O'Brien 2013; Hicks et al. 2015; Biggers and Hanmer 2017). New Hampshire's 2012 photo identification requirement came as a result of state Republicans gaining a majority of the New Hampshire House in 2010, the first time since 1911. Although Governor John Lynch, a Democrat, had vetoed a first attempt at a voter identification requirement, the Republican led legislature passed a second bill that Governor Lynch let become law without his signature.

The Rhode Island legislature passed a voter identification law in 2011 requiring a photo ID. The effort was led by the Democratic Secretary of State Ralph Mollis, approved by the Democratic legislature and signed into law by an independent Governor, Lincoln Chafee. Rhode Island's Democratic Party marched in an altogether different direction than the dominant policy views of national Democrats, being the only case of a Democratic-controlled legislature to introduce a restrictive voter ID measure between 2006 and 2016 that included support from two-thirds of the Democratic majority in the state's House and senate (Hicks, McKee, and Smith 2016). Rhode Island did not behave a "blue" way, nor was it "beyond blue" through Republican capture. Instead, it created a "new blue." The Rhode Island effort appears to be the result of a widely popular law proposed during a period of fiscal crisis when opposition to the law was not terribly effective. The law is also an example of reelection seeking politicians moving to reduce threats from challengers. In this case, according to Hicks et al. (2016), "Anglo Democratic legislators supported the measure as a means to tamp down the threat of a minority Democratic challengers in districts with significant minority (Black and Latino) populations," (Note 1, 426). Although there have been efforts to overturn the law since, they have all been defeated (Moakley 2011).

Teaching Civics in K-12 Schools

If the degree to which people participate is a measure of the health of the democracy, then whether or not the state requires that young people learn how democracies work is a further measure of the state's commitment to democracy and to preparing young people to become informed and active citizens. Civic education requirements are yet another example of the highly decentralized nature of American democracy. Some states have mandatory classes, others do not. And within the mandatory classes, the length, rigor, and focus varies from state-to-state and even from community-to-community (Shapiro and Brown 2018). Civic education is ostensibly designed to cultivate a sense of engaged citizenship and efficacy that stimulates political involvement over the life course (but see Litt 1963). Civic learning and engagement is a lifelong endeavor, as are the development of civic knowledge, civic skills, and dispositions. Nationally, civic education has become an afterthought (Cho 2021). Instead, today's national education policy has focused attention and investment in STEM fields, including science, technology, engineering and math. Nationally, the United States spends about $50 of federal funds per student per year on STEM and only five cents per year on civic education (Adams 2019).

Civic education and literacy neither begins nor ends with state curricular requirements. But because states play a critical role in education policy, including establishing and overseeing curricula, standards, and procedures, states have genuine power to invest in and provide investments and standards for civic education.

Five of the six New England states provide little to no formal civics education and five of the six do not require a full year of civic education, a fact at odds with the idealized view of New England as a place dedicated to participatory democracy. The majority of the region has failed to invest in civic education; the public commitment to educating the next generation of citizens is illusory. According to a report, "The State of State Standards for Civics and U.S. History in 2021" produced by the Thomas B. Fordham

Institute, Massachusetts was among the top five states in the country, earning a grade of A-. Vermont, New Hampshire, and Maine earned failing grades, Rhode Island received a D-, and Connecticut received a D+. Massachusetts requires that all eighth-grade students take a full-year civics course and provides rigorous and thoughtful sequencing. Vermont, by contrast, does not have any civics requirement at all (joining eight other states in the United States) and does not require high school students to take courses in either civics or US History. In 2021, Rhode Island passed a law requiring civics proficiency which can be demonstrated through a student-led civics project in either middle or high school (Gagosz 2021). But, like Vermont, Rhode Island does not require a US History or Civics course.

The most rigorous civics education provides a yearlong course that includes a focus not just on knowledge, including comparing the United States to other democracies, but also on building skills for "agency in civic engagement" (Shapiro and Brown 2018). Such programs clearly articulate what students should know, emphasize skills essential to informed citizenship including critical thinking, problem analysis, and evaluating, interpreting, and arguing, and "champion essential civic dispositions" (Fordham Institute 2021, 14).

Requiring a class called "civics" is not the only path toward civics education. Multiple alternative strategies exist, ranging from "including questions about knowledge of the mandated civic pedagogical practices in teacher licensure exams, tying civic teaching strategies to teacher evaluation frameworks, and creating a student civics accomplishment badge" (Tichnor-Wagner, Kawashima-Ginsberg, and Hayat 2020). While Vermont does not have a state-level civics requirement, in part because local districts set their own graduation requirements and write their own curricula, it does require that all high school seniors be able to explain "how the U.S. Constitution establishes a system of government that has powers, responsibilities, and limits that have changed over time and that are still contested" (Duffort 2021). Yet being able to explain constitutional structure does not help young people learn the nuts and bolts of how to actually vote, how to organize and mobilize like-minded citizens, how to have important intergroup dialogue, or how to help shape policies and procedures of the community. These are the skills that participatory democracy demands. The New England states, save Massachusetts, do not take a rigorous approach to civic education.

The low levels of participation and representation in town meetings and the challenges the New England states have in promulgating democracy at the local level belie the images of "New England Yankees," noted in the introduction of this volume and chapter—of a populace defined by "thrift, localism and civic participation regardless of racial or ethnic background" (Fried and O'Brien, this volume). The New England states are engaged in national elections but have opted out of local politics. Save Massachusetts, the five other New England states are not paying it forward to the next generation in investing in the education system to prepare young people for citizenship. The New England states are indeed "More than Yankee" in this way. And yet, strikingly, at the national level, voter participation in national elections has been high. Moreover, laws promoting voter access help the New England states rank fairly high on measures of convenience voting.

Conclusion

The casual observer might look to the New England states as a regional block of progressivism vis-à-vis voting rights, a place where democracy's promise of citizen engagement and full participation was evident in both cultural norms and legal statute. The region's high level of turnout during presidential elections over the last quarter century, along with its long-standing use of the town meeting, produce a superficial patina of widespread citizen involvement and participation. Yet, when we peel back the onion and inspect the region's commitment to expanding access to voting and promoting participation, a more nuanced picture comes into focus, one that is neither beyond blue nor pure blue.

Along nearly every policy dimension outlined in this chapter on civic participation in New England, whether it be voting rights or civic education or broad voter participation, there are significant outliers as well as points of convergence. Maine and Vermont are the only two states in the country in which individuals convicted of a felony never lose their right to vote, even while they are incarcerated and regardless of the offense. New Hampshire is the only New England state without some form of early voting. Rhode Island (along with 11 other states, all outside New England) has among the longest voter registration requirements of thirty days, followed by Massachusetts which has a ten-day requirement. The remaining New England states all have same-day registration. Massachusetts ranks at the bottom of the states nationally for electoral competitiveness in state legislative elections; New Hampshire ranks second in the nation for competitiveness. They are almost exactly inverted when it comes to legislative professionalism. Massachusetts ranks at the top for civics education, receiving an A- from the Fordham

Institute, while all the rest of the New England states receive either Ds or Fs. While the town meeting is widely used across the region, like many other states in the nation, participation in local elections is low.

As is evident, it is hard to fit all six New England into a neat box and draw broad generalizations. Changes to voting laws, levels of political participation, and intensity of civic engagement occur as a result of a complex mix of partisan tactics, political culture, and external factors such as changes in the economy or demographic shifts. Similarly, levels of political engagement and civic participation can be influenced by factors such as social and economic inequality, educational attainment, and levels of trust in government institutions. These factors differ from state-to-state and from region-to-region. While there may be commonalities in political culture and governance structures across New England, it is important to recognize the unique factors that influence voting patterns and political participation in each state and community. On civic participation, New England does not speak with one voice.

Works Cited

Adams, Kimberly. 2019. "What Federal Funding for Civics Reveals about American Political Discourse." *Marketplace* (blog). November 6, 2019. https://www.marketplace.org/2019/11/06/what-federal-funding-for-civics-reveals-about-american-political-discourse/.

Educating for American Democracy (EAD). 2021. "Educating for American Democracy: Excellence in History and Civics for All Learners." *iCivics*. March 2, 2021. www.educatingforamericandemocracy.org.

Ballotpedia. n.d.. "Maine Same-Day Registration Veto Referendum, Question 1." 2011. https://ballotpedia.org/Maine_SameDay_Registration_Veto_Referendum,_Question_1_(2011).

Ballotpedia. 2022. "Annual State Legislative Competitiveness Report: Vol. 12, 2022." https://ballotpedia.org/Annual_State_Legislative_Competitiveness_Report:_Vol._12,_2022.

Bentele, Keith G., and Erin E. O'Brien. 2013. "Jim Crow 2.0? Why States Consider and Adopt Restrictive Voter Access Policies." *Perspectives on Politics* 11, no. 4: 1088–1116.

Berry, William D., Michael B. Berkman, and Stuart Schneiderman. 2000. "Legislative Professionalism and Incumbent Reelection: The Development of Institutional Boundaries." *American Political Science Review* 94, no. 4: 859–74.

Biggers, Daniel R., and Michael J. Hanmer. 2017. "Understanding the Adoption of Voter Identification Laws in the American States." *American Politics Research* 45, no. 4: 560–88.

Bryan, Frank M. 2010. *Real Democracy: The New England Town Meeting and How It Works*. Chicago: University Of Chicago Press.

Carey, John M., Richard G. Niemi, and Lynda W. Powell. 2000. "Incumbency and the Probability of Reelection in State Legislative Elections." *The Journal of Politics* 62, no. 3: 671–700.

Cho, Isabella. 2021. "Danielle Allen Calls for Expansion of U.S. 'Civic Infrastructure' At Kennedy School Panel." *The Harvard Crimson*. https://www.thecrimson.com/article/2021/3/25/allen-civic-infrastructure-panel/.

DeSantis, Victor, and Tari Renner. 1997. "Democratic Traditions in New England Town Meetings: Myths and Realities." Paper presented at the *Annual Convention of the Midwest Political Science Association*, Chicago.
DeSantis, Victor, and David Hill. 2004. "Citizen Participation in Local Politics: Evidence from New England Town Meetings." *State and Local Government Review* 36, no. 3: 166–73.
Duffort, Lola. 2021. "A Civics Graduation Requirement? Vermont Already (Kind of) Has One." *VTDigger*. February 2, 2021. https://vtdigger.org/2021/02/02/a-civics-graduation-requirement-vermont-already-kind-of-has-one/.
Litt, Edgar. 1963. "Civic Education, Community Norms, and Political Indoctrination." *American Sociological Review* 28, no. 3: 69–75.
National Conference of State Legislatures. 2022a. "Felon Voting Rights." https://www.ncsl.org/research/elections-and-campaigns/felon-voting-rights.aspx.
National Conference of State Legislatures. 2022b. "Voter ID Laws." https://www.ncsl.org/research/elections-and-campaigns/early-voting-in-state-elections.aspx.
National Conference of State Legislatures. 2023. "Early In-Person Voting." https://www.ncsl.org/elections-and-campaigns/early-in-person-vo.
Edison, Jaden. 2022. "CT Approves Early Voting Ballot Question, Paving Path to New Law." *Connecticut Mirror*, November 9, 2022. https://ctmirror.org/2022/11/09/ct-early-voting-in-person-ballot-question/.
Field, Jonathan Beecher. 2019. *Town Hall Meetings and the Death of Deliberation*. University of Minnesota Press.
Gagosz, Alexa. 2021. "Civics Proficiency Now a Requirement for All Rhode Island Public School Graduates—The Boston Globe." *Boston Globe*. July 19, 2021. https://www.bostonglobe.com/2021/07/19/metro/civics-proficiency-now-requirement-all-rhode-island-public-school-graduates/.
Gerber, Alan S., Donald P. Green, and Ron Shachar. 2003. "Voting May Be Habit-Forming: Evidence from a Randomized Field Experiment." *American Journal of Political Science* 47, no. 3: 540–50.
Hicks, William D., Seth C. McKee, Mitchell D. Sellers, and Daniel A. Smith. 2015. "A Principle or a Strategy? Voter Identification Laws and Partisan Competition in the American States." *Political Research Quarterly* 68, no. 1: 18–33.
Hicks, William D., Seth C. McKee, and Daniel A. Smith. 2016. "The Determinants of State Legislator Support for Restrictive Voter ID Laws." *State Politics & Policy Quarterly* 16, no. 4: 411–31.
Highton, Benjamin, and Raymond E. Wolfinger. 1998. "Estimating the Effects of the National Voter Registration Act of 1993." *Political Behavior* 20, no. 2: 79–104.
Hogan, R.E., 2004. "Challenger Emergence, Incumbent Success, and Electoral Accountability in State Legislative Elections." *The Journal of Politics* 66, no. 4: 1283–1303.
Hopkins, Daniel J. 2018. *The Increasingly United States: How and Why American Political Behavior Nationalized*. Chicago: University of Chicago Press.
Jenkins, Shannon, Douglas D. Roscoe, and David Broges. 2016. "Voters in Representative Town Meeting Elections." *New England Journal of Political Science* 9, no. 2: 134–163.
Marschall, Melissa, and John Lappie. 2018. "Turnout in Local Elections: Is Timing Really Everything?" *Election Law Journal: Rules, Politics, and Policy* 17, no. 3: 221–33.
Schumacher, Shannon, and Aidan Connaughton. 2020. "From Voter Registration to Mail-in Ballots, How Do Countries Around the World Run Their Elections?" Pew Research Center. October 30, 2020. https://www.pewresearch.org/short-reads/2020/10/30/from-voter-registration-to-mail-in-ballots-how-do-countries-around-the-world-run-their-elections/.

Statista. 2022. "Median Household Income in the United States in 2021, by State (in 2021 U.S. Dollars)." US Census Bureau. https://www.statista.com/statistics/233170/median-household-income-in-the-united-states-by-state/.

Statista. 2021. "Percentage of The Population Aged 25 and over Who Have Completed a Bachelor's Degree or Higher in the U.S. In 2020, by State." US Census Bureau. https://www.statista.com/statistics/725331/us-population-that-held-bachelors-degree-by-state/.

Moakley, Maureen. 2011. "Voter ID in Rhode Island." *New England Journal of Political Science* 6, no. 2: 358–70.

Palmer, Kenneth. 2010. "Maine's Paradoxical Politics." *Maine Policy Review* 19, no. 1: 26–34.

Rigby, Elizabeth, and Melanie J. Springer. 2011. "Does Electoral Reform Increase (or Decrease) Political Equality?" *Political Research Quarterly* 64, no. 2: 420–434.

Robinson, Donald. 2011. *Town Meeting: Practicing Democracy in Rural New England*. Amherst and Boston: University of Massachusetts Press.

Schraufnagel, Scot, Michael J. Pomante, and Quan Li. 2022. "Cost of Voting in the American States: 2022." *Election Law Journal: Rules, Politics, and Policy* 21, no. 3: 220–28.

Shapiro, Sarah, and Catherine Brown. 2018. "The State of Civics Education." *Center for American Progress*. https://www.americanprogress.org/article/state-civics-education/

Tichnor-Wagner, Ariel, Kim Kawashima-Ginsberg, and Noorya Hayat. 2020. "The State of Civic Education in Massachusetts." CIRCLE Tisch College of Civic Life. https://circle.tufts.edu/sites/default/files/2021-01/MA_DESE_civics_full_report.pdf.

Townsend, Rebecca, and Carmin C. Reiss. 2022. "An Enduring System of Local Deliberative Democracy: The 21st Century Legal and Normative Structure of Massachusetts Town Meeting." *Journal of Deliberative Democracy* 18, no. 1: 1–10.

Uggen, Christopher, Ryan Larson, and Sarah Shannon. 2016. "Million Lost Voters: State-Level Estimates of Felony Disenfranchisement." Washington DC: The Sentencing Project. https://www.sentencingproject.org/app/uploads/2022/08/6-Million-Lost-Voters.pdf.

Uggen, Christopher, Ryan Larson, Sarah Shannon, and Robert Stewart. 2022. "Locked Out 2022: Estimates of People Denied Voting Rights." https://www.sentencingproject.org/reports/locked-out-2022-estimates-of-people-denied-voting-rights/.

White, Ariel. 2019. "Misdemeanor Disenfranchisement? The Demobilizing Effects of Brief Jail Spells on Potential Voters." *American Political Science Review* 113, no. 2: 311–24.

Zimmerman, Joseph Francis. 1999. *The New England Town Meeting: Democracy in Action*. Bloomsbury Publishing.

Zuckerman, Michael. 2019. "Mirage of Democracy: The Town Meeting in America." *Journal of Public Deliberation* 15, no. 2, Article 3. https://delibdemjournal.org/article/id/603/.

CHAPTER 10

PRESIDENTIAL POLITICS AND INFLUENCE, NEW ENGLAND STYLE(S)

Dante J. Scala
Professor of Political Science
University of New Hampshire

Like the tides, American presidential politics do not stand still. Affected by population growth, demographic shifts, and the Electoral College, different states and regions rise and fall in their power to influence who wins presidential nominations and the presidency itself. Most states are caught in the undertow. Doomed to be uncompetitive, they get far less attention from the media and campaigns and are left to float adrift in the backwaters.

Such has been the fate of most of New England in the early twenty-first century. Not only is New England far from Hartville, Missouri, the population center of the twenty-first-century United States (United States Census Bureau 2022), which continues to grow in the South and the West at the expense of the Northeast. The region is also distant from the nation's increasingly multiracial demographic profile. Although New England has become more diverse over the past decade, whites continue to comprise the great majority of the population—roughly 80 percent in southern New England, and more than 90 percent in the northern portion (Barndollar 2021; Quarshie and Slack 2021; United States Census Bureau 2023).

Yet New England's presidential influence has not been peripheral. Instead, in February 2023, former Ambassador to the United Nations (and South Carolina Governor) Nikki Haley visited Exeter, New Hampshire, soon after announcing her presidential run as a Republican. Thanks to New Hampshire's first-in-the-nation primary, at least some New Englanders can weigh in at the crucial early stages of the presidential nomination process, leaving their imprint on the major-party nominees who face the nation months later.

As this chapter discusses, while most of New England is now deeply blue in presidential elections, the New Hampshire primary still garners great interest from national political elites as an early bellwether. A blow to New Hampshire's influence in presidential contests, and thus that of New England, came when the Democratic National Committee (DNC) voted in 2023 to move South Carolina ahead of New Hampshire on the primary calendar at

President Joe Biden's behest. Then Biden chose not to appear on the New Hampshire Democratic primary ballot when New Hampshire Democratic Party officials defied the DNC and still held their presidential primary first.

Moreover, the legendary narrative of the independent Yankee holding presidential hopefuls to account misses more complicated realities. Granite State Republicans have proven quite influential in crowning frontrunners, while their Democratic counterparts often succeeded in defining insurgent alternatives. Local elites present the primary as a model of small-scale, deliberative democracy, but the nationalization of the nomination process has weakened the leverage New Hampshire once employed to press candidates on issues. Thus presidential politics in New England is clearly more than blue and more than Yankee.

New England in the Electoral College

New England's modest cache of thirty-three electoral votes has become less important in general elections because it now typically votes as a solidly Democratic bloc. Indeed, as Table 10.1 shows, Democratic presidential nominees have dominated the New England states from 2000 to 2020. No Republican presidential candidate has won more than four electoral votes in New England since 2000, when George W. Bush carried New Hampshire with a plurality of 48.1 percent (Leip 2023).

New Hampshire remains a swing state, albeit one with a decided Democratic tilt. While the state flipped three times from 1992 to 2004, it has remained in the Democratic column since John Kerry's victory. No subsequent Republican candidate has matched the 48.9 percent Bush received in 2004 (Leip 2023; Scala 2022).

Outside New Hampshire, only Maine's rural Second Congressional District[1] qualifies as a presidential battleground; Donald Trump earned his only electoral vote from New England in 2016 and 2020 by winning there. As a state, Maine is the second-least Democratic in New England behind New Hampshire. The Democratic presidential nominee has failed

---

[1] Maine is one of two states (along with Nebraska) that does not award all its electoral votes to the winner of the statewide popular vote. Each of Maine's two congressional districts is allocated one of its four votes, so the loser of the statewide popular vote may still earn one vote by winning the popular vote in one of the districts. For more on Maine as a swing state, see Melcher and Fried (2022, 163–192).

TABLE 10.1: Democratic Nominees' Vote Share
in Presidential Elections, 2000–2020

YEAR	CONNEC-TICUT	MAINE	MASSA-CHUSETTS	NEW HAMPSHIRE	RHODE ISLAND	VERMONT
2020	59	53	66	53	59	66
2016	55	48	60	47	54	57
2012	58	56	61	52	63	67
2008	61	58	62	54	63	67
2004	54	54	62	50	59	59
2000	56	49	60	47	61	51
AVERAGE VOTE SHARE, 2000–2020	57	53	62	51	60	61

Source: Dave Leip's Atlas of U.S. Presidential Elections. All numbers rounded to nearest whole percentage.

to carry a majority twice here, in 2000 and 2016; the average vote share of the Democratic nominee from 2000 to 2020 was 53 percent.

The remaining four New England states—Connecticut, Massachusetts, Rhode Island, and Vermont—are automatically assigned to the Democratic column every four years. On average, the Democratic nominee has won between 57 percent and 62 percent of the vote in these states this century. Over the last six presidential elections, the Democratic presidential nominee has carried less than 55 percent of the vote in these states just four times.[2]

In short, New England's thirty-three electoral votes are an important component of the Democratic presidential electoral coalition, providing almost the entirety of Joe Biden's 306–232 margin of victory in 2020. But the region's general lack of competitiveness means that those thirty-three votes do not translate into a proportionate amount of influence in presidential elections. Looking ahead to autumn 2024, it is very unlikely New England will garner the same amount of attention from presidential campaigns as, say, Pennsylvania and Wisconsin (29 electoral votes, combined) or Georgia and Arizona (27 electoral votes, combined).

---

[2] In 2000, Gore won just 51 percent of the vote in Vermont, but nonetheless enjoyed a 10 percent margin of victory over Bush; 7 percent of Vermont voters cast ballots for Nader. Kerry only carried 54 percent of the vote in Connecticut in 2004. Hillary Clinton won just 54 percent in Rhode Island in 2016, and just under 55 percent in Connecticut. All presidential election statistics taken from Dave Leip's Atlas of U.S. Presidential Elections.

But even though New England suffers from relative neglect during the general election season, the region (at least one state within it) becomes the center of the American political universe every four years. That is because New Hampshire has held the first-in-the-nation presidential primary for more than a century. The Granite State's place at the front of the nomination calendar is stereotypically depicted as imposing an idiosyncratic "Yankee" imprint on presidential campaigns; the laconic citizen in the plaid shirt, stoically listening to the flashy presidential candidate from somewhere else, then cutting him or her down to size with a wry comment.

Yet the institution of the New Hampshire primary has also been "more than Yankee." This small state has been an incubator for national political trends that challenged the status quo, from Progressivism to Populism. And the Granite State's conception of itself (and self-justification for its exalted status) has rested on two rival notions of democracy; deliberative democracy, which focuses on rational argumentation among the citizenry as a means to the common good, and plebiscitary, which emphasizes the importance of direct participation through voting. These two concepts rest uneasily inside the singular New England institution; the New Hampshire presidential primary, which represents the New England town meeting writ large, exported for national consumption. The resulting tensions, increasingly apparent this century, tell the story of presidential politics and influence, New England style.

The New Hampshire Primary
THE ORIGINS OF THE NEW HAMPSHIRE PRIMARY

The Granite State has long embraced "democratic participation" as a core principle (Wright 1987, 87), and town meeting as that principle's emblem. "True town meeting is the purest form of democracy," wrote a representative of the New Hampshire Local Government Center, "as individuals gather to debate, discuss and decide upon matters that impact their lives and community" (French 2007). Town meeting first occurred in the early seventeenth century, in the very first New England settlements. In New Hampshire, town meeting was likely first held during the 1620s in the settlements of Dover and Portsmouth (French 2007).

Long before the dawn of the presidential primary, New Hampshire's town meeting was the center of national attention—then, as now, because of its early place on the political calendar. Through much of the nineteenth century (until 1878), the Granite State held its state elections on Town Meeting Day, the second Tuesday in March, thus providing the national media with an early barometer of public opinion (Brereton 1987, 2–3).

New Hampshire is not typically listed among the Progressive movement's vanguard at the turn of the twentieth century, although it did get a nod of approval from the progressive periodical *Outlook* (Wright 1987, xviii). The Granite State's historic preference for small government ran counter to the Progressive principle that the capacities of the state should be enhanced in order to address new social and economic issues of the day. But the specter of special interests certainly animated early twentieth-century Granite State politics. And New Hampshire reformers' solution to that problem—more democracy—was at the heart of Progressivism, and provided the catalyst for the eventual creation of the presidential primary.

New Hampshire's Progressive movement arose from within the Republican Party, the dominant force in early twentieth-century Granite State politics. Within the state GOP, reformers sought to expunge their party of the influence of the Boston and Maine Railroad. One of the chief venues of that influence was the party's nominating convention; the railroad's agents used the "proxy" in order to obtain control of the votes of delegates in exchange for various favors (Wright 1987, 70–71; Brereton 1987, 3). In true Progressive fashion, the reformers sought to improve the nomination process by making it more transparent and more democratic. During the 1909 legislative session, they created a direct primary law empowering party members to vote for nominees (Wright 1987, 95).

In 1913, New Hampshire Democrats extended this new institution to encompass the selection of presidential nominees. Two years later, New Hampshire unwittingly locked in long-term gains by making a penny-wise, short-term decision; to avoid the costs of running more than one event, the legislature pushed the primary forward two months in order to hold it on Town Meeting Day (Brereton 1987, 3–4). This decision to hold an early primary was of little import in 1916, when the Granite State held its first presidential primary. (It did not hold the first-in-the-nation primary until four years later.) By this time, Progressive efforts at reform were losing steam. Candidates could not earn enough delegates by winning primaries to become the de facto nominee. The result was a nomination process in which party bosses still largely decided the outcome at the national party convention. This remained true until the 1972 election cycle, when Democratic Party-led reforms transformed the nominating process, making voters' participation in primaries and caucuses critically important.

The first few decades of the primary were unremarkable. New Hampshire voters did not even cast ballots for candidates until 1952; prior, voters cast ballots for prospective convention delegates, who had publicly committed to a candidate or remained uncommitted (Brereton 1987, 4). The lackluster beginnings of the primary reached a nadir in 1948, when the contest failed to produce a clear victor between Republican rivals Thomas Dewey and Harold Stassen. The following year the state legislature added a "beauty contest" to the primary—candidates could put their names on the primary ballot, and voters could support these candidates directly (Brereton 1987, 4). This legislative alchemy, coupled with the early date of the event, converted a sleepy affair into a spectacle for the national political media's consumption. The 1952 Republican primary, which displayed Dwight Eisenhower's political potential, amply demonstrated the potential of the event. When the nomination process finally was put in the hands of primary and caucus voters for the 1972 cycle, the influence of New Hampshire (and New England) was cemented.

After 1972, other New England states considered adopting a regional New England primary, to be held on the same day as New Hampshire or shortly thereafter. The idea never gained unanimous approval, but Massachusetts and Vermont did move their primaries forward to early March (Brereton 1987, 169–171). The New Hampshire state legislature reacted to the threat to the primary's first-in-the-nation status with legislation that granted the Secretary of State, New Hampshire's chief elections officer, discretion to move the primary to keep it ahead of other states. Jim Splaine, a longtime state legislator from Portsmouth, was one of the architects of this law, as well as a subsequent measure in 1995 which specified that the primary must be held at least seven days before any other (Splaine n.d.; Palmer 1997, 149–150).

Since the 1970s, New Hampshire's Secretary of State has employed these statutory powers to protect the primary's status, even scheduling the event in the second week of January in the 2008 and 2012 cycles and on January 23 in the 2024 cycle. But New Hampshire's neighbors have not made another concerted effort to supplant its place at the front of the nomination calendar. Like states from other regions, however, they have occasionally moved up their events in order to have some influence on the outcome, a phenomenon known as "frontloading" (Mayer and Busch 2004).

For example, while New Hampshire held its 2000 primary February 1, all other New England states set their events on March 7, known as "Super Tuesday" because more than a dozen states held their nomination events that day (The Green Papers 2023). Four years later, New Hampshire moved up several days on the calendar, and Maine's caucuses leaped a month to February; all others retained their dates in the first week of March. When the Granite State moved to January 8 in 2008, Massachusetts joined a host of other states in voting February 5 (The Green Papers). Over the last quarter-century, New Hampshire, Maine, Massachusetts and Vermont have most consistently shifted their events forward to maximize their influence, while Connecticut and Rhode Island gave up on such efforts after 2008.

During the late twentieth century, New Hampshire's reputation as an incubator for presidents reached its apogee. John Sununu, three-term governor and patriarch of one of the Granite State's most successful political families, famously remarked that while Iowa picked corn, New Hampshire picked presidents (Pindell 2015). Sununu's comment encapsulated an enduring narrative of the primary; that Granite State voters are unusually perceptive, prescient and persistent, scrutinizing candidates multiple times before granting their support.

The embodiment of New Hampshire's version of deliberative democracy was town meeting—or more accurately, the "use of 'town meetings' as strategic devices in political campaigns," wrote Frank Bryan in his authoritative work on New England town meeting (51). Bill Clinton's 1992 campaign, for example, televised half-hour "town halls" with voters in the week before the primary (Healy 2016). Two cycles later, John McCain held more than 100 such meetings in the Granite State en route to his upset of George W. Bush in the New Hampshire GOP primary (Dickerson 2016). These town meetings burnished the reputations of candidates and voters alike, although at least sometimes there was less here than met the eye. "Standing before a crowd of ordinary people fielding questions in a seemingly ad hoc format is powerful imagery," wrote Bryan—and in addition, "Citizen-delivered questions are easier to handle than those offered up by seasoned reporters" (Bryan 2004).

Similarly, Governor Sununu's boast ultimately rang a bit hollow after Clinton, and then Bush, lost the New Hampshire primary but nonetheless captured the presidency. The real influence of the first-in-the-nation primary has been more nuanced, and has varied by political party.

NEW ENGLAND'S INFLUENCE ON REPUBLICAN PRESIDENTIAL POLITICS, 2000–2020

John McCain, Mitt Romney, Donald Trump; solve the riddle of what this unlikely trio has in common, and you will better understand the early twenty-first century history of Republican presidential nomination contests in New

England. Why did this region with a reputation for ideological moderation become the launching pad for McCain and Trump, two opposing figures who each sought to disrupt the status quo inside their party? This question is of more than regional import; as a result of New Hampshire's unique position, New England Republicans are, in effect, able to bat above their weight in terms of presidential influence. On the one hand, there is no question that the centers of power of the Republican Party sit in the South and the West, far from its ancestral home in New England. However, even though the fortunes of the GOP have waned significantly in the region, New England Republicans still possess considerable leverage in the presidential nomination process. McCain, Romney, and Trump were all able to parlay success in New England into the ultimate prize of the nomination itself.

McCain's 2000 New Hampshire campaign—the Vietnam War hero turned maverick senator, the dozens of town hall meetings, the candidate's bull sessions with the media on his campaign bus, the "Straight Talk Express"—is now part of Granite State primary lore. But the Arizona senator's success in New Hampshire (and most of New England) in 2000 and 2008 should not be attributed solely to his campaign or larger-than-life personality. McCain's insurgency had ideological roots which found New England soil especially accommodating, as Table 10.2 shows. The Arizona senator adopted a set of policy positions that sharply contrasted with George W. Bush, governor of Texas and eventual nominee. McCain supported campaign finance reform, even appearing with Democratic presidential candidate Bill Bradley to tout the issue. He advocated for a balanced federal budget, opposing tax cuts for the wealthiest. And while Bush wore his religion on his sleeve (naming Jesus Christ as his favorite political philosopher), McCain singled out evangelical Pat Robertson for his negative influence on the GOP. The Arizona senator's fiscally conservative, socially moderate brand resonated with New England Republicans, who have been among the most likely to report that they were moderate, even liberal. Almost half of New Hampshire Republican presidential primary voters identified as such in 2000 exit polls, and other New England states contained similarly high percentages of centrists (Olsen and Scala 2015, 35–37, 42–43).[3]

---

[3] New Hampshire allows "undeclared" voters, who refrain from identifying with a political party, to vote in either major-party primary, then revert to undeclared status. Most undeclared voters are in fact partisans, but a minority do identify as true independents; they are more likely to identify as moderates than Republicans who declare their partisanship.

TABLE 10.2: Presidential Nomination Results in New England States, 2000–2016

DEMOCRATIC

	CONNECTICUT	MAINE	MASSACHUSETTS	NEW HAMPSHIRE	RHODE ISLAND	VERMONT
2020	Joe Biden	Biden	Biden	Bernie Sanders	Biden	Sanders
2016	Hillary Clinton	Sanders	*Clinton*	Sanders	Sanders	Sanders
2008	Barack Obama	Obama	Clinton	Clinton	Clinton	*Obama*
2004	John Kerry	*Kerry*	*Kerry*	*Kerry*	*Kerry*	Dean
2000	Al Gore	*Gore*	*Gore*	*Gore*	*Gore*	*Gore*

REPUBLICAN

	CONNECTICUT	MAINE	MASSACHUSETTS	NEW HAMPSHIRE	RHODE ISLAND	VERMONT
2016	Donald Trump	Ted Cruz	Trump	Trump	*Trump*	*Trump*
2012	Mitt Romney	*Romney*	*Romney*	*Romney*	*Romney*	*Romney*
2008	John McCain	Mitt Romney	Romney	*McCain*	*McCain*	*McCain*
2000	McCain	George W. Bush	McCain	McCain	McCain	McCain

Sources: The Green Papers; Politico, "Maine Presidential Caucuses Results" https://www.politico.com/2016-election/primary/results/map/president/maine/
N. B. Eventual nominee in italics. Barack Obama was the presumptive nominee in 2012. Bush and Trump were presumptive nominees in 2004 and 2020, respectively.

Exit polls from 2000 to 2012 reveal a bloc of voters with a distinctive set of candidate preferences and issue priorities. They are, first and foremost, most likely to describe themselves as independent-minded, and seek candidates who profess to be the same. While they are not gadflies, they tend to be attracted to candidates who are self-proclaimed tellers of difficult truths that challenge party orthodoxy.

They are much more secular than more conservative primary voters, and steer clear of candidates who are the champions of religious conservatives. Moderate and liberal voters prefer someone who is both more secular and less fiscally conservative than their somewhat conservative cousins (Olsen and Scala 2015, 37).

McCain did well not only in New Hampshire, on which he pinned all his hopes for launching a viable run.[4] Even after he lost a decisive battle to Bush in South Carolina, other New England Republicans nonetheless rallied to his failed cause. McCain won five of six New England primaries that year, thanks in large part to his performance among moderate and liberal Republican primary voters; according to 2000 exit polls, McCain won 59 percent of moderate and liberal voters in Connecticut; 55 percent in Maine; 75 percent in Massachusetts; 74 percent in Rhode Island; and 72 percent in Vermont (Olsen and Scala 2015, 44).

Eight years later, McCain began the 2008 nomination season as the supposed favorite, but his attempt to build a frontrunning campaign collapsed in summer 2007. Unsurprisingly, when all seemed lost for McCain, he returned to New Hampshire, the scene of his greatest success, to attempt to rebuild. He faced a crowded primary field, in which two candidates appeared especially formidable; Rudy Giuliani, then hailed as "America's Mayor" after the events of September 11; and Mitt Romney, the former governor of Massachusetts. But Giuliani's campaign sputtered in the Granite State and he eventually abandoned it in favor of Florida. Romney proved a far more serious foe, but New Hampshire came through once more for the Arizona senator because of his enduring popularity among moderate and liberal Republican primary voters. McCain carried almost half of such voters en route to a narrow 5-point victory (Olsen and Scala 2015, 46–50). Romney succeeded in winning contests in Maine and his home state of Massachusetts before dropping out of the nomination fight.

Four years later, in 2012, Romney returned for another bid as the heavy favorite in New Hampshire, where he had acquitted himself well in a losing effort four years earlier. And once again, he faced a challenge to his left for moderate and liberal primary voters, albeit a less formidable one than McCain. Jon Huntsman, former governor of Utah and President Obama's ambassador to China, entered the race as a moderate alternative and focused his efforts in New Hampshire. Huntsman was a case study in how a certain type of presidential candidate took the wrong lessons from McCain's example. He correctly identified New Hampshire as a promising site for a moderate Republican candidacy, but focused so much on a Granite State breakthrough that it curtailed his ability to attract the wider coalition of voters necessary to

---

[4] The Arizona senator elected not to compete in the Iowa caucuses, the first event on the nomination calendar.

win the nomination. For such candidates, New England becomes a cul-de-sac. Huntsman found small niches of voters in the New Hampshire electorate (such as opponents of the Tea Party, and those who liked the job President Obama was doing) but finished third overall and ended his campaign soon afterward (Olsen and Scala 2015, 54–56).

The runner-up to Romney in New Hampshire was not one of his better-known rivals, such as former Speaker of the House Newt Gingrich or former Pennsylvania Senator Rick Santorum, the winner of the Iowa caucuses. Instead, it was Ron Paul, a 76-year-old Texas congressman, who finished a distant second with 23 percent of the vote. Paul's two runs for the Republican nomination in 2008 and 2012 highlighted another species of New England Republicanism—Libertarians. Paul was a hero to libertarians for his vociferous criticism of the Federal Reserve and support for a return to the gold standard, but his presidential candidacy caught (a modest amount of) fire because of his stance on foreign policy. Paul's firm opposition to the Iraq War and his general support for non-interventionism struck a chord in 2008 among moderate and liberal Republican primary voters, many of whom had doubts about US involvement and downplayed the threat of terrorism. Four years later, the Texas congressman again found support among this slice of the electorate; young, moderate, independent voters (Olsen and Scala 2015, 49–50, 54). Paul was able to claim victory in Maine's Republican caucuses. Although he narrowly lost the non-binding portion of the caucuses to Romney, his supporters later succeeded in capturing most of Maine's twenty-four delegates at the state party convention (Associated Press 2012; *New York Times* 2012).

On the face of it, the 2016 New Hampshire Republican presidential primary closely resembled its predecessor; one candidate seized a sizable lead months ahead of the contest, and never relinquished it.[5] But while Romney's victory in 2012 never seemed in serious doubt, many veteran observers of New Hampshire politics (including the author of this chapter) waited for the wheels to come off the 2016 campaign of Donald Trump. But instead, after Trump lost the Iowa caucuses to Texas Senator Ted Cruz, the Granite State provided a safe haven for the candidate then known as a reality star mogul. His 20-point victory bolstered his campaign, paving the way for a South Carolina triumph that made him the favorite for the GOP nomination in 2016.

---

[5] Compare this graph of New Hampshire Republican primary polling during the 2012 cycle (https://www.realclearpolitics.com/epolls/2012/president/nh/new_hampshire_republican_presidential_primary-1581.html) to the 2016 cycle (https://www.realclearpolitics.com/epolls/2016/president/nh/new_hampshire_republican_presidential_primary-3350.html).

One reason for doubting Trump was the candidate's flouting of the traditional rules for success in New Hampshire. Per conventional wisdom among local political elites, successful campaigns were built on candidate accessibility—specifically, the willingness to engage voters in thoughtful give-and-take at town hall meetings. Trump's 2016 campaign ignored this article of faith, instead holding large rallies drawing hundreds and hundreds. "We always prided ourselves on insisting on retail campaigning. Donald Trump has turned tradition on its head," explained Donna Sytek, former speaker of the New Hampshire House of Representatives (Goldmacher 2015). Entering the final month of the New Hampshire campaign, observers theorized that perhaps Trump had created a reservoir of support that was wide but neither deep nor abiding.

Local conservative elites aimed to cut Trump down to size, but found themselves daunted by a political phenomenon that confounded Republican leaders across the nation. The *New Hampshire Union Leader*, famed for making Ed Muskie cry in 1972, compared him to the bully Biff from the movie *Back to the Future* (Gass 2015). Former governor John Sununu described the mogul as "a loser all his life" (Naft 2016).[6] But local Republican leaders were uneasy. Two weeks before the primary, the New Hampshire Republican Party held a "First-in-the-Nation Presidential Town Hall." Byron York, the chief political correspondent for the conservative *Washington Examiner*, found local political elites bewildered by the Trump phenomenon:

In one of my first conversations at the Radisson, with two Republican activists, I asked a simple what's-up question about Trump. Both immediately responded in exactly the same way: "I don't know anybody who supports him." They're politically active and aware, but they said they have no contact in their daily lives with even a single person who supports their party's front-runner.

After that conversation, I began to ask everyone I met: Do you know anyone who supports Donald Trump? In more cases than not—actually, in nearly all the cases—the answer was no (York 2016).

Trump's 2016 victory by nearly 20 points in New Hampshire is sometimes attributed to the inability of Republican elites and voters to rally around an alternative. This reasoning assumes that Trump was a polarizing primary candidate who attracted a significant portion of voters but repelled most

---

[6] Sununu, whose son Chris was the Republican nominee for governor in 2016, supported Trump once he became the nominee.

others. This assumption is plausible, but New Hampshire exit poll data[7] suggests Trump was more of a consensus candidate, attracting support across socioeconomic and ideological boundaries in that contest. He definitely was the favorite of Republicans without a college degree (47 percent support), but also attracted a significant portion of the highly educated (33 percent, almost twice the portion that went to former Ohio Governor John Kasich, the 2016 runner-up). His support across gender and age groups was roughly equal. And while Trump pursued quite conservative policy goals while in office from 2017–2021, as a candidate in New Hampshire he won pluralities across the ideological spectrum (32 percent of moderates, 38 percent of somewhat conservative voters, and 36 percent of very conservative voters).[8] Trump's 2016 victory in the Granite State was a portent of his popularity throughout the Northeast, including other New England states. With the exception of the Maine caucuses (where he finished second to Ted Cruz), Trump swept the region en route to the nomination.[9]

NEW ENGLAND'S INFLUENCE ON DEMOCRATIC PRESIDENTIAL POLITICS, 2000–2020

Unlike their Republican counterparts, New Hampshire Democrats often have chosen presidential candidates who failed to capture their party's nomination. Instead, the frigid Granite State often has provided a hothouse for Democratic insurgents to grow, from Eugene McCarthy and George McGovern to Bernie Sanders. New Hampshire Democrats have not chosen a president since they plucked Jimmy Carter from obscurity in 1976. (One could make the case that Bill Clinton, the self-proclaimed Comeback Kid, saved his 1992 presidential campaign in New Hampshire by exceeding expectations and finishing second, but former Massachusetts senator Paul Tsongas was the actual winner of that primary.) Half a century ago, New Hampshire Democrats put their primary in the national spotlight not by choosing winners (i.e., eventual nominees), but by defining the opposition to the status quo. In 1968, the election cycle prior to the advent of the modern presidential nomination process, McCarthy, a US Senator from Minnesota, entered the primary to deliver a message denouncing American military

---

[7] For exit poll data, see https://www.cnn.com/election/2016/primaries/polls/nh/Rep.
[8] I wrote at length on Trump's ability to blur ideological lines in "The Fuzzy Frontrunner," for the *Routledge Handbook of Primary Elections*, first edition, edited by Robert G. Boatright, 290–306. New York: Routledge, 2018.
[9] Trump's closest call was in Vermont, where he only defeated Kasich by 3 percentage points.

involvement in Vietnam. The intended recipient of that message, President Lyndon Johnson, chose not to place his name on the primary ballot (although a write-in campaign was eventually staged). McCarthy lost the primary to Johnson, but the media trumpeted the president's small margin of victory as a sign of his weakness. Just three weeks later, Johnson told the nation he would retire, and Granite State voters were credited with sending a message to the powerful political elite. Four years later, the same pattern held when McGovern, another insurgent from the Left, came closer than expected to defeating Muskie in the Maine senator's neighboring state.

In the first primaries of the twenty-first century, however, New Hampshire Democrats rallied behind establishment candidates, easing their path to the nomination. But more recently, New Hampshire became a satellite of the Bernie Sanders insurgency, and further removed from the national party's center of gravity. This was most glaring in 2020, when the fifth-place finisher in New Hampshire, former Vice President Joe Biden, ultimately became the Democratic nominee.

From 1972 until 2000, the implications of the results of the New Hampshire Democratic primary were fairly predictable. The Granite State offered an early glimpse of how two important constituencies in the Democratic Party assessed the candidates. White working-class Democrats sought a candidate who spoke to "lunch pail" issues such as jobs, economic security, and the cost of living; these candidates tended to emerge from the party establishment, such as former Vice President Walter Mondale in 1984 or Vice President Al Gore in 2000. In contrast, white Democrats with higher socioeconomic status (i.e., the college-educated voters described by journalist Ronald Brownstein [1992] as "Volvo Democrats") gravitated toward candidates who delivered a message of reform and promised to change the party's direction, such as McGovern in 1972, Gary Hart in 1984, or Bill Bradley in 2000. Through the decades, "reform" candidates have tended to perform especially well in New Hampshire, but their strong Granite State performance failed to translate into "momentum" in later contests because they were unable to attract working-class voters. In contrast, candidates who accumulated support across socioeconomic lines in New Hampshire were better able to build majority coalitions in the latter stages of the nomination process (Scala 2003).

In the 2000 and 2004 nomination contests, Progressive insurgent candidates hit high-water marks in New Hampshire, but failed to win outright. Instead, establishment candidates achieved hard-fought victories. In both cases, other New England states ratified the front-runner in subsequent contests, as Table 10.2 shows. In 2000, Bradley took the role of reformer versus Gore, who carried the baggage of the Clinton presidency into his presidential candidacy. But Bradley's popularity among New Hampshire's elite voters was not enough to defeat the vice president, who did far better among working-class Democrats. Gore then proceeded to sweep the rest of New England. A similar pattern unfolded in 2004, albeit with a New England twist. Vermont Governor Howard Dean, self-proclaimed candidate of "the Democratic wing of the Democratic Party," seized on anti-Iraq War fervor and small-dollar fundraising to become the early front-runner. Massachusetts Senator John Kerry struggled to gain traction and ultimately made his stand in the Iowa caucuses. Kerry's gamble paid off, and New Hampshire Democrats ultimately "dated Dean," but finally committed to the Massachusetts senator, who subsequently sailed to the nomination. Along the way, he swept all other New England contests, with the exception of Dean's home state.

Of all the Democratic nomination contests in the twenty-first century, New England was most closely divided in 2008, when Illinois Senator Barack Obama emerged as the leading challenger to New York Senator and former First Lady Hillary Clinton. In New Hampshire, where the two senators built formidable campaigns and clashed over the Iraq War, Obama's and Clinton's supporters took on familiar profiles. Obama, the self-proclaimed reformer, led in municipalities with higher levels of income and education, while Clinton had the upper hand in working-class areas of the state (Scala 2008). Unlike previous reform-minded candidates, however, Obama ultimately had more staying power by fusing together a unique coalition of white voters with high socioeconomic status and Black voters. The two senators fought to a virtual draw across the nation and in New England, where they evenly split the six contests.

Eight years later, Clinton returned to New Hampshire for a second run at the Democratic nomination, this time facing just one significant opponent—Independent Bernie Sanders running in the Democratic primary. The Progressive from Vermont, whose presidential campaign appeared quixotic to some, turned out to have a host of advantages in New Hampshire. Besides being a fellow New Englander, Sanders broke the mold of the reform-minded candidate with his crossover appeal to working-class voters.[10] Sanders was an avowedly Populist Progressive, advocating for a higher minimum wage, free public higher education, and single-payer health care (Detrow 2020). In addition, as Clinton's only challenger, Sanders was the sole beneficiary of negative feelings among Democratic primary voters toward the eventual

---

[10] 2016 New Hampshire primary exit polls can be found at https://www.cnn.com/election/2016/primaries/polls/nh/Dem.

nominee. He won New Hampshire by more than 20 percentage points, and proceeded to carry most New England states during the surprisingly lengthy nomination contest.

In a much larger Democratic 2020 field, Sanders's support in New Hampshire proved durable enough to achieve a narrow victory. He successfully staved off a challenge on the left from Massachusetts Senator Elizabeth Warren, who finished with just 9 percent of the vote in her neighboring state. To Sanders's right, former Vice President Joe Biden stumbled badly on the heels of a disappointing performance in the Iowa caucuses, finishing fifth behind South Bend Mayor Pete Buttigieg and Minnesota Senator Amy Klobuchar. Biden wasted no time putting the Granite State behind him, moving on to South Carolina before the primary concluded. Biden's early departure was met with derision, but proved pragmatic. South Carolina once again was decisive, as it had been in 2008 and 2016—in this case, dramatically so for Biden, whose candidacy seemed doomed weeks earlier. After capturing the first southern primary, Biden returned to New England and won a majority of contests.

The 2024 New Hampshire Primary

The 2024 New Hampshire primary unfolded under the shadow of the greatest threat ever to its status at the head of the nomination process. Citing concerns about the lack of representation of voters of color at the beginning of the nomination process, President Joe Biden requested in late 2022 that the South Carolina primary be moved to the front of the calendar. (Perhaps not coincidentally, South Carolina Democrats saved Biden's 2020 presidential bid by delivering a much-needed victory in their primary after early stumbles in New Hampshire, Iowa, and Nevada) The Democratic National Committee approved Biden's proposal, relegating New Hampshire to follow South Carolina three days later, voting the same day as Nevada. New Hampshire's Secretary of State, following state law, disregarded the Democrats' calendar and scheduled the primary on January 23, 2024, in order to keep it first.

New Hampshire Democratic leaders found themselves at an impasse with Biden and the national party. On the one hand, they felt blindsided by the president's decision and felt bound to defend their primary's status; but on the other, they remained loyal to the leader of their party, especially in the face of Trump's efforts to regain the White House. Local Democrats such as Kathy Sullivan, the former head of the New Hampshire Democrats, led a write-in campaign for the president when he refused to put his name on the primary ballot; a super PAC organized on Biden's behalf spent more than $1.2 million on advertising (Epstein 2024; Novelo 2024). Biden faced challenges from Minnesota Congressman Dean Phillips, who personally spent $5 million to make the case that Biden's age made him a weak candidate for reelection; author Marianne Williamson, who ran for the nomination in 2020, also put her name forward. The write-in effort was successful, inasmuch as Biden's performance (64 percent of the 124,000 votes cast) avoided unfavorable comparisons to Lyndon Johnson, whose write-in campaign in 1968 only earned 50 percent, and led to his decision not to run again for the presidency (*New York Times* 2024; McArdle 2018). Moreover, a grassroots effort focused on the Israel-Hamas war and US foreign policy to write in "ceasefire" yielded little (Brooks 2024).

For New Hampshire Republicans, it was business as usual—at least to a point. The national Republican Party declined to follow the Democrats, leaving the Granite State in its traditional place on the calendar, behind the Iowa caucus and ahead of the South Carolina primary. Granite Staters had plenty of opportunities to assess Trump's rivals, while the former president occasionally dropped in to hold large rallies. Polling in the year prior to the primary largely mirrored national surveys. Florida Governor Ron DeSantis began 2023 in an apparently strong position to challenge Trump, but then faded; ultimately, the challenger chose to focus on Iowa in a failed attempt to win over conservative evangelicals. Ultimately Nikki Haley, former governor of South Carolina and US ambassador to the United Nations during the Trump administration, emerged as the former president's chief opponent. Haley held many "town hall" meetings in New Hampshire, and then gained national momentum from strong performances in debates (which Trump refused to attend). After she earned Governor Chris Sununu's endorsement and former New Jersey Governor Chris Christie dropped out, Haley became the "moderate" alternative to Trump, putting together a coalition of moderates and independents. But Trump retained the loyalty of most Republicans and conservatives, and won the primary, 54 percent to 43 percent (*New York Times* 2024). Eight years earlier, Trump and his followers crashed the New Hampshire Republican Party; in 2024, they simply were the party.

Conclusions

The strongly Democratic tilt of New England mostly confines the region to the periphery of national presidential elections, a distant wavelet on the outskirts of the powerful tidal pulls. The tides, however, have a quite eccentric force—for one week every four years, the region became the power center of the American political universe, as New Hampshire citizens cast ballots that influence the outcome of both major parties' nomination contests. However, because of the decision of national Democrats to end New Hampshire's status as having the first-in-the-nation primary, that quadrennial event now faces the most significant threat ever in its century-long history. At the same time, this reinforced the importance of the New Hampshire Republican presidential primary in a very blue region during the presidential election season.

In addition to the specific threat from the DNC, New Hampshire (and New England) face a more diffuse one—the nationalization of the nomination process itself. Once upon a time, New Hampshire voters (and those few members of the national political press who ventured north) had an exclusive view of presidential candidates' first steps toward the nomination. Lesser-known candidates hoped that a surprise finish in the Granite State would deliver their campaigns momentum and a deluge of donors. Nowadays, the early pressure on candidates to build national name recognition and enormous donor bases makes "breakout" moments imperative months before New Hampshire votes. And thanks to cable television and the Internet, interested voters across the country have a front-row seat to watch the nomination process, right alongside citizens of New Hampshire. (Town meeting, once a local institution, then a campaign stratagem, has become part of cable TV programming.) More and more often, candidates have been able to skip traditional small gatherings and house parties, and move straight to larger events. In fact, the winners of the 2020 New Hampshire primary, Bernie Sanders and Donald Trump, ran campaigns centered around enormous meetings and rallies. And in 2024, Trump felt no particular need to change his approach and place himself under voters' scrutiny; he even skipped the traditional debate held the week before the primary (and when Haley refused to participate without Trump, the event was canceled).

The New Hampshire primary is still democratic in process—but it seems more plebiscitary of late, and a little less Yankee and deliberative.

Works Cited

Associated Press. 2012. "Paul Wins Most of Maine's delegates." May 7, 2012. https://www.politico.com/story/2012/05/paul-wins-majority-of-maine-delegates-075964.

Barndollar, Hadley. 2021. "What Does the 2020 Census Say about New England? The Region Is More Populated, Diverse." *Providence Journal*, August 18, 2021. https://www.providencejournal.com/story/news/2021/08/18/census-2020-ma-nh-vt-ri-ct-data-new-england-more-populated-diverse-race-age/8152565002/.

Brereton, Charles. 1987. *First in the Nation: New Hampshire and the Premier Presidential Primary.* Portsmouth: Peter E. Randall.

Brooks, David. 2024. "Voter Turnout Beats Record in NH GOP Primary." *Concord Monitor*, January 24, 2024. https://www.concordmonitor.com/presidential-primary-new-hampshire-53808362.

Brownstein, Ronald. 1992. "Fewer 'Volvo Voters' Offer Tsongas a Lift in the South." *Los Angeles Times*, March 8, 1992. https://www.latimes.com/archives/la-xpm-1992-03-08-mn-6099-story.html.

Bryan, Frank M. 2004. *Real Democracy: The New England Town Meeting and How It Works.* Chicago: University of Chicago Press, 2004.

Dave Leip's Atlas of U.S. Presidential Elections. "2000 Presidential General Election Results—New Hampshire." https://uselectionatlas.org/RESULTS/.

Detrow, Scott. 2020. "8 Key Moments That Helped Define Bernie Sanders' Presidential Runs." National Public Radio. April 9, 2020. https://www.npr.org/2020/04/09/830728501/8-key-moments-that-helped-define-bernie-sanders-presidential-runs.

Dickerson, John. 2016. "When the Straight Talk Express Rolled Through New Hampshire." *Slate*, February 9, 2016. https://slate.com/news-and-politics/2016/02/john-dickerson-revisits-john-mccains-new-hampshire-primary-victory.html.

Epstein, Reid J. 2024. "He's Not on the N.H. Ballot, but Biden's Allies Hope He'll Still Win." *New York Times*, January 22, 2024. https://www.nytimes.com/2024/01/22/us/politics/biden-write-in-new-hampshire-democrats.html.

French, AnnMarie. 2007. "The Evolution of Town Meeting." New Hampshire Municipal Association, *Town & City Magazine*, February 2007. https://www.nhmunicipal.org/town-city-article/evolution-town-meeting.

Gass, Nick. 2015. "New Hampshire Paper Compares Trump to Biff from 'Back to the Future.'" *Politico*, December 28, 2015. https://www.politico.com/story/2015/12/donald-trump-biff-tannen-back-to-the-future-217161.

Goldmacher, Shane. 2015. "Trump Treads on Tradition in New Hampshire." *Politico*, December 2, 2015. https://www.politico.com/story/2015/12/donald-trump-new-hampshire-retail-politics-216338.

Healy, Patrick. 2016. "Resurrection: How New Hampshire Saved the 1992 Clinton Campaign." *New York Times*, February 8, 2016. https://www.nytimes.com/interactive/2016/02/08/us/politics/bill-hillary-clinton-new-hampshire.html.

Mayer, William G., and Andrew E. Busch. 2004. *The Front-Loading Problem in Presidential Nominations.* Washington, D.C.: Brookings Institution Press, 2004.

McArdle, Terence. 2018. "Eugene McCarthy vs. LBJ: The New Hampshire Primary Showdown that Changed Everything 50 Years Ago." *Washington Post*, March 12, 2018. https://www.washingtonpost.com/news/retropolis/wp/2018/03/12/eugene-mccarthy-vs-lbj-the-new-hampshire-primary-showdown-that-changed-everything/.

Melcher, James P., and Amy Fried. 2022. "A State Divided: Maine and Its Continued Electoral Vote Split." In *Presidential Swing States*, third edition, edited by David Schultz and Rafael Jacob, 163–192. New York: Lexington Books.

Naft, Jeff. 2016. "Donald Trump Slammed as 'Loser All His Life' by Former New Hampshire Gov. John Sununu." ABC News, February 5, 2016. https://abcnews.go.com/Politics/donald-trump-slammed-loser-life-hampshire-gov-john/story?id=36736314.

Novelo, Allison. 2024. "How Much Did Candidates, PACs Spend on the New Hampshire Primary? See what Trump, Haley and Biden invested." CBS News, January 25, 2024. https://www.cbsnews.com/news/how-much-candidates-spent-2024-new-hampshire/.

Olsen, Henry, and Dante J. Scala. 2016. *The Four Faces of the Republican Party: The Fight for the 2016 Presidential Nomination.* New York: Palgrave Macmillan.

Palmer, Niall. 1997. *The New Hampshire Primary and the American Electoral Process.* Westport, Conn.: Praeger.

Pindell, James. 2015. "NH Will Weed Out Presidential Candidates." *New Hampshire Magazine,* June 24, 2015. https://www.nhmagazine.com/nh-will-weed-out-presidential-candidates/.

Quarshie, Mabinty, and Donovan Slack. 2021. "Census: US Sees Unprecedented Multiracial Growth, Decline in the White Population for First Time in History." *USA Today,* August 12, 2021. https://www.usatoday.com/story/news/politics/2021/08/12/how-2020-census-change-how-we-look-america-what-expect/5493043001/.

Scala, Dante J. 2022. "Set in Granite: New Hampshire as a Presidential Bellwether." In *Presidential Swing States,* third edition, edited by David Schultz and Rafael Jacob, 51–78. New York: Lexington Books.

———. 2018. "The Fuzzy Frontrunner." In *Routledge Handbook of Primary Elections,* first edition, edited by Robert G. Boatright, 290–306. New York: Routledge, 2018.

———. 2008. "Why New Hampshire wasn't all bad for Barack Obama." January 17, 2008. https://graniteprof.typepad.com/graniteprof/2008/01/why-new-hampshi.html.

———. 2003. *Stormy Weather.* New York: Palgrave Macmillan.

Splaine, James R. n.d. "The Story of the 1975 Law Requiring the New Hampshire Presidential Primary to be First in the Nation." New Hampshire Department of State. https://sos.nh.gov/media/53hje5j3/the-nh-law-behind-the-first-in-the-nation-presidential-primary.pdf.

The Green Papers. n.d. "Election 2000: Primary, Caucus, and Convention Phase." https://www.thegreenpapers.com/PCC/PCC.html.

———. n.d. "Election 2004: Primary, Caucus, and Convention Phase." https://www.thegreenpapers.com/P04/.

———. n.d. "Election 2008: Primary, Caucus, and Convention Phase." https://www.thegreenpapers.com/P08/.

———. n.d. "Election 2012: Presidential Primaries, Caucuses, and Conventions." https://www.thegreenpapers.com/P12/.

———. n.d. "Election 2016: Presidential Primaries, Caucuses, and Conventions." https://www.thegreenpapers.com/P16/.

———. n.d. "Election 2020: Presidential Primaries, Caucuses, and Conventions." https://www.thegreenpapers.com/P20/.

New York Times. 2012. "Maine Republican Caucuses." https://www.nytimes.com/elections/2012/primaries/states/maine.html.

———. 2024. "New Hampshire Republican Primary Election Results." January 26, 2024. https://www.nytimes.com/interactive/2024/01/23/us/elections/results-new-hampshire-republican-primary.html?action=click&pgtype=Article&state=default&module=election-results&context=election_recirc&region=NavBar.

———. 2024. "New Hampshire Democratic Primary Election Results." January 26, 2024. https://www.nytimes.com/interactive/2024/01/23/us/elections/results-new-hampshire-democratic-primary.html?action=click&pgtype=Article&state=default&module=election-results&context=election_recirc&region=NavBar.

United States Census Bureau. 2023. "QuickFacts: Vermont; Rhode Island; New Hampshire; Maine; Massachusetts; Connecticut." https://www.census.gov/quickfacts/fact/table/VT,RI,NH,ME,MA,CT/PST045221.

United States Census Bureau. 2022. "2020 Center of Population Press Kit." https://www.census.gov/newsroom/press-kits/2021/2020-center-of-population.html.

Wright, James. 1987. *The Progressive Yankees: Republican Reformers in New Hampshire, 1906–1916*. Hanover, NH: University Press of New England.

York, Byron. 2016. "GOP Fear and Loathing in New Hampshire." *Washington Examiner*, January 24, 2016. https://www.washingtonexaminer.com/byron-york-gop-fear-and-loathing-in-new-hampshire.

CHAPTER II

DEMOGRAPHIC CHANGE AND
POLITICAL POWER IN NEW ENGLAND

Luis Jiménez
Associate Professor of Political Science
University of Massachusetts Boston

The story of New England politics has been, and continues to be, one of new groups of people arriving and subsequent conflict, accommodation, incorporation, or domination, depending on the group, the time period, and the varied political landscapes across states. Some groups—e.g., religious minorities in Connecticut—brought a shift in the region's priorities and the role of government. Others—like the Irish—led to a reinforcement of the political culture and revitalization of older political patterns.

This chapter surveys how these dynamics are playing out since the turn of the millennium, concentrating concentrates on the three fastest growing minorities in the region—African Americans, Latinos, and Asian Americans. It explores the demographic picture in New England and how it has evolved in the past five decades. It then explores how changing demographics affect the political landscape, why demographic shifts in New England do not necessarily replicate national trends, and why political power for some underrepresented groups in New England—African Americans, Latinos, and Asian Americans—falls short of expectations based on their proportion of the regional population. Finally, it compares how these underrepresented groups are doing materially to the dominant white group, showing how Latinos have improved dramatically in some New England states and how Asian Americans retain an educational advantage over Latinos and African Americans and sometimes the region's white demographic majority.

The Political History of New England is One of Demographic Change

The story of arrivals changing the political landscape of the region began with the foundation of the New England colonies by the Puritans along the coast. It then continued with the creation of the future states. Three of the six states in the region—Connecticut, Rhode Island, and New Hampshire—originated largely as a result of disagreements between new waves of Puritans and the leaders of the Massachusetts Bay Colony, the former of whom decided to make separate colonies that would not answer to Boston (Shearer 2004). Maine's newcomers' distrust of Massachusetts played a role in its final separation in 1820 from the Massachusetts Bay Colony. But Maine's original distinctiveness, along with that of Vermont, developed because of their frontier status and the land disputes that developed between the English and French. In the case of Vermont, these overlapping claims between New York and New Hampshire, and the arrival of new settlers, is what eventually led to its formation as an independent political unit (Shearer 2004).

Subsequently, while the American Revolution upended the political landscape by forming a United States, individual state politics did not always change as much as one might think. Connecticut, for instance, did not draft a new constitution and maintained a colonial charter that favored its pre-revolutionary institutions, especially its established Congregational Church. This only changed in 1818 when the number of non-Congregationalists arriving from neighboring states grew large enough to fund the Toleration Party. This party was vital in establishing a new constitution, one that clearly separated church and state (Janis 2021). Something similar happened in Rhode Island. In 1793, a British immigrant, Samuel Slater developed the first mechanized textile mill in Pawtucket—a key spark in the American Industrial Revolution—which made the state an attractive destination for thousands of newcomers. Rhode Island, however, continued to restrict suffrage to landowners even after most other states had allowed universal suffrage for white men. Discontent with the restrictions eventually led to an armed insurrection in 1842. Led by Thomas Dorr, and strongly supported by newly arrived Irish immigrants, the rebellion proved military unsuccessful, but it convinced decisionmakers to write a new constitution that dramatically expanded the right to vote (McLoughlin 1976).

The great potato famine in Ireland and the continued industrialization of the region continued to bring fresh waves of Irish immigrants to New England. This in turn would trigger a nativist backlash and the consolidation of the Know-Nothing Party, a xenophobic, anti-Catholic outfit that had massive clout in the region for a short period of time. The height of their power came in the mid 1850s when they dominated the Massachusetts (1854), Rhode Island (1854), Connecticut (1855) and New Hampshire elections (1855) with landslides that netted them the governorship of all four states and large parts of the various legislatures. Given the relatively smaller numbers of Irish immigrants in Maine and Vermont, the Know-Nothings did not experience similar electoral success in those states, but this did not necessarily mean the Irish were more welcome. In Vermont, local newspapers called for the deportation of all Irish (Bushnell 2016) and in Maine, Catholic churches were burned in Lewiston and Bath. At least one Catholic priest who was tarred and feathered and run out of town (Palmer et al. 2009, 11). Within a few years, the government inexperience of the Know-Nothings and internal divisions within the movement doomed it to irrelevance. The Irish, however, would continue to come and would eventually come to be a major force in New England politics, electing the first Irish mayor of Boston in 1885 and Irish governors in Rhode Island (1907), Massachusetts (1913), Connecticut (1925), and New Hampshire (1937).[1]

As manufacturing evolved from textile mills into more complex and more labor intensive industries using machine tools, industrial operations began to concentrate in Connecticut, Massachusetts, and Rhode Island. This altered New England's economic landscape and its appeal to potential migrants. The southern portion of New England subsequently attracted fresh waves of people including Italians, Portuguese, and Eastern Europeans who tended to settle in urban areas, creating an urban/rural cleavage in states where the new immigrants gravitated disproportionately into the orbit of the Democratic Party dominant in cities. In contrast, the northern parts of New England, especially Vermont, were far more agricultural and rural. Maine and New Hampshire did have some manufacturing cores in Portland and Portsmouth, but these were not large enough to dictate state politics, especially because the largest group of immigrants in northern New England—French Canadians— did not flock to cities. This limited the political participation of French Canadians in New England and sometimes brought them into conflict with other Catholics during this period over the resources and role of the Catholic Church (Palmer et al. 2009). Indeed, well into the mid-twentieth century, the French in the region practiced *La Survivance*, a strategy to maintain their way of life and prevent assimilation, which in turn preserved a political culture that impeded them from "[ever using] their numerical power to its full potential beyond local politics" (Palmer et al. 2009, 13).

The Great Depression and immigration restrictions confined new arrivals to New England to a trickle well into the 1970s (Daniels 2002). Since then,

---

[1] Both Massachusetts and New Hampshire technically had governors whose parents were Irish immigrants (Brothers John and James Sullivan in 1789 and 1807 respectively), but these positions did not come as a result of the Irish being an important part of an electoral coalition.

however, fresh waves of immigrants have once again begun to transform New England. Given that they are sometimes racially distinct from prior immigrant waves, however, contemporary migrants face varied political welcomes. The state they opt to live in, and whether in a rural or urban environment, prove to be key factors in political incorporation.

Obstacles to political power also differ widely across states and especially within the northern/southern New England cleavage explained above. This is in large part because as late as 2004 "the arrival of new populations may have had the effect of reinforcing the linkage between ethnicity and political identity for established white ethnic groups" (Gimpel and Tam Cho 2004, 992). This means that the political incorporation of new arrivals has been met with varying degrees of hostility. That is, as New England has grown to become more than Yankee, so have its politics, but in inconsistent ways across the region. Let us look in more detail at the three currently fastest growing populations—African Americans, Latinos and Asian Americans. Groups that encompass both long established generations as well as newcomers.

AFRICAN AMERICANS IN NEW ENGLAND

The first Black people that came to the region were enslaved individuals who had no choice in the matter. In New England, the first record we have of their arrival is in Boston in 1638. Soon they would become an integral part of the area's social and economic life. Newport, Rhode Island, for example, would become the center of the enslaved trade in New England bringing much prosperity to the town and the state (McLoughlin 1976). The forced servitude of kidnapped Africans, however, did not follow the same pattern as that of the American South, where enslaved people were mostly used as agricultural labor. Instead, the North employed these individuals in a variety of skilled jobs and as household servants. They were concentrated in cities and along the coast (Melish 1998). Once freed, the more diversified economy in the North would allow for a wider range of economic opportunities for African Americans compared to the South.

By the time of the American Revolution, it is estimated that there was one enslaved Black person for every four white families in New England (Melish 1998, 16). This fact did not immediately change after independence from Britain despite the passage of multiple laws allowing various degrees of freedom in the region—Massachusetts and New Hampshire in 1783 and Connecticut and Rhode Island in 1784. Despite these early partial laws, the abolition process was a gradual and protracted one that culminated with

Connecticut in 1848 (Melish 1998). Of course, freedom did not mean an end to discrimination. Racism and segregation would continue to be a fact of life for African Americans irrespective of their legal status. And thus, Black politics in New England well into the 1970s would be about trying to counter the region's version of Jim Crow, especially securing voting rights, access to public education, and safe housing (Archer 2017; Miletsky 2022).

The specific form of Black activism varied overtime—particularly the degree to which it favored electoral incorporation or more radical options. Prior to the Civil War, New England was a hotbed of abolitionism and radical Black liberation politics. At one point in the 1840s, for example, Sojourner Truth, Frederick Douglass, and John Brown all lived in Massachusetts. Likewise, the Underground Railroad, a network of safehouses that provided enslaved people an escape route to free states or Canada, had a dense presence in New England. Indeed, it had enough public support in some parts of the region, namely Vermont, that the Underground Railroad was very much out in the open—standing sharp contrast to its necessarily clandestine nature in the rest of the country (Broderick 2005).

Later, just as had happened in New England, the federal abolition of slavery and even the passage of the Fourteenth, Fifteenth and Sixteenth Amendments could not overcome the discrimination faced by African Americans in the country. As a result, a number of important civil rights organizations emerged at the turn of the twentieth century. These included the National Association of Colored Women's Clubs and the National Association for the Advancement of Colored People the (NAACP), both of which were created with strong leadership from the Bay State. The former was co-founded by Josephine St. Pierre Ruffin, a longtime anti-slavery activist from Boston while the latter was established by two men with important Massachusetts ties. The first was W. E. B. Du Bois, one of the most prominent African American activists at the time, a Great Barrington native, and the first Black person to earn a PhD from Harvard. The second was Moorfield Storey, a white lawyer from Boston, who became the organization's first president. The NAACP was too accommodationist for some, however. William Monroe Trotter, another Massachusetts native and early Du Bois collaborator, abhorred the idea of an organization for the advancement of Black people that included both white participation and leadership. Displeased at the organization's direction, Trotter organized a competing outfit in 1908, the National Equal Rights League, which had similar goals to the NAACP, but more aggressive tactics and a policy of actively blocking white membership.

This period also brought the beginning of the Great Migration, a process where a significant number of Black people living in the South moved North in search of jobs and a better life. This brought tens of thousands of African Americans to New England between 1910 and 1940, especially to places like New Haven, Providence, and Boston. Far fewer made it up to Maine, but this did not prevent a backlash from developing. In the 1920s, for example, the new Black arrivals, combined with the perceived Catholic threat from French Canadians, sparked the largest Ku Klux Klan chapter in New England. The Klan was so strong politically that when Ralph Owen Brewster supported ending funding for parochial schools (French Canadian), they helped elect him governor of Maine in 1925 (Palmer et al. 2009). The Klan's power would dissipate by the 1930s, but African Americans and others would continue facing discriminatory policies and practices in the state well into the future (Myall 2020).

Historically, despite resource constraints and low numbers relative to the total population, African Americans were able to punch above their weight politically because of key alliances with the larger population who were sympathetic to their struggle. This was especially so in New England where Black causes had much larger visibility and saliency than would have otherwise been the case due to the resources, public writing, and speeches by white allies like Prudence Crandall, Harriet Beecher Stowe, and William Lloyd Garrison. This continued at the turn of the twentieth century and later during the civil rights of the 1960s and 1970s especially as African Americans began decisively shaping electoral politics as they started to gravitate toward the Democratic Party. Aligning with a political party, however, was not without drawbacks. For example, the Black community helped elect New Haven's youngest mayor, Richard Lee, a Democrat, in 1954. His tenure began with promise when he appointed the city's first Black corporation counsel—the individual in charge of dealing with civil rights claims against the city. Soon after, however, the mayor's urban renewal programs created housing shortages that negatively affected African Americans in the city and the mayor moved to weaken any Black opposition to his policies through marginalization and the cooptation of Black leadership (Williams 2001). Elsewhere, Black support for the Democratic Party did not mean their preferred policies would be enacted. Boston, for example, would see struggles, especially around education, well into the 1970s (Miletsky 2022).

Around this time, the region began to see the arrival of new waves of Black people who were not descendants of the enslaved in the United States, but rather came from the Caribbean or from Africa itself. The two primary groups numerically were Haitians and Cape Verdeans who came to the United States seeking economic opportunity and, particularly in the case of the former, escaping political violence and instability under the twin Duvalier dictatorships of father and son. They settled disproportionately in Massachusetts, particularly Boston (Halter 2008), and have retained distinct mobilization patterns around a political identity coalesced around Haitianess rather than blackness (Halter 2008; Jackson 2011).

Meanwhile, in the last forty years, African Americans have been expanding their footprint in electoral politics, often as Democratic Party nominees. At the local level, Black mayors have won office in New England since 1981. Examples include Hartford (1981) and New Haven (1990) in Connecticut; Newport (1981) in Rhode Island; and Cambridge in Massachusetts (1992). Their presence in state legislatures has a much longer history especially in Vermont, Massachusetts, and Rhode Island where Black lawmakers have existed since 1836 (Alexander Twilight, Vermont),[2] 1866 (Edward G. Walker and Charles L. Mitchell, Massachusetts), and 1885 (Mahlon Van Horne, Rhode Island). The other three New England states would not elect a Black legislator until late in the twentieth century starting with Connecticut in 1958 (Wilfred X. Johnson), followed by Maine in 1972 (Gerald Talbot), and New Hampshire in 1975 (Henry B. Richardson).

Getting elected to higher office as a Black individual has been fairly rare in New England, though, when it occurred, both political parties can claim Black representation. The first elected Black lawmaker to the US Congress from Massachusetts was a Republican, Edward Brooke[3] (elected in 1969) as was Connecticut's first Black member of Congress, Gary Franks (elected in 1991). Since then, both of these states have sent Black Democrats to DC—as of 2024 two Black women, Ayanna Pressley and Jahana Hayes, are serving in the respective states. Rhode Island elected its first Black member of Congress, Gabe Amo, in a 2023 special election but Maine, Rhode Island, and Vermont still lack their first Black member of Congress. This is partly a reflection of their demographic makeup of these states as each has a Black population below 2 percent, with Maine having the highest at just 1.9 percent of the population.

---

[2] Alexander Twilight was the first Black person elected to Vermont's state legislature, as well as also the *only* Black person to be elected to a state legislature anywhere in the country before the Civil War. In that, he was an outlier, and still is, given that today Vermont has not a single Black state legislator.
[3] This was Edward Brooke, the first Black senator from Massachusetts. The first Black person elected to the House was Ayanna Pressley in 2019.

Winning statewide office is also rare for African Americans: only Connecticut (1963-treasurer), Vermont (2004-auditor), and Massachusetts (2006-governor, 2022-attorney general) have elected a Black person in a statewide contest. Of these, the most visible has undoubtedly been Deval Patrick as Governor of Massachusetts. Beyond that, the other important position of note is Supreme Court Justice as they can also shape policy through the courts. African Americans have served in four states in New England, starting with Connecticut in 1987, followed by Massachusetts in 1997, Rhode Island in 2021, and finally Maine in 2022. As it happens, appointment of these positions has been evenly split between Democratic and Republican governors.

LATINOS IN NEW ENGLAND

People from Latin America have a much more recent history in the region than African Americans. Although records of small groups of Cubans go as far back as the turn of the twentieth century in Massachusetts, sizable waves of Latinos did not arrive until the mid-twentieth century (Torres 2006). The largest of these were Puerto Ricans in the 1950s and 1960s, the majority of whom settled first in New York City and then began moving to neighboring states to escape the overcrowding of the city. Given its proximity to New York City, Connecticut became the New England state with the most Puerto Ricans in the region as well as the New England state with the largest number of Puerto Ricans as a percentage of the total population (Collazo, Ryan and Bauman 2008). These newcomers to Connecticut settled disproportionately in Hartford, Bridgeport, and Waterbury with smaller numbers further afield in the Massachusetts cities of Boston, Springfield, Lawrence, and Holyoke as well as Providence, Rhode Island (Jiménez 2022).

The next major wave of Latinx migration to New England was that of Dominicans who began to arrive in the United States in sizable numbers in the 1960s after the United States invaded the Dominican Republic following the toppling of strongman Rafael Trujillo in 1961. They too first concentrated in New York. And just like the Puerto Ricans before them, and responding to similar incentives and opportunities like jobs in less crowded cities, Dominicans moved out of New York City in large numbers in the 1980s and settled in three main states in New England—Connecticut, Massachusetts, and Rhode Island. Lawrence, Massachusetts, has the highest portion of Dominicans as a percentage of the total population in the country. As of 2020, this was 51.5 percent of the population. The city with the second highest percentage in the United States, Providence, RI, stood at a mere 19 percent.

Since the arrival of Dominicans, there have been new waves of Central Americans to New England in the 1980s, Colombians and Ecuadorians in the 1990s, and Venezuelans in the 2010s. All four groups migrated as a result of changing dynamics in their home countries including economic insecurity and violence. Unfortunately, these conditions have remained constant, especially in Central America and Venezuela, so migration flows from these countries continue. Just like the previous two waves of Latino immigrants to New England, the newcomers gravitated toward southern New England, except for Ecuadorians who have tended to shun Rhode Island. Today, Central Americans alone make up a noticeable percentage of people in southern New England—standing at 2.7 percent, 1.91 percent, and 1.36 percent of the overall population in Rhode Island, Massachusetts, and Connecticut, respectively (US Census 2020a). Colombian numbers are much smaller but are still a noteworthy at 0.88 percent and 0.87 percent in Rhode Island and Connecticut and a mere 0.2 percent in the Bay State (US Census 2020a). The equivalent numbers for Ecuadorians are 0.68 percent, 0.53 percent, and 0.11 percent in Connecticut, Massachusetts, and Rhode Island respectively (US Census 2020a).

Politically speaking, Latinos faced different obstacles to African Americans. They certainly encountered discrimination and suffered some of the same indignities and disadvantages that Blacks had been historically working to counter, but their path to collective action followed a different pattern. The main problem continues to be that Latinos do not necessarily see themselves as a coherent group with a shared destiny working for mutually beneficial goals. In the parlance of Political Science, they often do not feel a sense of linked fate.

There are multiple reasons for this. The first are national differences. Despite sharing a language—and sometimes barely, as any Spanish translator will tell you—the distinct histories and cultural norms of the various origin countries in Latin America mean that newcomers to New England tend to have dissimilar political cultures. These makes trying to unify around specific shared political goals difficult. The second is that a dark-skin color is easily identifiable in society where whiteness has traditionally afforded advantages. The complex history of racial-mixing in Latin America has meant that Latinos come in a wide variety of shades, which in turn means that individuals may not respond collectively to their racialization. That is, some might choose to pass for white or prefer to mobilize around political issues salient to the majority rather than their own group.[4] Finally, with neither language nor

---

[4] The term for this phenomenon is colorism. For a discussion of it worldwide see Kamilah Woodson's edited book, *Colorism, Investigating a Global Phenomenon*.

race as guaranteed beacons to create an identity around, *Latinidad* (shared Latino identity) becomes a socially constructed and amorphous idea—which further complicates it being used as a way to recognize oneself as sharing a destiny, a sense of linked fate, with others in the Latino community.

Another major problem is that a significant portion of the Latino community has lacked citizenship and, sometimes, even legal residency in the United States. This makes influence via electoral politics a difficult lift as a sizable portion of the community is legally barred from voting. Indeed, given that the number of potential Latino voters has historically been far fewer than the number of *Latino individuals*, attempts to mobilize the Latino community have a reduced electoral payoff. Thus, political parties were slow to court this community, translating to a very different path to incorporation within the Democratic Party compared to African Americans.

For all these reasons, early political mobilization efforts by Latinos in New England tended to be by individual national groups, especially Puerto Ricans who had enjoyed American citizenship since 1917. These efforts were not necessarily even about local issues per se, but about concerns regarding Puerto Rico itself, such as the use of the Vieques Island by the US Navy as a testing ground (Barreto 2006). Specific local concerns did echo those of African Americans around education and housing, however, which is where early mobilization was also concentrated (Jiménez 2021). Much later, as groups became more established, enjoyed educational gains, and began to recognize their shared challenges some broader pan-Latino institutions were instituted. These acted as mutual-aid organizations and advocates for immigrants who might or might not engage directly in politics such as Progreso Latino in Rhode Island (1977), Centro Latino in Massachusetts (1989), Unidad Latina en Acción in Connecticut (2002), Centro Latino de New Hampshire (2002), and Mano en Mano in Maine (2005).

Because of the obstacles outlined above, it took much longer for Latinos to find success in electoral politics and current representation still lags far behind their percentage of the population in each New England state. Their political incorporation has been concentrated at the local level, especially in city councils and school committees in southern New England. Mayorships are rare but grew in number since the 2000s (Jiménez 2021). Here too the wins concentrate in states where Latinos enjoy higher numbers—Connecticut, Massachusetts, and Rhode Island. The first mayor to be elected in New England was Eddie Pérez, a Puerto Rican man who won Hartford's top office in 2001. Almost a decade later, Massachusetts elected its first Latino mayor, when William Latingua became mayor of Lawrence in 2010. That win was followed by Providence, RI, electing a Latino mayor in 2011 and Holyoke, MA, doing the same in 2021. Since Connecticut and Rhode Island saw the first Latino mayors elected in their state, both Hartford and Providence have sent two additional Latinos to the office. One of them, Jorge Elorza, became the first mayor of Central American descent in New England when he won in 2015. Latina mayors are even less common in New England, but Central Falls, RI, elected the first Latina Mayor in New England in 2021, Maria Rivera.

Meanwhile, statewide positions prove extremely elusive. There have only ever been two Latinx individuals elected to the constitutional offices in New England. The first was John Sununu, a man born to a Salvadoran mother who was elected governor of New Hampshire in 1983 and Nellie Gorbea, a Puerto Rican woman, who was elected as Connecticut's secretary of state in 2011. Incidentally, Sununu is a superb example of the complexity of Latinidad discussed earlier. Given that both of his parents were culturally Greek Orthodox, it is not clear whether he "counts" as Latino. Certainly, his ascent in politics and that of his son—who is the governor of New Hampshire through at least 2024—was entirely divorced of reference to his Salvadorian roots. Only two Latinx individuals have ever been appointed state Supreme Court Justice. Both women: Carmen Elisa Espinosa in Connecticut in 2013 and Dalila Argaez Wendlandt in Massachusetts in 2020.

In terms of party identification, Latinos in New England have tended to gravitate toward the Democratic Party for similar reasons to their Black counterparts. Yet, Republicans have recently began to make inroads with Latinos. Trump expanded his vote share in Latino strongholds within Massachusetts such as Fall River, Lawrence, and New Bedford in 2020. Former Massachusetts Republican Governor Charlie Baker even gained important Latino endorsements for his re-elect such as that of the Dominican mayor of Lawrence, MA, Dan Rivera. These shifts combine with Latinx's population gains within the region to indicate that neither party can ignore the group nor can they take a Latinx vote for granted.

ASIAN AMERICANS IN NEW ENGLAND

Asian people also have a long history in New England. The earliest numerically sizable groups were Chinese laborers who were brought to work in various jobs in the mid-nineteenth century (National Park Service 2021). Recruited from other parts of the country, especially California, their numbers were never as large in New England as they were in California, but they were large enough to establish a number of Chinatowns around New England including Boston,

Portland, and Providence.[5] Their presence in the United States triggered a furious backlash and for the next several decades Congress passed increasingly restrictive immigration laws starting with the Chinese Exclusion Act in 1882 and later the Asiatic Barred Zone of 1917 which expanded prohibitions well beyond the Chinese. This severely limited the number of Asians that could come to New England, but Boston's Chinatown survived despite growth restrictions and attempts to disband it (National Park Service 2021).

Substantial waves of immigration from Asia would not begin again until after World War II when some of the anti-Asian immigration restrictions were relaxed. Following the Chinese Revolution in 1949, however, as US national politics moved into the Cold War, anti-communist immigration regulations were adopted. In New England, this meant that the Chinese that did come to the region were primarily from Hong Kong or Taiwan—thus possessing distinct countries of origins, political experiences, and cultural traditions from the Chinese who had previously come to New England (Global Boston 2021). Later, in 1965, the US Congress abolished national quotas which once again made New England an attractive destination to people from across the Asian continent. The new waves were not limited to Chinese, residents of Hong Kong, or Taiwanese people. Indians, Pakistanis, Vietnamese, and others joined them. In contrast to previous migrants, however, they settled disproportionately in Massachusetts—especially after the 1990s when the state's high-tech economy began to flourish. Another difference was that the Asian immigrants of the 1990s tended to be wealthier and better educated than previous waves. (Global Boston 2021).

Similar to Latinos, the barriers for Asian American political incorporation and influence are considerable. The factors precluding Latinos from seeing themselves as a people with shared fate are far more prominent among the Asian diaspora. For one thing, national differences are far more pronounced among Asian immigrants since they do not even share an imagined moment of political unity, given they were never under a single authority as opposed to the majority of Latinos who were part of Spanish Crown domains—including even Brazilians from 1580 to 1640. Language is also a barrier for political mobilization among Asian Americans. The differences are not merely within Spanish language or across Spanish and English languages, as is the case for

---

[5] Portland and Providence Chinatowns survived in diminished form until the middle of the 20th century. You can visit archives documenting their history for Providence (https://richinesehistory.com/index.html) and Portland (https://cafammaine.org/portland-walking-tour/).

Latinos, but instead across dozens of distinct languages spoken with little to no overlap. Thus, not surprisingly, and similar to Latinos, early political engagement among Asian Americans tended to be along singular national group identities—particularly the more temporally established Chinese (Lee 2015).

The political concerns of Asian Americans in New England were also similar to that of Latinos and Blacks on some counts—namely, housing and education. In Boston for example, there were a number of community organizations that developed directly as a result of urban revitalization projects surrounding Chinatown. These included the Chinese American Civic Organization in 1967 (later renamed Asian American Civic Organization) and the Asian Community Development Organization in 1987. Mutual-aid societies developed especially among the Chinese who had a long history in the region. And similarly as it happened with Latinos, once Asian Americans became more assimilated and recognized, the recognition of some shared challenges emerged. As such, organizations shifted to broader Pan-Asian outfits that provided broader services to their communities and directly advocated for their political interests. Examples include the Asian American Resource Workshop Organization in Massachusetts (1979), the Asian Pacific American Coalition of Connecticut (2008), and Unified Asian Communities in Maine (2020).

In contrast to the numbers among African American and Latinx populations, Asian Americans have not gravitated as disproportionately toward the Democratic Party. One might think this level of relative independence might provide Asian Americans some leverage in furthering their political goals as it would create a healthy competition between the Republicans and Democrats for Asian communities votes. This has not been the case in New England. Prominent scholar Thomas Kim contends this is because Asian Americans retain a racialization as perpetual foreigners, which significantly increases the cost of courtship for both parties, limiting their appeal as swing voters (2007). It follows from this argument, that even if Asian Americans overcame their within-group organizing constraints, neither Republicans nor Democrats would court them electorally with the intensity that their numbers in the state population would suggest.

This argument may be somewhat overstated, but it is true that in contrast to Blacks and Latinos, a significant portion of Asian Americans must navigate associations with China, even if they are not ethnically Chinese or lack any relation to the country. This is significant because the visibility and power of the People's Republic of China as a nation-state far surpasses any country that might be linked to Blacks or Latinos in the current political moment. This in turn means that any threat, slight, or concern related to China in American foreign policy is all too often then projected by the American public onto all Asian Americans in the United States regardless of whether or not an Asian individual has any actual connection to China. Look no further than the early stages of the COVID pandemic for evidence of when Asian Americans were accused of carrying the virus, or being responsible for it, merely because they were read as Chinese.

Asian American do have one significant organizing advantage, however: educational attainment. The rates of college graduation for Asian Americans surpasses those of African Americans, Latinos, and even the white majority in every state in New England. This is particularly impressive in the highest two—Massachusetts and New Hampshire—where 61.8 percent and 58.5 percent of Asian Americans possess a college degree, respectively (US Census Bureau, Educational Attainment in the US). This is critical because education is an important determinant of both political participation and organizing success (Brady, Verba, and Schlozman 1995).

Electoral successes nonetheless remain uneven at best. Asian Americans have been elected to school committees in Massachusetts since the 1980s (Center for Women in Politics and Policy 2015) but higher offices in New England too often elude. The first Asian American mayor in New England, for example, did not win until 2008 when Cranston, RI and Fitchburg, MA elected Allan Fung and Lisa Wong, respectively. No other state followed, but Massachusetts did elect the most visible Asian American politician in the region, the mayor of Boston, Michelle Wu, the daughter of Taiwanese immigrants, in 2021. Massachusetts then followed the next year with the election of Sokhary Chau, as the mayor of Lowell. This was historic not just because he had come to the US as refugee, but also because Chau became the first Cambodian person to be elected to a mayor's office not just in New England, but anywhere in the United States.

Asian state legislators are more numerous in all New England states, except for Maine. The first Asian American was elected to the state legislature in New Hampshire in 2000, followed by Connecticut in 2006, Vermont in 2009, Massachusetts in 2011, and Rhode Island in 2022. One of these legislators, Kesha Ram, a Vermont representative, and woman of Indian descent, would go onto the Vermont Senate, the first woman of color to be elected to the upper house in the state (Syed 2020).

Asian Americans winning statewide office is extremely rare in New England. William Tong stands alone in the region as Connecticut's Attorney General in 2018. Even *candidates* for statewide positions are rare. Allan Fung is the rare exception to this rule as he was the Republican nominee for governor of Rhode Island, though he lost by at least 5 points. Twice.

Asian Americans have served as Supreme Court Justices in Massachusetts in 2017 and Vermont in 2022. Interestingly, and despite the difficulties inherent in coalition building, Asian Americans have partnered with Latinos to use the courts to expand access to the ballot box in Lowell, MA as well as in the state of Connecticut.[6]

The Current Demographic Picture

As seen in Figure 11.1, since the 1970s, African Americans, Latinos, and Asian Americans have all seen significant growth in the region. According to the US Census, in 1975, over 95 percent of the population in New England classified itself as white, 45 years later, less than 75 percent did. Of course, the non-white populations have not been evenly distributed across the region. In fact, the newcomers generally recreated the same pattern that previous waves of immigrants developed at the turn of the twentieth century—southern New England saw the largest absolute increases because of migrant networks and the availability of jobs.

Breaking the demographic shifts down by state, Latinos in Connecticut

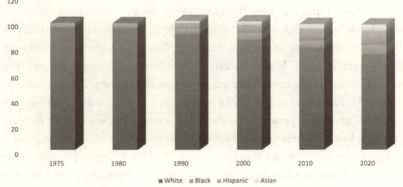

FIGURE 11.1. New England's changing demographics, 1975–2020.

---

[6] The cases in question (Hout v. Lowell, 2019, DOJ v. Connecticut, 2015) reached memorandums of understanding after Lowell and Connecticut were found to violate aspects of the Voting Rights Act of 1965 and National Voter Registration Act of 1993.

saw the biggest single group increase as a proportion of the total population, doubling their share between 1990 and 2020 ending at 17.3 percent of the state's population (US Census 2020a). As an overall percentage of the state population Connecticut is followed by Rhode Island (16.7%), Massachusetts (12.6%), New Hampshire (4.2%), Vermont (2.1%), and Maine (1.9%) (US Census 2020a). The group with the largest rate of growth in any New England state, however, is Asians in New Hampshire who increased their percentage of their population five times between 1990 and 2020—although from a low base of 0.6 percent.

Northern New England is far whiter than the southern part, but even the whitest states in the region are dotted with important communities of color. The area around Lewiston, Maine, for example, has a large number of Black people who came as refugees from Somalia and now make up around 7 percent of the total population of the city. Communities in New Hampshire bordering Massachusetts boast a sizable number of Latinos so that in 2020 they made up 7.9 percent of the total population of Hillsborough County. Another example is Burlington, Vermont, where Asians make up 6.4 percent of the population. If previous patterns of migration repeat themselves, it is likely these pockets will attract others and thus further diversify northern New England.

These increases in population and demographic representation in office have not necessarily meant vast improvement in material conditions. For instance, as is clear from Table 11.1, while some groups in some states have a lower percentage of people below the poverty line than they did thirty years ago, as a whole, the picture is rather mixed. Only one state, Rhode Island, has seen the poverty rate go down for all three groups so that in 2020, there were 2.5 percent, 3.4 percent, and 16 percent fewer African Americans, Latinos, and Asian Americans living in poverty in the Ocean State. In Vermont and Maine the opposite is true—all three groups have a higher percentage of people below the poverty line between 1990 and 2020. In part, this is because some are refugees or newer migrants who are less likely to be economically established. In contrast, Massachusetts has seen the most dramatic drop in poverty for a single group. In 2020, 11.8 percent Latinos in the state living below the poverty rate, a 23.9 percent drop from the equivalent numbers in 1990.

Likewise, if we look at household median income for Asian Americans, Blacks, and Latinx in each state as presented in Table 11.2, it is clear that the 2008 financial crisis seriously disrupted the earnings of all three groups and

TABLE 11.1. Percent Below Poverty in New England for Selected Demographic Groups, 1990–2020

BELOW POVERTY	WHITE	BLACK	LATINO	ASIAN
CONNECTICUT				
1990	2.7	17.8	27.6	6.5
2000	7	29.6	24.7	
2010	5.9	22.1	23.6	8.6
2020	5.9	17.5	21	8.8
Change	3.2	-0.3	-6.6	2.3
MAINE				
1990	7.9	12.3	13.5	10.7
2000	7.1	20.8	19.8	
2010	12	46.5	30.6	10.4
2020	10.4	31.1	16.9	13
Change	2.5	18.8	3.4	2.3
MASSACHUSETTS				
1990	4.8	20.6	35.7	15.6
2000	5.3	21.2	29.8	
2010	7.7	24.4	31.3	13.3
2020	6.7	17.6	11.8	23
Change	1.9	-3	-23.9	7.4
NEW HAMPSHIRE				
1990	4.3	11.1	9.9	8.9
2000	10.5	27.7	18.7	9.9
2010	7.6	25.8	13.8	16.3
2020	6.8	18.5	14.8	8.4
Change	2.5	7.4	4.9	-0.5
RHODE ISLAND				
1990	5.2	23	26.5	29.3
2000	8.9	29.6	36.1	
2010	9.4	36.5	30.3	13.5
2020	8	20.5	23.1	13.3
Change	2.8	-2.5	-3.4	-16
VERMONT				
1990	6.9	17.6	10.6	6.4
2000	6.2	19.7	17.5	
2010	10.3	24.2	16.1	14.4
2020	12.2	32.2	27.6	20
Change	5.3	14.6	17	13.6

Source: US Census Bureau. 2020c. "Income and Poverty By State"

TABLE 11.2. Median Household Income in New England in 2020 dollars, 1990–2020

	WHITE	BLACK	LATINO	ASIAN
CONNECTICUT	MEDIAN INCOME			
1990	85,954	55,467	49,734	96,158
2010	85,015	47,128	44,415	89,304
2020	90,941	50,905	48,715	101,418
MAINE	MEDIAN INCOME			
1990	55,249	51,980	57,168	55,094
2010	55,155	34,684	32,237	58,165
2020	60,207	41,174	55,821	57,868
MASSACHUSETTS	MEDIAN INCOME			
1990	75,411	50,300	39,061	68,724
2010	77,853	48,730	36,836	83,239
2020	91,759	54,835	48,450	102,235
NEW HAMPSHIRE	MEDIAN INCOME			
1990	72,037	62,686	69,146	85,074
2010	72,600	58,786	60,832	90,200
2020	79,050	59,261	63,535	79,154
RHODE ISLAND	MEDIAN INCOME			
1990	65,550	40,350	39,730	50,284
2010	68,688	33,255	37,712	63,914
2020	76,742	47,723	43,609	82,252
VERMONT	MEDIAN INCOME			
1990	59,112	56,682	57,712	55,096
2010	59,034	67,186	35,412	42,785
2020	64,412	37,489	49,349	57,756

Source: US Census Bureau. 2020c. "Income and Poverty by State."

some of them have yet to regain the financial terrain they lost. Compared to 1990, Latinos and African Americans have lost ground in every single state except for Massachusetts and Rhode Island. In contrast, Asian Americans have done much better. Their median income was higher in 2020 in every state except for New Hampshire. Massachusetts is the only state in New England where all three groups have seen their median income increase.

A more persistent problem in the region has been access to housing.

Ownership and rental costs have risen exponentially as supply has not kept up with demand—even in more rural states like New Hampshire—which "has created an affordability and availability crisis, particularly among . . . first-time homebuyers" (New Hampshire Realtors 2021). Indeed, during this period, the only state to see Asian Americans, Blacks, and Latinos experience a higher rate of homeownership was Massachusetts, and even then, by a paltry increase 0.06 percent for African Americans, and a more respectable 1.42 percent for Latinos, and a more significant 3.85 percent for Asian Americans. This still places all 3 groups well below the 70 percent home ownership among whites in Massachusetts—Asian Americans 54.47 percent, Blacks at 35.4 percent, and Latinx at 28 percent.

African Americans are the least likely to own a home today in *every* other state in New England (United States Census 2020b). Maine and Vermont are particularly awful for Black homeownership with a mere 25.25 percent and 21.11 percent rate, respectively (United States Census 2020b). Improving on this is crucial because home ownership is the single most important contributor to wealth for most Americans and thus, should it continue, these groups will be disadvantaged compared to the white majority for decades to come on the vital wealth metric.

Conclusion

The demographics of New England have changed dramatically in the last fifty years. A region that was over 90 percent white in 1975 is now much more diverse overall as 74 percent of residents to the region report they are white non-Hispanic in 2020. This shift is attributable to consistent growth among African Americans, Latinos, and Asian Americans in the region. Just as previous waves of immigrants, such as the Irish, slowly shaped the politics of the region, the newcomers are doing the same. In recent times, their concerns have slowly coalesced around discrimination and material concerns such as housing and education, while the political landscapes they have had to navigate differ by state. Timing of their arrival, locale of selected residence, and numbers have been key in shaping strategies for political influence.

Electorally, for example, African Americans have the longest and broadest record in the region largely because of their incorporation as a key constituency within the Democratic Party. Latinos have been the second most successful when it comes to political incorporation, although their representation is far below what their numbers in the New England population would suggest. This is because of the inherent difficulties of organization within the group discussed, as well as their much later and incomplete incorporation into the Democratic Party coalition. Asian Americans face even higher obstacles to collective action. Their lower relative numbers in New England couple with high salience of association with the powerful nation-state of China so that a perceived foreignness complicates their incorporation into the two-party American system. Nonetheless, Asian Americans continue to gain political space in the region, especially as they tend to have higher income and education compared to Blacks and Latinos in New England.

The present demographic picture shows Asian Americans, Blacks, and Latinx are gaining relative to the white majority in every state and raising their educational attainment overall. Material conditions in southern New England are improving—especially for Latinos in Massachusetts—but either stalling or deteriorating in northern New England with the exception of Asian Americans. Despite some progress in home ownership rates, and even among Asians and Latinos who have seen the most economic gains among the groups centered here, Asian Americans, Blacks, and Latinos in New England still typically trail the white majority on economic measures, especially home ownership. This stems from persistent obstacles in New England, like high housing costs and low availability, as well as some the political obstacles outlined here. The history of the region suggests that these figures will improve as the numbers of African Americans, Asian Americans, and Latinos grow, especially if, as they become more established, they manage to become a key part of the region's electoral coalitions. The exact pace and pattern are yet to be determined, but New England as a whole should do well to take note of their potential.

Works Cited

Archer, Jim. 2017. *The Struggle for Equal Rights in Antebellum New England*. Oxford: Oxford University Press.

Brady, Henry, Sidney Verba, Kay Lehman Schlozman. 1995. "Beyond SES: A Resource Model of Political Participation." *American Political Science Review*, 89, no. 2: 271–294.

Bushnell, Mark. 2016. "Then Again: Immigrants Helped Vermont Boom." *VTDigger*. Retrieved January 8, 2023. Available at: https://vtdigger.org/2016/09/11/immigrants-helped-vermont-boom/.

Center for Women in Politics and Public Policy. 2015. "Profiles in Leadership: Women of Color Elected to Office in Massachusetts" (2015). University of Massachusetts Boston and Women's Pipeline for Change Center for Women in Politics and Public Policy Publications. Paper 27.

Collazo, Sonia, Camille Ryan and Kurt Bauman. 2010. "Profile of the Puerto Rican Population in the United States and Puerto Rico: 2008." Presented at the Annual Meeting of the Population Association of America Dallas, TX April 15–17. Available at: https://www.census.gov/content/dam/Census/library/working-papers/2010/demo/collazo-ryan-bauman-paa2010-paper.pdf.

Daniels, Roger. 2002. *Coming to America: A History of Immigration and Ethnicity in American Life*. New York: Harper Perennial.

Gimpel James and Wendy Tam Cho. 2004. "The Persistence of White Ethnicity in New England Politics." *Political Geography*. 23, no 8: 987–1008.

Global Boston. 2021. "Chinese." https://globalboston.bc.edu/index.php/home/ethnic-groups/chinese/.

Halter, Marylin. 2008. "Cape Verdeans in the US." In *Perspectives on Cape Verdean Immigration and Diaspora*, edited by Luís Batalha and Jørgen Carling, 35–46. Amsterdam: Amsterdam University Press.

Jackson, Regine. 2011. "The Uses of Diaspora Among Haitians in Boston." In *Geographies of the Haitian Diaspora*, edited by Regine Jackson, 135–162. New York: Routledge.

Janis, Mark Weston. 2021. "Connecticut 1818: From Theocracy to Toleration." *Connecticut Law Review*. 52, no. 5: 1701–09.

Jiménez, Luis. 2022. "Latinx in Massachusetts Politics." In *The Politics of Massachusetts Exceptionalism: Reputation Meets Reality*, edited by Jerold Duquette and Erin O'Brien, 233–254. Boston: University of Massachusetts Press.

Kim, Thomas. 2007. *The Racial Logic of Two-Party Politics: Asian-Americans and Party Competition*. Philadelphia: Temple University Press.

Lee, Erika. 2015. *The Making of Asian-America: A History*. New York: Simon and Schuster.

McLoughlin, William. 1976. *Rhode Island: A History*. New York: W. W. Norton and Company.

Melish, Joanne. 1998. *Disowning Slavery: Gradual Emancipation and "Race" in New England: 1780–1860*. Cornell: Cornell University Press.

Myall, James. 2020. "Race and Public Policy in Maine: Past, Present, and Future." *Maine Policy Review* 29, no. 2. Retrieved: January 10, 2022. Available at: https://digitalcommons.library.umaine.edu/mpr/vol29/iss2/4/.

National Park Service. 2021. "An Early History of Boston's Chinatown: Boston National Historical Park." Retrieved January 8, 2022. Available at: https://www.nps.gov/articles/000/boston-chinatown.htm.

New Hampshire Realtors. 2021. "Market Data" Retrieved January 14, 2023. Available at: https://www.nhar.org/resource/market-data.

Palmer, Kenneth, Thomas Taylor, Marcus Librizzi and Jean Lavigne. 2009. *Maine Politics and Government*. Lincoln: University of Nebraska Press.

Shearer, Benjamin. Ed. 2004. *The Uniting States: The Story of Statehood for the Fifty United States*. Westport, CT: Greenwood Press.

Syed, Maleeha. 2020. "Kesha Ram Becomes First Woman of Color in Vermont Senate: Here's What to Know." Burlington Free Press. Retrieved January 18. Available at: https://www.burlingtonfreepress.com/story/news/2020/11/04/vermont-election-results-kesha-ram-elected-state-senate-first-woman-color/3716467001/#.

Williams, Yohuru. 2001. "No Haven: From Civil Rights to Black Power in New Haven, Connecticut." *The Black Scholar* 31, no. 3–4: 54–66.

Woodson, Kamilah. 2020. *Colorism: Investigating a Global Phenomenon*. Santa Barbara, CA: Fielding University Press.
United States Census. 2020a. "Detailed Demographic and Housing Characteristics." Retrieved from: https://data.census.gov/.
———. 2020b. "Home Ownership by State." Retrieved from: http://data.census.gov/.

CHAPTER 12

GENDERING YANKEE INGENUITY

Electing Women in New England[1]

Jane JaKyung Han and Erin O'Brien
PhD Candidate | Associate Professor of Political Science
University of Massachusetts Boston

New England is a relatively good place for women seeking elected office. Breaking a glass ceiling decades ago in 1948, Margaret Chase Smith, a Republican from Maine, became the first woman elected to the US House and Senate. Elaine Noble, a Democrat from Massachusetts was the first out gay or lesbian individuals elected to the state legislature in 1974. Today, national political figures like Senators Susan Collins (R-ME), Elizabeth Warren (D-MA), and Jeanne Shaheen (D-NH) come from the region as do influential officials like Congresswoman Ayanna Pressley (D-MA). New England is the only region where each state has, or has had, a female governor. Among those is Gina Raimondo (D), the former Governor of Rhode Island and Biden Administration Commerce Secretary. As of 2024, three New England states rank among the top ten states for the percentage of women in their state legislatures: Vermont (#5), Maine (#7), and Rhode Island (#8). Five of the six New England states are in the top half of states when it comes to electing women to the state legislature (CAWP 2024). Regionally, only the Southwest rivals New England on this metric.

This does not make New England a utopia from the perspective of electing women. Vermont was the last state in the union to send a woman to Congress, only rectifying this in 2022 with the election of Democrat Becca Balint (Shivaram 2022). Massachusetts ranks among the bottom half of states in sending women to the state legislature (O'Brien 2022; CAWP 2024) and only popularly elected a female governor in November 2022. Moreover, the women elected in New England are not racially diverse but are overwhelmingly white.

---

[1] The authors thank Jaymin Ding for his assistance with scraping data from the election archives websites of the New England states to construct a large portion of the database. His work facilitated the speedy collection of data and provided validity checks for the database. A prior version of this chapter was presented at the 2023 Annual Meeting of the New England Political Science Association, winning the John C. Donovan Prize for Best Paper by a Faculty Member.

This chapter both documents and explains these realities. We find that "blue" is central to understanding women's electoral success in today's New England. The women the region elects are overwhelmingly Democrats. But, as the title of this volume signals, that does not tell the whole story—it takes "more than blue" to understand the substantial variation among the New England states when it comes to electing women.

To see how far women have come in being elected to office requires a close, deep look at multiple offices. After discussing how having women in elected office matters for public policy and democratic legitimacy, we present data on the make-up of each New England state's congressional delegations, statewide constitutional officers, and state legislatures. We compile the gender breakdown for each state as well as the party affiliation and race/ethnicity of the women currently in these offices, comparing these numbers to the United States congressional averages, which serve as a benchmark. However, what is happening now is only a snapshot and may, in fact, be anomalistic. Thus, the second section of the chapter compiles and discusses an over 100-year database of the percentage of women serving in each state's legislature since suffrage. The last third of the chapter tests whether or not the degree of professionalization of the legislature and degree of party competition explain the variation exhibited among the New England states. What emerges is a full portrait of each New England state's tendencies in electing women as well as a methodologically robust examination of why the states differ in their propensity to send women to elected office.

Why Does Women's Representation Matter?

Some readers might wonder why women's representation matters. If elected officials are charged with representing their districts, and the residents of said districts both choose their leaders and have this choice honored, why do the demographics of elected officials matter? The answer involves descriptive and substantive representation (Dodson 2006; Reingold 2012; Dolan, Deckman, and Swers 2021). Descriptive representation encompasses the impacts of seeing women in office. Having more women in office, especially in top offices, can help counter gendered political socialization (Bos et al. 2021) and policy outcomes are viewed as more legitimate by the people the more legislative body or executive office approximates the population. Substantive representation is also advanced as women enter elected office—especially as they reach a critical mass. Female legislators, like all politicians, are motivated by re-election and represent their geographic districts (MacDonald and O'Brien 2008). Beyond these considerations, women legislate differently. They ask previously unvoiced questions in committee, prioritize different policy issues, and advance "women's interests" beyond their district (Swers 2002). So having gender parity in elected office is far more than just a "feel good" proposition—substantive changes occur when women are elected. The variation among the New England states in women's elected representation matters, therefore, for both political socialization and public policy.

The State of Women in New England Elected Offices
NEW ENGLAND'S CONGRESSIONAL REPRESENTATION, 2023

Getting elected to Congress is the penultimate goal of many politicians—one of three equal federal branches of government, prestigious, and able to influence the national policy agenda. Plus, many politicians reason, it is a good route to the White House.

There is substantial variation among the New England states when it comes to gender and their congressional delegations. Because the delegations are small—especially in Maine (4), New Hampshire (4), Rhode Island (4), and Vermont (3)—the percentages can shift dramatically with the addition or loss of one female member of Congress. Hence, these numbers are best paired with other offices to get a fuller picture. But Congress is the highest legislative body in the United States and whom a state sends there matters a great deal for descriptive and substantive representation.

As the first column of Table 12.1 shows, as of 2023 one New England state sends no women to Congress—Rhode Island. New Hampshire sends a majority female delegation to DC (75%), Maine has gender parity (50%), the Massachusetts delegation is just over one-third female (36.4%), and the Vermont delegation is exactly one-third. These four states exceed the percentage of women in the US Congress in 2023 (27.9%) while Connecticut nearly parallels the congressional average with 26.6 percent of its chamber being female.

The first row under each state in Table 12.1 provides the party breakdown of the female members of Congress from that state and the second row shows their race or ethnicity. This compilation makes evident that the women New England sends to Congress are overwhelmingly white Democrats. Only Maine sends a Republican to Congress and that same women, Senator Susan Collins, is also the only Republican woman in the New England congressional

TABLE 12.1. New England Women's Representation in
Congress and Statewide Executive Office, 2023

	CONGRESSIONAL DELEGATION	STATEWIDE EXECUTIVE OFFICE
CT	26.6% (2/7)	33% (2/6)
party	2Ds	2Ds
race/ethnicity	1 bl, 1 wh	1 bl, 1 wh
ME	50% (2/4)	20% (1/5)
party	1D, 1R	1D
race/ethnicity	2 wh	1 wh
MA	36.4% (4/11)	83.3% (5/6)
party	4Ds	5D
race/ethnicity	1 bl, 3 wh	1 bl, 4 wh
NH	75% (3/4)	0% (0/3)
party	3D	n/a
race/ethnicity	3 wh	n/a
RI	0%	20% (1/5)
party	n/a	1D
race/ethnicity	n/a	1 afro-la
VT	33% (1/3)	33.3% (2/6)
party	1D	2D
race/ethnicity	1 wh	2 wh
U.S.	27.9% (149/535)	30.3% (94/310)
party	106D, 42R, 1Ind	52D, 40R, 2NP
race/ethnicity[1]	10 as-am/pi, 27 bl, 19 la, 2 nat-am, 1 m-e, 94 wh	4 as-am/pi, 10 bl, 8 la, 1 nat-am, 72 wh

Data source: Center for American Women and Politics (CAWP). 2022. "State Fact Sheets 2022." New Brunswick, NJ: Center for American Women and Politics, Eagleton Institute of Politics, Rutgers University-New Brunswick. https://cawp.rutgers.edu/facts/levels-office/state-legislature/women-state-legislatures-2022

[1] Numbers exceed total "n" as some women identify with more than one racial or ethnic group.

delegation. The Democratic Party bias among female members of Congress in New England is more pronounced than Congress as a whole—91.7 percent Democrats in New England while 71.1 percent of the female members of Congress are Democrats.

Ten of the twelve female members of Congress from New England are white and two are Black. Three of the four whitest states in the nation are in New England—Vermont (95.6%), Maine (95.4%), and New Hampshire

(93.7%) (World Population Review 2022). That the women these states send to Congress are white is thus reflective of the vast majority of their population. But Rhode Island, Connecticut, and Massachusetts are comparatively more diverse with 79.4 percent, 77.5 percent, and 77.8 percent of the population being white. Still, Rhode Island's first ever female member of Congress is white. Connecticut and Massachusetts both send one Black female to the House—Jahana Hayes and Ayanna Pressley, respectively. The relative whiteness of New England's population compared to other regions of the country is important context, but it is still the case that in 2023 just 16.6 percent of the women sent to Congress from New England are of color while that figure for the whole of the US Congress is 39.6 percent.

NEW ENGLAND WOMEN'S REPRESENTATION IN STATEWIDE EXECUTIVE OFFICES, 2023

The number of constitutional officers differ by state with Connecticut, Massachusetts, and Vermont having six while Maine and Rhode Island have five, and New Hampshire just three. At a minimum, all include the governor, attorney general, and Secretary of State. But except for Maine where the governor runs statewide while the other constitutional officers are selected by a combined vote of the state legislature, each officer runs statewide and serves in the executive branch. The second column of Table 12.1 provides the gender breakdown of each New England state's executive officers.

It is evident that gender representation in statewide executive offices is not a mirror image of a state's congressional delegation. The caveat that comparisons are influenced by the small numbers of statewide elected offices is again relevant. That said, these too are top spots with substantial ability to affect policy in each state. Who is occupying them matters. And while Rhode Island and Vermont send no women to Congress, 40 percent and 50 percent of their executive officers, respectively, are female. Connecticut and Massachusetts also perform better for women's representation when it comes to constitutional officers rather than congressional delegations—Connecticut marginally (33% vs. 26.6%) and Massachusetts substantially (83.3% vs. 36.4%). Maine and Massachusetts are the only two New England states with a sitting female governor as of 2024. New Hampshire's small congressional delegation is 75 percent female, but none of the Granite State's constitutional officers are female.

Another takeaway from Table 12.1's compilation of statewide executive officers is that the Democratic dominance among female elected leaders in

New England holds. Of the eleven women serving as executive officers, all are Democrats.

Women of color are underrepresented even when we take into account the relative whiteness of much of the region. Three women serving in the New England constitutional offices identify as women of color—Connecticut Secretary of State Stephanie Thomas (Black), Massachusetts Attorney General Andrea Campbell (Black), and Rhode Island Lt. Governor Sabina Matos (Afro-Latina). This translates to 9.6 percent of the region's statewide executive offices being held by women of color—and none in the corner office. For comparison, women of color make up the following percentages of the population in each state: Connecticut, 17.5 percent; Maine, 3.6 percent; Massachusetts, 14.9 percent; New Hampshire 5.1 percent; Rhode Island 14.7 percent; Vermont 3.7 percent (O'Brien 2022, 264). The United States is approximately 20.3 percent women of color.

NEW ENGLAND WOMEN'S REPRESENTATION IN STATE LEGISLATURE, 2023

We now turn to state legislatures. In many ways this metric is more compelling for comparison across states as the number of individuals who serve in the state legislature is far greater than the congressional delegations or constitutional officers. State legislative bodies reflect the regional particularities of a state, are comparable across states, and send substantial numbers of individuals to their chambers. They also regularly form the pipeline to more prestigious positions in the US Congress and the statewide constitutional offices (McGlen et al. 2010; Mariani 2008; Ransford, Hardy-Fanta, and Cammisa 2007, 31). Thus, these bodies tell us much about the state's preferences for electing women and whether or not women will be in the higher-ranking offices soon.

The 151st United States Congress is 28.2 percent female (CAWP 2024). The first column of Table 12.2 shows that every New England state legislature bests the congressional number. Vermont is tops in New England when it comes to electing women, 45 percent, with Rhode Island close behind, 44.2 percent, and Massachusetts comes in last with 31.5 percent. Compared to the percentages of women in the fifty state legislatures, all but Massachusetts exceeds the national average. Vermont, Rhode Island, and Maine are all in the top ten with New Hampshire and Connecticut ranking 17th and 18th, respectively. Massachusetts is 27th among the 50 states (CAWP 2023).

TABLE 12.2. New England Women's Representation in State Legislatures, 2022

	WOMEN[1]	WOMEN OF COLOR IN POPULATION[2]	WOMEN OF COLOR AS PERCENTAGE OF CHAMBER[3]	WOMEN OF COLOR AS PERCENTAGE OF WOMEN SERVING
CT	34.2% (64/187)	17.5	5.9% (11/187)	17.2% (11/64)
party	43D, 21R		10D, 1R	
ME	42.5% (79/186)	3.6	.54% (1/186)	1.3% (1/79)
party	54D, 24R, 1I		1D	
MA	29.5% (59/200)	14.9	5% (10/200)	16.9% (10/59)
party	54D, 4R, 1I		10D	
NH	34.4% (146/424)	5.1	1.4% (6/424)	4.1% (6/146)
party	96D, 50R		6D	
RI	44.2% (50/113)	14.7	9.7% (11/113)	22% (11/50)
party	45D, 5R		11D	
VT	41.7% (75/180)	3.7	1.7% (3/180)	4% (3/75)
party	57D, 13R, 5I		3D	

Data Sources:
1 Center for American Women and Politics (CAWP). 2022. "Women in State Legislatures 2022." New Brunswick, NJ: Center for American Women and Politics, Eagleton Institute of Politics, Rutgers University-New Brunswick. https://cawp.rutgers.edu/facts/levels-office/state-legislature/women-state-legislatures-2022
2 Figures for computing women of color in the state population are from U.S. Census Bureau QuickFacts.
3 Center for American Women and Politics (CAWP). 2022. Women Elected Officials Filter Tool. New Brunswick, NJ: Center for American Women and Politics, Eagleton Institute of Politics, Rutgers University-New Brunswick. Asian-American/Pacific Islander, Black, Latina, Middle Eastern/North African, Multiracial alone, Native American/Alaska Native/Native Hawaiian, other.

When women serve in New England state legislatures, they are most likely Democrats. But here there is variation among the six states. The first row under each state provides the party breakdown of the women in the state's legislature. Roughly two-thirds of the women serving are Democrats in Connecticut (69.6%), Maine (73.1%), and New Hampshire (66.5%). In Congress, 72.3 percent of the women serving are Democrats. This means the party imbalance is actually lower in Connecticut and New Hampshire compared to the United States Congress while Maine almost directly mirrors Congress. In Vermont, 85.2 percent of the women serving are Democrats. Massachusetts (92.1%) and Rhode Island (90%) witness near exclusive dominance of Democrats over Republicans among female legislators—far more than other New England states and the congressional percentage. Both states' legislatures are extremely unbalanced in favor of Democrats.

NEW ENGLAND WOMEN OF COLOR'S REPRESENTATION
IN STATE LEGISLATURE, 2022

Column two in Table 12.2 provides the percentage of the population in each state that is women of color. Column 3 examines the relative strength of women of color in New England state legislatures in 2022.[2] Compared to the percentage of women of color in the state (column 2), all New England states fall short in proportional representation in the legislature (column 3). Some shortfalls are more dramatic than others. Two states, Rhode Island and Vermont, are 1.5 times and 2 times short of proportional representation for women of color in the legislature compared to the population of women of color in the state.[3] Connecticut, Massachusetts are both 3 times short and New Hampshire 3.5 times. Maine has the greatest disparity at 7x—0.54 percent of the legislature is women of color while the state is 3.6 percent women of color; however, its Speaker of the House is a Black woman.

Table 12.2's column 4 presents the percentage of women of color serving *among* female state legislators. Unsurprisingly, the three whitest states in New England (and three of the top four whitest in the nation), have small percentages of women of color among the women serving—Maine, New Hampshire, and Vermont. Connecticut, Massachusetts, and Rhode Island—more diverse, and in the case of Connecticut and Massachusetts, more populous—elect more diverse women's caucuses.

Of the forty-two women of color serving in New England state legislatures, all but one is a Democrat—Connecticut State Representative Kimberly Fiorello, born in Seoul, South Korea, is a Republican. This means that 97.6 percent of the women of color serving as state legislators are Democrats.

What does all this suggest? Compared to other regions, New England is, on the whole, better at electing women. How effective the various New England states are, however, often depends on the level of office. States with parity or near parity for constitutional officers can have no women in the congressional delegation (Rhode Island and Vermont) while, in the case of Rhode Island, can also be best in the region for electing women to the state legislature. New Hampshire features three of four female members of Congress but no female statewide elected officials. Connecticut, Maine, and

---

[2] At time of writing, figures for new 2023 legislatures were not available.
[3] Because the percentages of women of color are so small in the states, we group them together in these calculations. This is *not* to say that the experiences of women of color are the same or interchangeable. It is simply the case that the "n" is so low of individual groups of women of color that presentation of the data necessitated grouping.

Massachusetts have rough parity between their congressional delegation and constitutional officers—but Massachusetts lags in electing women to the state legislature. When women are elected to any of these offices in New England though, they are most often Democrats. Underneath this trend, and especially in the state legislatures, we see that Massachusetts and Rhode Island elect female Democrats almost exclusively whereas the other New England states include some Republican representation—if not parity. Women of color are underrepresented across all offices even once we take into account the lack of diversity within some New England states.

State Legislatures across New England, 1921–2023

Do the above trends hold over time? Are they unrepresentative snapshots? To assess this possibility, and to garner a fuller understanding of New England's taste for electing women, we turn to a longitudinal database of all the women elected to each of the New England states legislature since suffrage.

Data from The Center for American Women and Politics (CAWP) at Rutgers University was used to compile our New England states' database. For years 1921–1973, the searchable database provided the raw number of female state senators and state representatives by state. Each woman was coded for their party affiliation, also recoverable via filters in the CAWP database. For years 1975–2023, CAWP provides summary fact sheets reporting the percentage of women serving by state for each session. These percentages were entered directly into the longitudinal database. The summary fact sheets, however, did not provide partisanship breakdowns nor race and ethnicity. For these additional considerations, we returned to the searchable database. For race and ethnicity, each state was searched separately so that all women who served and were coded by CAWP as "Asian American/Pacific Islander," "Black," "Latina," "Middle Eastern/North African," "Native American/Alaska Native/Native Hawaiian," "multiracial alone," "White," or "other" appeared.

The resulting longitudinal dataset provides the most comprehensive accounting of women in New England state legislatures since women won the right to vote. We prefer it to an analysis over time of local government officials because each state has a comparable legislature rather than the often-particularistic local government setups. As noted, state legislatures also send large numbers of senators and representatives to the state Houses whereas congressional delegations and constitutional officers are small in number and

Gendering Yankee Ingenuity 237

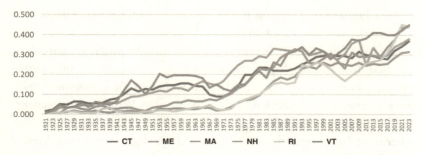

FIGURE 12.1. Percentage of Female State Legislators Across New England, 1921–2023.

thus subject to far more unique electoral considerations beyond the state's taste for electing women over time.

Figure 12.1 presents the percentage of women in each of the New England state legislatures since suffrage. This more robust data source helps us discern several trends among the six states. First, no state has reached 50 percent parity in over one hundred plus years since women gained the right to vote. Second, while there is a gentle upward slope over the course of the panel, progress is not a clear linear path. States hover around the same percentage for years. Take Connecticut for an example—between 1997 and 2007 it remained around 30 percent. From 1995 to 2017, Massachusetts held close to 25 percent. Steep improvement is not the norm.

Third, New Hampshire and Vermont generally lead the pack in electing women over the course of the one hundred years depicted. New Hampshire experiences dramatic gains and losses between 2009 to 2023 though while Vermont continues to be a leader over most of the full panel.

Fourth, Rhode Island and Massachusetts are laggards. For almost the whole of the 102-year panel, these 2 states register the lowest percentage of female legislators. Maine too ran with these back-of-the-pack states until the late 1960s when it began electing women at rates more commensurate with the New England states.

Fifth, Rhode Island has experienced a dramatic turnaround as of late. In 2013, 27.4 percent of the Rhode Island legislature was female. In 2015, the exact same percentage held, and in 2017 there was a slight uptick to 31 percent. In 2019, however, the percentage jumped to 37.2 percent and in 2021 it reached 44.2 percent and held there in 2023. This places Rhode Island second in New England and seventh in the United States for electing women to their legislative branch as of 2022.

The last takeaway from Figure 12.1 is central to the puzzle we unpack in the final third of this chapter. Figure 1 shows us that there is substantive variation among the six states in electing women to the legislature despite sharing many regional political sensibilities. By 1949, Vermont, Connecticut, and New Hampshire had legislatures at or above 10 percent female. The other three New England states are in low single digits with Massachusetts and Rhode Island hovering near zero. Through the post war years and into the mid-1960s, the gap between Massachusetts, Rhode Island, and the other New England states expands. In 1981, Massachusetts and Rhode Island finally cross 10 percent while New Hampshire's legislature is 30 percent female, and all other New England states are above 20 percent. The late 1990s through most of the 2000s sees growth among all the New England states, and a few years of more compression between them, but by 2023 the gap is back up to almost fifteen points between the top New England state, Connecticut (45%), and the bottom state in the region, Massachusetts (31.5%). This gap between percentages of women in the state legislature is all the more seismic when we highlight that the ceiling for the percentage of women in New England legislatures is 45 as of 2023. From the vantage point of regional comparison, the biggest story is that New England does not perform as a block over the 102-year timespan when it comes to electing women.

Representational Variation in New England: Legislative Professionalization and Electoral Competition

The final third of this chapter assesses why there is such variation among the New England states. The first explanation, which holds in part for New England, is that there is an inverse relationship between a state legislature's professionalization and the presence of women (Ransford, Hardy-Fanta, and Cammisa 2007). Said differently, the less prestigious the position, the more likely one is to see women. Women's path toward political incorporation has seen this elsewhere—women are disproportionately responsible for the more mundane, less prestigious campaign work or overrepresentation on PTAs rather than top spots like superintendent or mayor (Evans, 1980; McGlen et al., 2010).

State legislatures are not created equal. Professional legislatures are "associated with unlimited professional sessions, superior staff resources, and sufficient pay to allow members to pursue legislative service as their vocation" (Squire 2007, 211). Squire's seminal measure of legislative professionalism include salary and benefits, time demands of legislative service, and staff and other resources. Where these component parts are high, the incentive to serve is greater, members are incentivized to build legislative skills, legislation gets more focused attention and is more apt to tread into complicated matters, and staff and legislator turnover is lower (Squire 2007, 213).

Based on this metric, Squire's (2017) latest ranking of the New England states for professionalism is Massachusetts (#2), Connecticut (#13), Rhode Island (#28), Vermont (#33), Maine (#41) and New Hampshire (#50). This means that Massachusetts is the second most professional, resource-rich, state legislature in the country and New Hampshire is dead last.

The National Conference of State Legislatures (NCSL) also developed a measure of the "capacity of legislatures to function as independent branches of government, capable of balancing the power of the executive branch and having the information necessary to make independent, informed policy decisions . . . . [It] consider[s] the amount of time legislators spend on the job, the amount they are compensated, and the size of the legislature's staff" (NCSL 2021). The NCSL is a five-tiered, colored scale ranging from green (full-time, well-paid, large staff) to gold (part-time, low pay, small staff). It places the New England states in essentially the same order as Squire—Massachusetts in light green (a two on five-point scale), Connecticut in gray (a three on a five-point scale) and the other four New England states all "gold lite" which amount to a four on the five-point scale.

The professionalization explanation seemingly does an effective job explaining why Massachusetts consistently ranks last in New England for electing women to the state legislature. Simply put, the job is attractive. It pays well and is relatively resourced. Given the long history of sexism in the United States, it is thus not particularly surprising that the New England state with the objectively best working conditions is the same one that has been most resistant to incorporating women. Connecticut's current position of second from the bottom for electing women is, likewise, in keeping with the professionalism explanation. Connecticut and Massachusetts do the worst in electing women in New England, in part, because their legislatures are the most professionalized and, thus, attractive to work in. Over the course of the over one hundred-year panel, the general trend of New Hampshire and Vermont leading the way for electing women is also in keeping with these states' low legislative professionalism scores. As of 2023, the four best states for electing women to the state legislature in New England are the ones ranked 28th (Rhode Island), 33rd (Vermont), 41st (Maine) and 50th (New Hampshire) for legislative professionalism. Women are more apt to win when the job is not as lucrative, resourced, or full-time.

But legislative professionalism as the explanation for variation among the NE states in electing women to the state legislature is not consistent with all the data points. For instance, there has been a dramatic recent shift in Rhode Island's propensity to elect to women to the state legislature even as its legislative professionalism score is but twenty-eight out of fifty states. This suggests that legislative professionalism is indeed a key factor in explaining the differences between the percentages of women in New England state legislatures but that it is not complete.

To more fully understand the presence of women elected officials in the region, we turn to the role of electoral competition. A prominent scholarly strain of work on political parties finds that electoral competition encourages parties to expand their electoral base by mobilizing new constituencies (Key 1949; Schattschneider 1942, 59; Schattschneider 1960, 95; Rosenstone and Hansen 1993). So, when Democrats and Republicans are evenly matched, they fight to expand their base with untapped constituencies.[4] Running more diverse candidates is a popular strategy for doing so (Sanbonmatsu 2002).

Yes, Democrats dominate in modern New England but there is variation in how electorally competitive the GOP is in each state. We hypothesize that, over time, where electoral competition is stronger, those states will be more likely to see women win legislative office. Importantly, the party competition hypothesis holds regardless of which party is ascendant—it is simply the fact that in New England the Democratic Party is more dominant in the modern era. This hypothesis is counterintuitive to those who view the Democratic Party as more responsive to "women's interests." That is true on policy outputs (Swers 2002) but, perhaps, not candidate selection. Democrats are more likely to elect women than Republicans *but*, we hypothesize, they are most likely to do so at the state-level when they experience electoral threat at the ballot box by a competitive state GOP.

---

[4] An opposing perspective is that tight electoral competition encourages demobilization of the other party's core constituencies (Piven, Minnite, and Groarke 2009; Piven and Cloward 1988; Keyssar 2011).

OUR DATABASE: NEW ENGLAND LEGISLATIVE RACES & THE ELECTORAL COMPETITION HYPOTHESIS

To formally test this hypothesis, we looked at the election margins in all district-level legislative races in the six states from 1990–2022 (with the exception of Vermont, for which 2022 election data was unavailable). Election margins, the percentage vote difference between two candidates, are recognized measures of electoral competition (Mayhew 1974; Holbrook and Dunk 1983) with the most advantageous indicator too accounting for whether or not the race was contested (Holbrook and Dunk 1983). Therefore, district-level data for each of the six New England states was compiled for votes cast for each candidate, total votes cast in each district race, and whether or not the race was contested. From there, the percentages of votes cast for the top two candidates was subtracted from one another creating the election margin. For district races featuring only one candidate, the percentage was 100 percent. Districts were also coded according to whether any female candidates ran for legislative office in each general election from 1990–2022. Names of female candidates, the district races and years in which they ran for office, party affiliation, and their election results were confirmed using CAWP's State Legislative Women Nominees Database (1992–2021), CAWP's searchable Database on Women Elected Officials by Position, and Ballotpedia.

Using this data, we performed two logistic regressions to determine what factors increase the likelihood of a female candidate *running for state legislature* at the district-level and the likelihood of a *women being elected to state legislative office*. Regression analysis offers the most rigorous test of the electoral competition hypothesis as it examines what effect, if any, electoral competition has for women running and winning while simultaneously controlling for an array of factors also related to why women run and win. Said differently, the advantage of regression analysis is that if electoral competition emerges as statistically significant, we know it does so even when we take into account the independent effect of the following: level of office being sought, whether or not there was an opponent in the previous district race, the party that won the seat in the previous cycle,[5] and state. We hypothesize that districts with higher levels of electoral competitiveness in the prior general election will have higher likelihoods of being represented by a woman as well as having

---

[5] Some districts in New Hampshire and Vermont elect more than one candidate to office. For these districts, the winning party was assigned to the candidate with the highest number of votes.

female candidate vie for that office (see methodological appendix for more detail on variable construction and modeling decisions).

The results are consistent with the electoral competition hypotheses. New England districts that exhibit more party competition are more likely to see women run for legislative office.[6] Importantly, as we see in column 2 of Table 12.3, this holds true for both those seeking office *and* those elected. For every 1 percentage point *decrease* in the electoral gap between the top two candidates of differing parties from the prior election cycle, there was a 0.37 percent higher likelihood that a woman would win the seat. Women are more likely to run, and win, in New England where the two parties are more evenly matched.

Digging further into the state-level data from the logistic regression confirms the trends we saw among New England states for electing women in stunning fashion. Compared to districts in Massachusetts, districts in other New England states have higher likelihoods of women running for office: 50 percent higher likelihood for Connecticut, 75 percent for Maine, 250 percent for New Hampshire, 11 percent for Rhode Island, and 169 percent for Vermont. The same is true for women being elected to office: 15 percent higher likelihood for Connecticut, 14 percent for Maine, 128 percent for New Hampshire, 27 percent for Rhode Island, and 124 percent for Vermont. These likelihoods provide more context for the patterns uncovered in the longitudinal analysis: Massachusetts performs comparatively poorly in eliciting female candidates as well as in electing them compared to the other New England states. Reminder: What state is worst in state legislative competitiveness in New England? Massachusetts—the 46th among the 50 states (Ballotpedia). New Hampshire, by contrast, is second among the fifty states for state legislative competitiveness—and is 128 percent more likely to elect a woman than Massachusetts.

What does the rest of Table 12.3 tell us? First, compared to races for the state Senate, races for the state House have higher likelihoods of female candidates running as well as being elected to office. This is likely because the Senate is more prestigious than the House, making it more attractive to

---

[6] For every 1 percentage point decrease in the electoral gap between the top two candidates of different parties from the prior election cycle, there was a higher likelihood (1%) that a woman would run for district office. The predicted probabilities of a women running for a seat in the MA statehouse in a district in which a Democrat had been elected in the prior general election drops from 0.43 for very competitive races (difference in percentage of votes = 0) to 0.38 for less competitive races (difference in percentage of votes = 20).

TABLE 12.3: Logistic Regression Coefficients – District Level

VARIABLE	FEMALE CANDIDATE (STANDARD ERROR)	FEMALE ELECTED OFFICIAL (STANDARD ERROR)
Electoral Competition $_{t-2}$ (Difference in % of votes – top 2 parties)	0.9898093*** (0.0010472)	0.9963061*** (0.0012013)
Office (House relative to Senate)	1.039874 (0.0450148)	1.211982*** (0.0555255)
Opponent $_{t-2}$ (Uncontested Race vs. Contested)	0.6591039*** (0.0586471)	0.8625318 (0.08408)
Winning Party $_{t-2}$ (Relative to Rep Party)		
Democratic	1.093451** (0.0413855)	1.48498*** (0.0591091)
Independent	1.250262 (0.2869988)	1.255236 (0.2949021)
Other	0.7909684** (0.0754629)	1.173296 (0.1125375)
State (Relative to Massachusetts)		
Connecticut	1.503336*** (0.0842648)	1.154948** (0.0714792)
Maine	1.74901*** (0.1000556)	1.136201** (0.0720009)
New Hampshire	3.495179*** (0.2174491)	2.277542*** (0.1486471)
Rhode Island	1.111893 (0.069525)	1.270892*** (0.0832331)
Vermont	2.691599*** (0.1801906)	2.241769*** (0.1558573)
Electoral Competition $_t$ (Difference in % of votes – top 2 parties)		0.9939833*** (0.0011892)
Opponent $_t$ (Uncontested Race vs. Contested)		0.81931** (0.0795388)
Constant	1.023199*** (0.1245093)	0.4886732 (0.0744299)
N	15,430	15,430

Note: * = $p < 0.10$; ** = $p < 0.05$; *** = $p < 0.01$

men—especially when combined with the fact that women tend to run later in life, making it more difficult to achieve top offices. Second, female candidates are more likely to run for office in district races which were previously uncontested. Taken together with the previous finding on electoral competition, this result indicates that women in New England are more likely to enter those races they think they can win, running in previously contested districts with very narrow margins of victory or previously uncontested districts. Third, the data reveals too that compared to districts that voted Republican in the prior general election year, districts that voted Democratic have higher likelihoods of women running (9.3% higher) and winning office (48.5% higher). This suggests that in New England, for the time period examined, Democratic districts are more inviting to female candidates. This aligns well with what we saw in the party breakdowns among Democratic and Republican women in all levels of office within New England. There are far more female elected officials among Democrats than Republicans.

NEW ENGLAND LEGISLATIVE RACES AND THE PROFESSIONALIZATION HYPOTHESIS

We demonstrated how state rankings suggest that, in general, the more professional the New England legislature, the lower percentage of women among its officeholders. But does this result hold up in our more compelling statistical analyses? Short answer: yes.

To formally test the professionalization hypothesis via the regression analysis tool, we collected data on the biennium salaries of legislators (i.e., base amount paid to legislators) from the Book of the States. We again constructed dependent variables that captured *women running in New England* (the ratio of total number of female candidates to district races for each state-year) and *women winning in New England* legislative races (percentage of district offices held by women for each biennium). Electoral competitiveness was again accounted for in the analyses.

Additional controls included the percentage of districts won by Democrats and percentage of districts won by Republicans in the previous election. This helps account for the fact that there are more female candidates who are Democrats than Republicans in New England. We also control for gender bias by including data from the US Census Bureau's American Community Survey on gender wage gaps, as measured by women's median earnings as a percentage of men's for each state's general election year (Altonji and Blank 1999; Bertrand 2011; Le Barbanchon and Sauvagnat 2022).

As hypothesized, an *increase* in salary is associated with a *decrease* in the ratio of female candidates running for office—as indicated by the negative sign on the biennium salary coefficient in Table 12.4. Depending on the

TABLE 12.4: Pooled OLS Regression Coefficients – State Level

VARIABLE	RATIO OF FEMALE CANDIDATES TO DISTRICT RACES * 100 (ROBUST STANDARD ERROR)	% OF DISTRICTS WITH FEMALE ELECTED OFFICIALS (ROBUST STANDARD ERROR)
Biennium Salary $_{t-2}$ (Base salary for 2 years, lagged)	-0.4141354** (0.1103379)	-0.1485016* (0.0638649)
% Competitive Races $_{t-2}$ (% races with margin of victory ≤ 10%)	0.5256615 (0.3520871)	0.3442549 (0.3175103)
% Races with an Opponent $_{t-2}$	-0.2391272 (0.2160564)	-0.1931332 (0.1225273)
% Dem Wins $_{t-2}$ (% of district races won by Democrats)	0.2669644* (0.1344431)	0.1242575 (0.1001487)
% Rep Wins $_{t-2}$ (% of district races won by Republicans)	-0.1053175 (0.1359665)	-0.0342052 (0.0802055)
Wage Equality (Women's as % of Men's Earnings)	0.437263 (0.2322222)	0.2506025 (0.1369851)
State (Relative to Rhode Island)		
Connecticut	35.96755*** (7.592069)	19.80416** (7.113909)
Maine	31.58133*** (6.228833)	17.59834** (6.08647)
Massachusetts	34.07876** (8.791609)	8.350136 (4.834069)
New Hampshire	16.5952** (4.661206)	0.7958407 (3.492597)
Vermont	18.36232*** (2.607928)	10.50453*** (2.572287)
% Competitive Races $_t$ (% races with margin of victory ≤ 10%)		-0.0813377 (0.1128732)
% Races with an Opponent $_t$		-0.1855919 (0.1218516)
Constant	-0.3783197 (18.01629)	17.6633 (8.404104)
N	71	71

Note: * = $p < 0.10$; ** = $p < 0.05$; *** = $p < 0.01$

state and year, a $10,000 increase in biennium salary—$5000 more for each term—could translate to seventeen to eighteen fewer female candidates running for district office. A similar relationship was found between legislative professionalism and females being in state legislative seats: higher salaries translate to lower percentages of districts with female elected officials. Hence, even with the inclusion of the control variables, legislative professionalization is negatively associated with women in New England both running for the state legislature and winning a seat.

The data also revealed a positive, though not statistically significant, relationship between electoral competition (percentage of races with margins of victory less than or equal to 10%) and election of women to legislative office: higher numbers of competitive races in previous elections lead to more women being elected to office in subsequent elections. This is also true for the ratio of female candidates to district races. This suggests that *both* electoral competition and legislative professionalization drive differences among the New England states.

Conclusion

As a region, New England is comparatively good for electing women. Democratic women that is. But is it a liberal oasis of gender equity? Hardly. Only New Hampshire has a majority female congressional delegation, and only Maine has exact gender parity among those it sends to Congress. Despite the fact women gained the right to vote just over a hundred years ago, no New England state legislature has gender parity. Only two states have female governors. All New England states have significant gaps between the percentage of women of color in their population and the percentage of said women in office. There is substantial variation among the New England states for electing women overtime, but Massachusetts is almost always back of the pack with Vermont and New Hampshire generally leading the way. From the twin perspectives of descriptive and substantive representation then, New England largely falls short. Improvement, yes, but the evidence does not suggest that New England is on a pre-ordained path to representational equity. When it comes to who New Englanders see in office, and thus perceive as "natural fits" for politics, men remain the default. And, with women but rarely achieving parity in office, we also know that the agenda space, the issues state governments or state delegations prioritize, remains more likely to be centered around traditionally male priorities.

Our rigorous empirical analyses revealed two reasons for why the variation exists among the New England states in electing women—legislative professionalization and electoral competition. The more resourced the state legislature, and hence more prestigious, the less likely one is to see female candidates running for, and being elected to, these spots. Massachusetts vies for last in show over the 102-year panel and is worst in New England in 2024. Massachusetts is also the highest in legislative professionalism. Additionally, where party competition is low, women are less likely to run and win legislative seats. So the variation among the New England states in electing women is, in no small way, attributable to the variation in GOP party strength across the region. Where New England is "more than blue," as measured by competitive elections between Democrats and Republicans, females are more likely to hold legislative seats.

In New England politics then, there is real irony in the fact that electing so many Democrats is, on average, better for representing women's interests, but it is also more likely that women run where Republicans continue to put up an electoral fight. And, in another irony all too familiar to women, the less prestigious and resourced the legislature, the more likely one is to see women in said offices. Yankee ingenuity involves making do with less by using one's wits—making it work despite lacking seemingly vital resources. In New England, women are more apt to be in elected positions that require using their Yankee ingenuity because the position they've won does not pay well nor provide full staff support. In electoral politics then, Yankee ingenuity is gendered.

APPENDIX
Methodology for Regression Analyses in Chapter 12

We performed two sets of logistic regressions to determine what factors increase the likelihood of a *female candidate running for state legislature* and the likelihood of a *women being elected to state legislature* at the district-level. In the first set (Table 12.3), we hypothesized that districts with higher levels of electoral competitiveness in the prior general election (as measured by lower differences in the percentage of votes cast between the top two candidates in a district) would have higher likelihoods of being represented by a woman as well as having female candidate vie for that office. Other control variables included office sought (state House or Senate) and dummy variables for the presence of an opponent in the previous district race, the party that won the seat in the previous cycle, and state. Some districts in New Hampshire and Vermont elect more than one candidate to office. For these districts, the winning party was assigned to the candidate with the highest number of votes. The percentage of votes won for each party does not reflect the total number of votes won by all candidates of each respective party but reflects the percentage of votes won by the candidate with the highest number of votes within each party. The difference in these percentages was used to measure electoral competitiveness. The regression model for women being elected to state legislature also included that district-year's overall level of electoral competitiveness and the presence of an opponent. Variables in the model denoted by t-2 subscripts represent values from the prior general election year.

$$\text{Female Candidate} = \beta_0 + \beta_1 \textit{ Electoral Competition}_{t-2} + \beta_2 \textit{ Office} + \beta_3 \textit{ Opponent}_{t-2} + \beta_4 \textit{ Winning Party}_{t-2} + \beta_5 \textit{ State}$$

$$\text{Female Elected Official} = \beta_0 + \beta_1 \textit{ Electoral Competition}_{t-2} + \beta_2 \textit{ Office} + \beta_3 \textit{ Opponent}_{t-2} + \beta_4 \textit{ Winning Party}_{t-2} + \beta_5 \textit{ State} + \beta_6 \textit{ Electoral Competition}_t + \beta_7 \textit{ Opponent}_t$$

In these models, 15,430 of all 17,081 observations—or district-level races—were used in the analyses. Because data from the previous general election cycle were used in the logistic regressions and because our observations begin from 1990, observations for 1990 for all state districts were dropped. If new districts had no parallel district reference in the previous election cycle, they could not be matched with lagged data for electoral competition, presence of an opponent, and winning party; these observations were dropped because of redistricting.

The second set of regression analyses (Table 12.4) formally tested the professionalization hypothesis. Using the New England districts database, collapsed to state-level, we constructed dependent variables that captured how many *female candidates ran for state legislature* (the ratio of total number of female candidates to district races for each state-year) and how many *women won NE legislative races* (percentage of district offices held by women for each biennium). We collected data on the biennium salaries of legislators (i.e., base amount paid to legislators). Though the aforementioned Squire Index incorporates three aspects of professionalism (i.e., salary and benefits, time demands of service, and staff and resources), Bowen and Greene (2014) have found that disaggregating the components of multidimensional scales and analyzing the components individually to be beneficial particularly since multidimensional scales such as the Squire Index are not updated annually. The US Inflation Calculator was used to calculate each year's base salary in 2010 dollars: https://www.usinflationcalculator.com/. Electoral competitiveness was accounted for again. First, by determining the percentage of districts for each state and year where the margin of victory between the top two candidates was less than or equal to 10 percent—the margin that typically defines a "competitive race" (Ballotpedia). Second, electoral competitiveness was accounted for by including data on the percentage of districts where candidates faced an opponent.

Additional controls included the percentage of districts won by Democrats and the percentage of districts won by Republicans in the previous election as well as gender bias (voter bias and gender socialization). For the latter, one-year estimates from the US Census Bureau's American Community Survey on gender wage gaps were used for each New England state, each general election year. The gender wage gap measured women's median earnings as a percentage of men's. We use a pooled OLS regression to determine whether the level of professionalism of New England state legislative offices correlates with fewer female candidates running for and winning state legislative office. Fixed effects and random effects regressions were run, but the Hausman specification test indicated that the random effects model was preferred. The Breusch-Pagan Lagrange Multiplier (LM) test indicated that there was no significant difference across the states (i.e., no panel effect). Therefore, the pooled OLS regression was used with clustered standard errors.

$$\text{Ratio of Female Candidates} = \beta_0 + \beta_1 \textit{ Biennium Salary}_{t-2} +$$
$$\beta_2 \text{ \% Competitive Races}_{t-2} + \beta_3 \text{ \% Opponent}_{t-2} + \beta_4 \text{ \% Dem Wins}_{t-2} +$$
$$\beta_5 \text{ \% Rep Wins}_{t-2} + \beta_6 \text{ Wage Equality} + \text{ß}_i \text{ States}$$
$$\text{\% Women in Office} = \beta_0 + \beta_1 \textit{ Biennium Salary}_{t-2} +$$
$$\beta_2 \text{ \% Competitive Races}_{t-2} + \beta_3 \text{ \% Opponent}_{t-2} + \beta_4 \text{ \% Dem Wins}_{t-2} +$$
$$\beta_5 \text{ \% Rep Wins}_{t-2} + \beta_6 \text{ Wage Equality} + \text{ß}_i \text{ States} +$$
$$\beta_7 \text{ \% Competitive Races (at 10\%)}_t + \beta_8 \text{ \% Opponent}_t$$

Because the 17,081 observations at the district-level were collapsed to the state-year level and lagged, there were only ninety-five units of observation (16 biennia for 5 states and 15 biennia for Vermont, since 2022 data was unavailable). Gender wage gap data was only available for biennia from 1998 to 2020, so the number of observations was further reduced to 71 (12 biennia for 5 states and 11 biennia for Vermont). 79.8 percent of the variance in the sample is explained by our model with statistically significant values for the biennium salary coefficient and state constants.

Works Cited

Bos, Angela, Jill Greenlee, Mirya Holman, Zoe Oxley, and J. Celeste Lay. 2021. "This One's for the Boys: How Gendered Political Socialization Limits Girls' Political Ambition." *American Political Science Review* 116, no. 2: 484–501.
Center for Women in American Politics (CAWP). 2024. "Facts: Women in State Legislatures 2024." Eagleton Institute of Politics, Rutgers University.
Center for Women in American Politics (CAWP). 2023. "Facts: Women of Color in Elective Office 2021." Eagleton Institute of Politics, Rutgers University.
———. 2023. "State Fact Sheet—Connecticut."
———. 2023. "State Fact Sheet—Maine."
———. 2023. "State Fact Sheet—Massachusetts."
———. 2023. "State Fact Sheet—New Hampshire."
———. 2023. "State Fact Sheet—Rhode Island."
———. 2023. "State Fact Sheet—Vermont."
———. 2023. "Women in the U.S. Congress."
Dodson, Debra. 2006. *The Impact of Women in Congress*. Oxford: Oxford University Press.
Dolan, Julie, Melissa Deckman, and Michele Swers. 2021. *Women and Politics: Paths to Power and Political Influence*. New York: Rowman and Littlefield.
Evans, Sara. 1980. *Personal Politics: The Roots of Women's Liberation in the Civil Rights Movement and the New Left*. New York: Vintage.
Key, V.O., Jr. 1949. *Southern Politics in State and Nation*. New York: Knopf.

Keyssar, Alexander. 2011. "How Americans Vote." *Election Law Journal: Rules, Politics, and Policy* 10, no. 4: 471–473.

MacDonald, Jason, and Erin O'Brien. 2011. "Quasi-Experimental Design, Constituency, and Advancing Women's Interests: Reexamining the Influence of Gender on Substantive Representation." *Political Research Quarterly* 64, no. 2: 472–486.

Mariani, Mack. 2008. "A Gendered Pipeline? The Advancement of State Legislators to Congress in Five States." *Politics & Gender* 4, no. 2: 285–308.

McGlen, Nancy, Karen O'Connor, Laura van Assendelft, and Wendy Gunther-Canada. 2010. *Women, Politics, and American Society*. New York: Longman.

National Conference of State Legislatures. 2021. "Full- and Part-Time Legislatures." https://www.ncsl.org/research/about-state-legislatures/full-and-part-time-legislatures.aspx.

O'Brien, Erin. 2022. "Women, Women of Color in Massachusetts Politics: Not So Exceptional." In *The Politics of Massachusetts Exceptionalism: Reputation Meets Reality*, edited by Jerold Duquette and Erin O'Brien, 254–281. Amherst and Boston: University of Massachusetts Press.

Piven, Frances Fox, and Richard Cloward. 1988. *Why Americans Don't Vote*. New York: Pantheon.

Piven, Frances Fox, Lorainne Minnite, and Margaret Groarke. 2009. *Keeping Down the Black Vote: Race and the Demobilization of American Voters*. New York: NYU Press.

Ransford, Paige, Carol Hardy-Fanta, and Ann Marie Cammisa. 2007. "Women in New England Politics." *New England Journal of Public Policy* 23, no. 1/2: 17–36.

Reingold, Beth. 2012. "Women as Officeholders: Linking Descriptive and Substantive Representation." In *Political Women and American Democracy*, edited by Christina Wolbrecht, Karen Beckwith, and Lisa Baldez, 167–180. Boston: Cambridge University Press.

Rosenstone, Steven, and John Mark Hansen. 1993. *Mobilization, Participation, and Democracy in America*. New York: Macmillan Publishing Company.

Sanbonmatsu, Kira. 2002. "Political Parties and the Recruitment of Women to State Legislatures." *The Journal of Politics* 64, no. 3: 791–809.

Schattschneider, E.E. 1942. "Party Government." *National Municipal Review* 31, no. 4: 220–42.

Schattschneider, E.E. 1960. *Semi-Sovereign People: A Realist's View of Democracy in America*. Boston: Cengage Learning.

Shivaram, Deepa. 2022. "Vermont Ends Streak as the Last State to Send a Woman to Congress." NPR. November 8. https://www.npr.org/2022/11/08/1134352130/vermont-balint-election-day-results-2022.

Swers, Michelle. 2002. *The Difference Women Make: The Policy Impact of Women in Congress*. Chicago: University of Chicago Press.

Squire, Peverill. 2007. "Measuring State Legislative Professionalism: The Squire Index Revisited." *State Politics & Policy Quarterly* 7, no. 2: 211–227.

Squire, Peverill. 2017. "A Squire Index Update." *State Politics & Policy Quarterly* 17, no. 4: 361–371.

World Population Review. 2022. "Whitest States 2022." https://worldpopulationreview.com/state-rankings/whitest-states.

CHAPTER 13

CONCLUSION

Amy Fried and Erin O'Brien
Professor of Political Science | Associate Professor of Political Science
University of Maine | University of Massachusetts Boston

The chapters in this volume examine the politics of New England—a section of the United States that has had an enormous impact on the development of the nation but has, until now, received relatively little scholarly attention in recent decades. Taken together, the authors inquire about the culture and demography of New England and its partisan slant, asking to what extent it is "more than Yankee" and "more than blue."

In the past, New England epitomized the culture and politics of Yankeeism—thrifty, pragmatic, blunt-talking but civil, caring for one's community, and civically involved while also respecting others' choices. "Good fences make good neighbors," as Robert Frost, a poet long associated with New England, put it in "The Mending Wall." When living in England, where he first published that poem, Frost wrote to a friend about his soon-to-be fulfilled wish to find "a farm in New England where I could live cheap and get Yankier and Yankier" (Paton 2018, 17). Despite many positives listed, the cultural trope of the New England Yankees was also associated with an exclusivity rooted in whiteness and maleness, especially in political power.

Has that Yankeeism persisted today? The answer is complicated. As Rachael Cobb writes, when it comes to civic participation, New England states have high voting rates during presidential elections, and nearly all have voting laws that make it easy to register to vote and to cast one's ballots. Two states, Maine and Vermont, are the only ones in the nation to allow felons to vote when incarcerated and all but two states allow voters to register on Election Day (Cobb, this volume). Most New England states do not require voter identification to cast one's ballot. Where they do exist, it is unusual in that the adoption of these laws spanned party lines, as they were passed under Democratic control in Rhode Island and Republican control in New Hampshire.

Direct engagement of citizens—in town meetings and similar settings—has been another aspect of New England Yankeeism. However, as Cobb explains, the New England town meetings touted by Alexis de Tocqueville garner little love and involvement, and local elections attract few voters. And, as Dante Scala shows, another quintessentially and beloved Yankee practice—the grilling of candidates in the first-in-the-nation New Hampshire primary—was bypassed by candidate Donald Trump in 2016, and given but passing attention in 2024, as the former president balanced court appearances and campaigning. Yet he still beat the second-place candidate in New Hampshire by 20 percentage points in 2016 and 11 percentage points in 2024. Although civility combined with straightforwardness is emblematic of Yankee culture, the strength of support for Trump and growing polarization and negative partisanship suggests that national trends are exerting a pull on the region's political culture. The state chapters on Connecticut, Maine, and Massachusetts all note how the GOP party organizations in these states have become dominated by Trump aligned or Trump sympathetic forces—largely to their electoral detriment.

The gendered aspect of Yankeeism has been challenged in New England—in part. As the analysis of Jane JaKyung Han and Erin O'Brien reveals, five of six New England states are in the top half of states when it comes to women in state legislatures and three are in the top ten. These women are disproportionately white and Democratic, yet deeply blue Massachusetts is in the bottom half of states in its percentage of female state legislators. What matters the most to how well women candidates do is how professional the state legislature is and if elections are more competitive. The less appealing the office, as measured by legislative professionalism, the more likely it is that a woman runs for office and wins elective office. Said differently, offices that require more Yankee ingenuity to get anything done because of a comparative lack of staff and salary supports, are the ones where women are more likely to hold the office.

While New England remains a very white region, its states have become more racially diverse; that's happened more in some places than others and along different timelines. At the same time, as Jiménez discusses, the immigration of new racial and ethnic groups is nothing new for New England. Whether those groups became politically powerful depended in large part on where they settled and how they connected to existing centers of power. Today, he shows, there is considerable variation in the political incorporation of Blacks, Latino, and Asian Americans within New England and in their partisan loyalties. Like what is seen nationally, Black and Latino voters are more Democratic, though the latter is slipping, while Asian Americans split their votes between major party candidates. Black candidates and officeholders have generally experienced more success, and hold more sway over the party, in large part, according to Luis Jiménez because there is less within group diversity in political identification—Latinos and Asian Americans understand themselves as coming from more diverse countries of origin and cultural traditions.

Beyond Yankeeism, New England's political imprint on the United States also has been quite strong. Over one hundred and fifty years before the First Amendment prohibited "respecting an establishment of religion, or prohibiting the free exercise thereof," Roger Williams founded what would become Rhode Island as a refuge for Jews, Quakers, and others seeking religious freedom. Generations of young children have drawn turkeys and Pilgrims' hats to celebrate Thanksgiving while the United American Indians of New England have protested it as a National Day of Mourning for fifty-two years in Plymouth, Massachusetts (United American Indians of New England 2022). Schoolchildren increasingly learn all these perspectives on the holiday and learn too about the Boston Tea Party and the creation of the Green Mountain Boys, in what is now Vermont, as key moments in resisting British colonial power, which ultimately led to the American Revolution and freedom from the king's rule. In the nineteenth century, Harriet Beecher Stowe, who was born in Connecticut, wrote the influential abolitionist novel *Uncle Tom's Cabin* in Brunswick, Maine in a home that was part of the Underground Railroad. In 2000, New Hampshire's four electoral votes literally picked the president, for without those, Republican George W. Bush would have lost the race (and there very well would have been no Florida recount and no recount-related court cases).

After the 2000 presidential race, New Hampshire and every other New England state voted Democratic statewide. And when New Englanders vote in US House and Senate races, the region has at least leaned Democratic since the start of the twenty-first century. After the 2022 midterms, while some House races were close, there were no Republican House members from New England. Moreover, there is only one Republican US Senator, Susan Collins of Maine, who was reelected in 2020.

However, as this book's chapters make clear, while there has been a transformation in partisanship over many decades from red to blue, New England is also more than blue. Not only do different parts of states have divergent political leanings, but, since 2000, New Englanders sometimes have chosen Republicans—typically center-right ones—to lead their states as governor and have given Republicans majorities in one or more chambers of their state legislatures.

To understand the broad sweep of political change in New England, as well as how it compares to other areas of the country, Amy Fried and Douglas B. Harris traced how well candidates from different political parties did from the early republic to 2020. They demonstrate that "New England's swing in party support has been at least as dramatic as what occurred in the former confederacy." Moreover, Fried and Harris argue that this shift occurred both because of what political leaders and strategists did in building Democratic coalitions, but also in reaction to what was going on with the Republican Party. Democrats like President Franklin D. Roosevelt and Maine's Ed Muskie reached out to new constituencies and gained their loyalty and support. What happened in New England reminds us that political parties cannot be healthy and successful over time if they just rely on their core supporters—their base—but also require attention to groups of voters that have not backed them before. Moreover, what leaders do in cultivating some can also backfire with others. For instance, Republicans' growing reliance on social conservatives and their use of racially oriented messages helped them shift the South and win elections, but their stances on these issues turned off voters in New England, a highly secular area of the nation.

But, as with much of American state politics, what is going on in New England politics varies by state. The states' histories, geographies, populations, laws, constitutions, and quirks all have local character. Even something as arbitrary as Rhode Island's small size, Maureen Moakley argues, affects how the state operates, with close relationships between elites of different sectors that sometimes bleed into all-too close connections and corruption in politics. Yet this tiny state finds its coziness challenged and changed by new groups of immigrants who have contributed to it addressing racial justice issues, as well as by progressives and professionals who reshaped laws on reproductive rights and countered long-standing fiscal concerns. As Scott McLean contends, Connecticut's suburbs have a major impact on elections in a state that used to choose Republicans and independents but is now mostly blue.

Maine is the largest geographically of the New England states, and, as James Melcher and Amy Fried show, its two congressional districts—one more urban and the other more rural—have moved apart politically. Mainers still bristle about the political involvement of people "from away," (i.e., out-of-staters). In contrast, politics in Vermont, another highly rural state, Paul

Petterson argues, was reshaped by the easier access enabled by the interstate highway system and the in-migration of those attracted to its recreational opportunities, cheap land, natural beauty, and sense of community. Unlike the other New England states, Vermont has no ocean coastline. Although there has been some pushback to these newer arrivals, mostly they have simply become Vermonters. Both Maine and Vermont have elected Democratic and Republican governors in the last two decades, but Maine's LePage was a product of the Tea Party and later associated with Trumpism, while Vermont's Phil Scott epitomizes moderate Republicanism. Meanwhile, Maine and Vermont have been quite blue in presidential races for quite a while (although Maine's Second Congressional District gave its electoral vote to Trump in 2016 and 2020; 2024 results forthcoming).

Massachusetts, with its vigorous technology and higher education sectors, is both cutting-edge in economics and learning, while resolutely old-school in its politics. From Boston Harbor to the Berkshires, like other states in New England, it has a strong sense of place, if an overemphasis on Boston to those Bay Staters outside the capital region. Bostonians like their prominence in state politics just fine. Er, wicked fine. As Jerold Duquette contends, insiders have cozy relationships in the state's legislature and governor's office while more diverse "outsiders" increasingly challenge these power centers—with significant success. While deeply blue in many respects, it has a history of selecting moderate Republican governors. And Duquette argues that the Massachusetts norm of legislative supremacy provides a healthy model for the nation's capital, both its imperial presidency and congressional dysfunction.

Located next to Massachusetts, with a small Atlantic shoreline, New Hampshire gained population for a time from what was called "Taxachussetts." Christopher Galdieri explains how these new residents remain concentrated on the New Hampshire/Massachusetts border with many still working in the Bay State. Nonetheless, they have been key players in the purpling of New Hampshire. It is hardly astonishing that a state whose motto is "Live Free or Die" retains its distaste toward income and sales taxes, but New Hampshire's state-level races are competitive even as Democratic presidential candidates have won every contest between 2004 and 2020. Galdieri notes that there are just too many elements of "New Hampshire weird" to draw major lessons for Washington DC—even though more than a few New Hampshirites think DC could learn a thing or two from them.

New England is a distinctive region with many variations across and within each state. Traditional Yankeeism does not dominate New England culturally as it once did, and the supremacy of rock-ribbed Republicanism is gone. While women and immigrants have gained office, their power has been constrained in many states. But as this volume shows, in many ways its tradition of vibrant, active, participatory politics still prevails.

Works Cited

Paton, Priscilla. 2018. "Going and Coming Back: The Many Houses of Robert Frost." *The Robert Frost Review*, no. 28: 11–25.

United American Indians of New England. 2022. "National Day of Mourning." Homepage. http://www.uaine.org/.

INDEX

Page numbers followed by an f indicate a figure.

abolitionism, 18, 26, 209–10
abortion. *See* reproductive rights
Adams, Charles, 18
Adams, John, 3, 16
Adams, John Quincy, 17
Affordable Care Act (2010), 96–97
African Americans: Caribbean and African immigrants, 212; communities of, 221; Democratic Party and, 211–12, 224; discrimination faced by, 210–11; enslaved brought to New England, 209; finances of, 223–24; Great Migration, 211; Underground Railroad and, 210, 254; voting rights for, 210
Aiken, George, 147–50, 153
American South, transformation of, 3, 7, 15–16, 209
Amo, Gabe, 134, 142, 212
Anderson, John, 63, 95
Anti-Masons, 17
Arthur, Chester, 3, 155
Arthur, Harold, 150
Asian Americans: Chinese laborers, 216–17; communities of, 221; elections and, 219–20; finances of, 223–24; housing and education concerns of, 218–19; languages of, 218; obstacles of, 217; political party affiliation of, 218; politics and, 225; relations with China, 218–19
Asian Community Development Organization, 218
Asiatic Barred Zone (1917), 217
Ayotte, Kelly, 108–9, 114–15, 121

Bailey, John, 39–40, 42, 49
Baker, Charlie, 90–93, 98, 168, 216
Baker v. Carr (1962), 151
Baldacci, John, 68, 71–73
Balint, Becca, 158, 228
Ballotpedia's 2022 Annual State Legislative Competitiveness Report, 172
Bangor Daily News, 174
Bankhead, William, 21–22
Barnum, P. T., 49

Barringer, Richard, 71
Bartlett, Josiah, 3
Bass, Charlie, 108, 116, 122
Bennett, Rick, 73–74
Benson, Craig, 107, 117
Beyle, Thad, 91
Biden, Joe: election (2020), 4, 44; in Massachusetts, 96; New England vote for, 187; in New Hampshire, 104, 109, 198, 200; New Hampshire primary and, 186, 201; in Vermont, 155–56, 159; vote splitting and, 63
Biden administration, 139, 228
Birmingham, Tom, 98
Bloomberg, Michael, 59
Blumenthal, Richard, 44–45
Blute, Peter, 96
Bolduc, Don, 116, 119
Boston Globe, 89
Bowles, Chester, 40
Bradley, Bill, 192, 198–99
Bradley, Jeb, 107, 116
Brazilians, 217
Brennan Center for Justice, 167
Brewster, Ralph Owen, 211
Brooke, Edward, 3, 96, 212
Brown, John, 127, 210
Brown, Scott, 96–97, 108, 114–15
Bryan, Frank, 150, 170, 191
Buckley, William F., 50
Bulger, William, 84–85, 92
Burns, Bob, 119
Bush, George H. W., 3, 37
Bush, George W.: election (2000), 110, 155; election (2006), 107; in New Hampshire, 186, 254; New Hampshire primary loss, 191–92, 194; presidency of, 114, 116, 158; Republican change, 45; in Vermont, 187n
Bush, Prescott, 49
Buttigieg, Pete, 200
Byrns, Joseph, 21

Cahill, Tim, 105
campaign financing, 51–52, 88–89, 134, 192

259

Campbell, Andrea, 233
Carter, Jimmy, 95, 197
Catholics and politics, 4, 19, 22, 25n, 40, 61, 82, 84, 130, 137, 208, 211. *See also* Irish immigrants
Cellucci, Paul, 98
Center for American Women and Politics (CAWP), 236, 241
Central Americans, 214
Chafee, John, 3, 114, 133
Chafee, Lincoln, 131, 133–35, 137–38, 178
Chau, Sokhary, 219
Chinese American Civic Organization, 218
Chinese Exclusion Act (1882), 217
Christie, Chris, 117, 201
Cianci, Buddy, 5, 129
Cicilline, David, 134–35
Citizens United v. F.E.C. (2010), 51
civics education, 179
Civil Rights Act (1964), 15n
Clay, Henry, 17
Clinton, Bill, 28, 50, 60, 107, 110, 155, 191
Clinton, Hillary, 44, 60, 104, 108, 110, 155–56, 187n, 199
Coakley, Martha, 98
Cobb, Rachael, 8–9, 11, 252
Coffin, Frank, 24
Cohen, Bill, 62
Collins, Susan, 4, 15, 59, 62–63, 69, 71, 75, 228, 230, 254
Colombians, 214
congressional elections: ethnic makeup of, 231–32; New England Democratic swing, 26–28, 29f, 30; women in government office, 230, 231f
Conley, Patrick, 129
Connecticut: African Americans in, 213; Asian Pacific American Coalition, 218; campaign financing, 89; challenge primary system, 37–38, 40–42, 49; Citizen Election Fund plan, 51; civics education, 180; colonial constitution and Congregational Church, 207; convenience voting, 173, 177; county government eliminated, 68; Democratic Party in, 5–6, 37, 39–46, 54–55, 208; diversity in, 46–47, 221, 235; Dominicans in, 213; electoral competition and, 242; enslaved people in, 209–10; ethnic makeup of, 8, 206; felon voting rights, 175–76; focusing events in, 53–54; gas tax holiday, 89; gubernatorial elections, 39–40, 47; identification requirements, 177–78; Know-Nothing Party in, 207; legislative professionalism in, 239–40, 244; local contested elections, 172; maverick tradition, 49–50, 52; millionaire mavericks, 38, 49–52; one person, one vote in, 9; online voter registration, 54; party identification, 41, 45, 47; party registration in, 41f, 42; poverty or wealth in, 43–45; public campaign financing, 51; Puerto Ricans in, 213; registration deadlines, 174; Republicans in, 37–39, 41–42, 44–46, 48, 51, 54–55; rural-urban divide, 208; Sandy Hook Elementary and gun control, 53; state constitutions, 38, 42; Toleration Party of, 207; unaffiliated voters, 40–42, 44, 46–48, 51, 53, 55; Unidad Latina en Acción, 215; urban suburban divide, 42, 45, 255; voter registration online and automatic, 176; women in government office in, 230, 232; women in state legislature, 233, 237–38; women voters in, 45, 48
Conte, Silvio, 96
Coolidge, Calvin, 3, 155
COVID pandemic, 54–55, 109, 115, 130, 139, 159, 219
Crandall, Prudence, 211
Cross, Wilber, 39, 49
Cruz, Ted, 104, 195
Cullen, Fergus, 120
Curtin, Ken, 62n, 64

Davis, Deane, 151, 153
Davis, John, 19
Day, Aaron, 115
Dean, Howard, 152, 155–57, 199
Delaware, 37
Democratic National Committee (DNC), 5, 185–86, 200, 202
Democratic Party: Austin-Boston alliance, 22; civil rights and, 24; convention delegation rules, 21; New England votes for, 18–21; party building, 4; solid South and, 20; transformation to, 6, 16, 26, 29, 31, 254; women in, 229–32, 234, 236, 247
Democratic- Republicans, 17
demographic changes: immigration and, 8; racial diversity and, 8, 224, 253–54
DeSantis, Ron, 11, 201
DeStefano, John, 48
Dewey, Thomas, 190
Diehl, Geoff, 93–94
disenfranchisement, 175–76

INDEX   261

diversity. *See* demographic changes
DiZoglio, Diana, 94–95
Dobbs v. Jackson Women's Health Organization (2022), 54, 120
Dodd, Thomas, 40, 49–50
Dole, Bob, 107, 110
Dorr, Thomas, 207
Douglas, James, 152, 159, 161
Douglass, Frederick, 210
Du Bois, W. E. B., 210
Duffey, Joseph, 50
Dukakis, Michael, 3, 82, 86–87, 106
Duquette, Jerold, 5–6, 9–10, 256
Duvalier, François (Papa Doc), 212
Duvalier, Jean-Claude (Baby Doc), 212

Ecuadorians, 214
Edwards, Eddie, 117
Eisenhower, Dwight D., 23, 28, 131, 190
Elazar, Daniel, 9, 61, 83–86, 126
elections, early republic and, 16–17
electoral college, 4, 17, 19–20, 27n8, 185–86
Elorza, Jorge, 216
Emerson, Lee, 150
Emerson, Ralph Waldo, 169
Espinosa, Carmen Elisa, 216

Farley, James, 21, 60
Federalists, 16–17
Flaherty, Charles, 92
Flanders, Ralph, 149
Foley, Tom, 48, 52
Fox, Gordon, 5
Franks, Gary, 212
Free Soil Party, 17–18
French Canadians, 208, 211
Fried, Amy, 4, 9–10, 255
Frost, Robert, 252
Fung, Allan, 135, 219–20

Galdieri, Christopher, 9–10, 256
Gallo, George, 51
Garcia, Marilinda, 117
Garrison, William Lloyd, 3, 211
Gibson, Ernest W., 149–50
Gingrich, Newt, 15, 195
Giuliani, Rudy, 194
Golden, Jared, 63, 65n, 71
Goldthwait, Jill, 73–74
Goldwater, Barry, 24–25
Gorbea, Nellie, 216
Gore, Al, 155, 187n, 198–99
Graham, Lindsay, 115

Grasso, Ella, 40
Great Depression, 20, 28, 39, 208
Great Society, 15, 30
Green, T. F., 130
Green Party, 63
Gregg, Judd, 114, 122
Grossman, Steve, 98
Guinta, Frank, 108–9, 116

Hackett, Luther, 152
Hale, John P., 18
Haley, Nikki, 104, 109, 185, 201
Han, Jane JaKyung, 9, 11, 253
Hancock, James, 3
Hansel, George, 119
Harris, Douglas B., 4, 10, 255
Hart, Gary, 198
Hassan, Maggie, 108–9, 115–17, 119, 121–22
Hayes, Jahana, 212, 232
Healey, Maura, 93–94, 98
Heppen, John, 5
Hodes, Paul, 108, 114, 116
Hoff, Philip, 151
Hong Kong, 217
Hooker, Thomas, 38
Hooker's Fundamental Orders (1639), 38
Hoover, Herbert, 19–20
Hopkins, David, 26–27
Hopkins, Harry, 22
Humphrey, Gordon, 106, 121
Huntsman, Jon, 194–95

Ickes, Harold, 22
Immigration Act of 1965, 140
initiatives, 61, 64–67, 95, 130
Irish immigrants, 16, 23, 82, 130, 207–8
Ivry, Elizabeth, 64

Jackson, Andrew, 17
Jefferson, Thomas, 16, 169
Jeffords, James, 153–54, 157–59
Jiménez, Luis, 8, 11
Johnson, Gary, 63
Johnson, Lyndon B., 24, 106, 198, 201
Journal of Deliberative Democracy, 170

Kasich, John, 108, 197
Kavanaugh, Brett, 69
Kennedy, John F., 3, 24
Kennedy, Patrick, 134
Kennedy, Ted, 96–97
Kerry, John, 3, 107, 155–56, 186, 187n, 199
Key, V. O., Jr., 17

Keyser, F. Ray, 151–52, 161
Kim, Thomas, 218
King, Angus, 62–63, 69, 72–74
King, Ed, 82
King, Rufus, 17
Klarides, Themis, 44–45
Klobuchar, Amy, 200
Know-Nothing Party, 207–8
Ku Klux Klan, 61, 211
Kunin, Madeline, 152, 154
Kuster, Ann McLane, 108–9, 116–17

Lacy, Karyn, 46
Lamont, Ned, 37, 47–48, 50–55
Lamontagne, Ovide, 117
Landon, Alf, 60
Langevin, Jim, 135
Lappie, John, 171
Latingua, William, 215
Latinos: citizenship and legal residency of, 215; communities of, 221; Democratic Party and, 216; dissimilarity of different groups, 214–15; finances of, 223–24; migration of, 213–14; obstacles of, 214; political wins, 215–16; politics and, 224–25
Leahy, Patrick, 153–54, 157–58, 161
Leavitt, Karoline, 117, 119
Ledbetter, Stewart, 157
Leddy, Bernard, 150
Lee, Richard, 211
legislative professionalism, 9, 11–12, 126, 131, 229, 247, 249, 253. *See also* women in government offices; *individual states*
LePage, Paul, 5, 60–61, 65–66, 69, 72–73, 75, 256
Levy, Leora, 44
liberalism, 5, 60, 157
libertarianism, 6
Libertarians, 6, 119, 127, 132, 195
Liberty Union Party, 147, 153–54
Lieberman, Joseph, 49–51
Lockard, Duane, 149, 161
Lodge, Henry Cabot, 3
Longley, James, 62
Lynch, John, 107–9, 117, 178
Lyons, Jim, 92

Machtley, Ronald, 134
Madison, James, 17
Magaziner, Seth, 135
Maine: African Americans in, 212–13; "from away," 10, 59, 61, 65, 67, 71, 255; campaign funding, 71; civics education, 180; Clean Elections policy, 8–9, 66, 89; conservative or liberal, 60; convenience voting, 177; Democratic Party in, 23–24, 60, 69, 71; demographics of, 60–61; diversity in, 221, 235; election laws, 62, 64–66; election winners, 70f; electoral college rules, 5; electoral competition and, 242; felon voting rights, 175, 181; gubernatorial elections, 23–24, 72–73; gun control in, 59; identification requirements, 177–78; independent candidates and voters, 63–64; Irish immigrants in, 208; legislative professionalism in, 239–40, 244; legislative shared governance, 73; local contested elections, 172; local government in, 68; Mano en Mano, 215; Medicaid in, 73; Native Americans in, 61; party competition in, 24; people's veto, 67, 71, 174; political culture of, 61–62, 64, 72–74; politics of, 255; poverty rate for non-whites, 221; rank choice voting (RCV), 65, 67, 137; Republican Party in, 23, 69, 72; Republicans in, 60; rural nature of, 208; rural-urban divide, 6, 59–60, 71; same-day registration, 174; same sex marriage, 67n; school district consolidation, 69; separation from Massachusetts, 207; statewide initiative votes, 64–66, 71, 73–74, 89, 168; term limits, 65; ticket splitting, 61–64, 75; turnout for state and federal elections, 172–73; two Maines, 71; Unified Asian Communities, 218; voter access expansion, 168; voter registration online and automatic, 176; white population of, 8; women in government office in, 230, 232; women in state legislature, 233
Maine League of Women Voters, 66
Mainers for Fair Bear Hunting, 67
Maine Sportsmen's Alliance, 66
Maisel, L. Sandy, 64
Mallary, Richard, 153
Malloy, Dannel, 48, 52–53
Malone, Joe, 96n
Man with A Plan (film), 157
Marschall, Melissa, 171
Martin, John, 65
Massachusetts: African Americans in, 213; Asian American Resource Workshop Organization, 218; Asian Americans in, 217, 219; ballot measures, 82, 88, 95; big three, 90–92, 100; campaign financing,

89; Centro Latino, 215; civics education, 180–81; competitiveness in politics, 81–82, 92–93; Cubans in, 213; Democratic Party in, 6–7, 82–83, 86, 95–97, 101, 208; diversity in, 221, 235–36; Dominicans in, 213; electoral competition and, 242; enslaved people in, 209; establishment and anti-establishment, 85–87, 97; ethnic makeup of, 8; federal elections, 95–96, 98; felon voting rights, 175–76; gas taxes in, 89; government transparency, 85, 87, 93–95; governors' powers and elections, 82, 84, 86–87, 90–92, 94, 97–98, 100; Haitian immigrants, 212; identification requirements, 177–78; independent candidates and voters, 82; Irish Catholics in, 82, 84, 206; Know-Nothing Party in, 207; legislative professionalism in, 81–85, 99n8, 100, 181, 239–40, 244, 247; legislative supremacy, 81, 83, 86, 89–90, 92, 94, 100; local contested elections, 172; local elections, 98–99, 101; Massachusetts Clean Elections Law, 89; one party rule in, 83; political civility of, 9; political culture of, 82–85, 100; political professionalism, 100; poverty rate for non-whites, 221; racial diversity and gender equity, 87–88, 93; registration deadlines, 174; Republican governors of, 5; Republican Party (MassGOP) in, 82, 92–93, 96–98; rural-urban divide, 208; town meetings in, 170–71; voter access expansion, 168; voter registration online and automatic, 176; voter registrations, 99, 101; VOTES act (2022), 168; women in government office, 230, 232; women in state legislature, 233, 237–38
Massachusetts Bay Colony, 207
Massachusetts Supreme Judicial Court, 8
Matos, Sabina, 135, 139, 233
Mayhew, David, 23, 97–98
McCain, John, 50, 108, 115, 191–92, 194
McCarthy, Eugene, 197–98
McCarthy, Joseph, 62
McCormack, John, 22
McGovern, George, 197–98
McKee, Dan, 135, 139
McKinley, William, 20
McLean, Scott, 5, 9, 11, 255
McMahon, Linda, 51
McMullen, Jack, 157
Meetup.com, 156
Melcher, James, 9–10, 255

"The Mending Wall" (Frost), 252
Messner, Bryant "Corky," 115–16
Meyer, William, 150
Michaud, Mike, 71, 73–74
Mileur, Jerome, 27n7, 98
Mills, Janet, 61, 72–73
The Mirage of Democracy (Zuckerman), 170
Mitchell, George, 3, 62
Moakley, Maureen, 5, 10–11, 255
Mollis, Ralph, 178
Mondale, Walter, 95, 198
Monroe, James, 17
Moore, Greg, 104
Morales, David, 137
Morning Consult Poll, 91
Morse, Chuck, 116
Mowers, Matt, 117
Muskie, Ed, 4, 16, 23–24, 31, 60, 62, 196, 198, 255

Nader, Ralph, 63, 107, 187n
National Abortion Rights Action League (NARAL), 44
National Association for the Advancement of Colored People the (NAACP), 210
National Association of Colored Women's Clubs, 210
National Equal Rights League, 210
National Voter Registration Act of 1993, 174, 220n
Native Americans and National Day of Mourning, 254
Nelson, Garrison, 148
New Deal, 15–16, 19–22, 28, 30–31
New England Clean Energy Connect project, 67
New England Yankee, 7–8, 31, 180, 252
New Hampshire: abortion issue in, 120; Asian American education success, 219; Centro Latino de New Hampshire, 215; civics education, 180; congressional elections in, 110, 112f–13f; convenience voting, 177, 181; "cost of voting" index, 169n; Democratic Party in, 104, 106–9, 118; diversity in, 104, 118–19, 221, 235; electoral competition and, 242; enslaved people in, 209; felon voting rights, 175; Free State Project, 6; geography of, 105; government structure, 121; gubernatorial elections in, 117, 118f; gun control in, 115; House of Representatives elections in, 116–17; Know-Nothing Party in, 207; legislative professionalism in, 172,

New Hampshire: (*continued*)
239–40, 244; legislature of, 107; local contested elections, 172; Old Man of the Mountain, 105; presidential elections in, 110, 111f; presidential primary and, 4–5, 7; Progressive movement in, 189; Republican Party in, 104, 106, 108–9, 119–21; rural nature of, 208; same-day registration, 174; Senate elections in, 114–16; state house swings in, 6; taxation, 105; ticket splitting, 104; Town Meeting Day, 188–89; turnout for state and federal elections, 172n, 181; voter access restrictions, 168, 173; voter identification requirements, 177–78; voter registration online and automatic, 176; weirdness of, 9, 104–6, 110, 256; white population of, 8; women in government office in, 230; women in state legislature, 233, 237–38

New Hampshire Local Government Center, 188

New Hampshire primary: Democrats and, 197–200; first- in- the-nation primary, 185–86, 188–91, 200, 202; grilling of candidates, 253; Republicans and, 191–96, 201–2; undeclared voters and, 192n

New Hampshire Union Leader, 196

Nicholl, Don, 23

Nixon, Richard, 15n, 50, 131, 153

Noble, Elaine, 228

non-white population: census increases, 220–21; changes to, 224–25; income and poverty of, 222f–23f; politics of, 224. *See also* African Americans; Asian Americans; Latinos

NORC/AP VoteCast survey, 47

Obama, Barack, 97, 108, 114, 116, 155–56, 159, 199

O'Brien, Erin, 9, 11, 88, 253

O'Brien, John, 157

O'Brien, Shannon, 98

O'Connor, John, 22

O'Neill, Tip, 3, 22

Outlook, 189

Palmer, Kenneth T., 172

Pappas, Chris, 117, 121–22

partisan transformations, 15–16, 27, 29

Patrick, Deval, 91, 93, 213

Patten, Roland T., 64

Paul, Ron, 195

Pence, Mike, 115

Pérez, Eddie, 215

Perot, Ross, 63, 107, 155

Petterson, Paul, 11, 256

Phillips, Dean, 201

Pierce, Franklin, 3, 17

Pinckney, Charles, 17

Poirier, Paul, 161

Poliquin, Bruce, 65n, 71

popular vote, 5, 6f

presidential election (1848), 18

presidential election (1852), 18

presidential election (1928), 4, 19, 82, 130

presidential election (2020), 3

presidential elections and primaries: Democratic Party and, 24–26; in Maine, 71; New England and Democrats, 185–86, 187f; nomination results, 193f; primary schedule, 185–86, 190; Republican candidates, 191–96; state results, 194; "Super Tuesday," 190; turnout for, 62. *See also* New Hampshire primary

Pressley, Ayanna, 3, 212, 228, 232

Proctor, Mortimer, 149

Progressive Democrats, 87, 198–99

Progressive Mass, 87

Progressive Party, 154

Prouty, Winston, 152

Providence Journal, 128

Puerto Ricans, 140, 214–16

Quinn, Robert, 129

Quinnipiac Polls, 45–48, 54

Raimondo, Gina, 135–39, 228

Ram, Kesha, 219

Rayburn, Sam, 22

Reagan, Ronald, 15, 23, 26, 31, 95, 131

Reagan administration, 154, 159

Reed, Jack, 134

regionalism, 10

regional patterns of politics, 27

Reich, Robert, 98

religion: evangelical Christians and, 25; freedom of religion, 125–27, 254; George W. Bush and, 192; Puritans and, 85, 125–26, 206–7. *See also* Catholics and politics

Rell, Jodi, 48, 51

reproductive rights, 44, 54, 137

Republican Party: beginnings of, 18; conservatism of, 4; early republic and, 17; evangelical Christians and, 25; extremism of, 15, 24, 26; in New England, 16, 18–19; one member from New England, 4;

social conservatism of, 14, 25, 29; South and, 3, 10, 15, 24–25, 29, 31; Southern strategy, 15, 25; theocracy and, 14; urban rural split and, 254; women in, 230
Rhode Island: Act on Climate, 137; African Americans in, 141–42, 213; Bloodless Revolution (1935), 130; civics education, 180; commerce and trade in, 126–27; constitution and right to vote, 207; convenience voting, 177; corruption in, 5; Democratic Party in, 6, 126, 130–31, 208, 236; diversity in, 126, 134, 140–41, 221, 235; Dominicans in, 213; election laws, 137; election results, 132f; electoral competition and, 242; enslaved people in, 209; ethnic makeup of, 8; felon voting rights, 175–76; freedom of religion, 126; geography and demography of, 125–26; gubernatorial elections, 135; history of, 126–27; House of Representatives elections in, 134–35; identification requirements, 177–79; Independent Man statue, 125, 143; Know-Nothing Party in, 207; labor unions in, 127–28, 138; Latinos in, 139–40, 213; legislative elections, 135–36; legislative professionalism in, 239–40, 244; local contested elections, 172; Mafia in, 129; Native Americans in, 142; political corruption in, 129; poverty rate for non-whites, 221; presidential elections, 131, 133f; Progreso Latino, 215; Providence Plantations, 142–43; Puerto Ricans, 140; registration deadlines, 174, 181; Reproductive Privacy Act, 136; Republican Party in, 126, 130; "Rogue Island," 125; rural-urban divide, 131–33, 208; Senate elections in, 133–34; small state politics, 128–29; turnout for state and federal elections, 172n; unaffiliated voters in, 131; undocumented population of, 141; voter registration online and automatic, 176; women in government office, 138–39, 230, 232; women in state legislature, 233, 237–38
Rhode Island Political Cooperative, 139
Ribicoff, Abraham, 40, 49
R- I- N- O, (i.e., Republican- In- Name- Only), 92
Rivera, Maria, 216
Robinson, Donald, 170
Rockefeller Republicans, 50
Roe v. Wade (1973), 44, 54, 120, 136
Rogers, Ernest, 39

Romney, Mitt, 89, 98, 108, 191–92, 194–95
Roosevelt, Franklin D., 4, 16, 19–24, 26n, 31, 60, 82, 106, 130, 255. *See also* New Deal
Roosevelt, Theodore, 18–19, 28, 60
Roraback, J. Henry, 39
Rowland, John, 89
Rudman, Warren, 106
Ruffin, Josephine St. Pierre, 210
Ruggerio, Dominick, 136

Salmon, Thomas, 152
Salvadore, 141, 216
Sanders, Bernie, 3, 5, 108, 147–48, 150, 153–58, 161, 197–200, 202
Sandoval, Dolores, 154
Santorum, Rick, 195
Scala, Dante J., 4, 7, 11, 253
Schlesinger, Alan, 51
Schneider, Claudine, 134, 138
Scott, Phil, 152, 159, 161
Sentencing Project, 175
Shaheen, Jeanne, 104, 107–9, 114–15, 121, 228
Shankman, Sabrina, 63
Shays, Christopher, 14, 31, 37
Shea-Porter, Carol, 108–9, 116–17
Shekarchi, Joe, 136–37
Sherman, Roger, 3
Shumlin, Peter, 152
Silver, Nate, 104
Slater, Samuel, 127, 207
slavery issue, 17–18
Smith, Al, 4, 19–20, 82, 129–30
Smith, Bob, 110, 114
Smith, Kevin, 116
Smith, Margaret Chase, 62, 71, 228
Smith, Peter, 153–54, 161
Snelling, Richard, 152, 154, 156–57, 161
Snowe, Olympia, 3, 62–63, 69, 71
Somalians, 60–61, 221
Souter, David, 106
South Carolina primary, 200
Splaine, Jim, 190
Squire's Index, 239, 249
Stafford, Robert, 28n, 150, 153–54
Stassen, Harold, 190
state and federal elections, 172
"The State of State Standards for Civics and U.S. History in 2021," 179
Stefanowski, Bob, 47–48, 52, 55
Stevenson, Adlai, 62
Stone, Lucy, 3
Storey, Moorfield, 210

Stowe, Harriet Beecher, 211, 254
Sullivan, Kathy, 200
Sundquist, James L., 18
Sununu, Chris, 104–5, 108–9, 115–17, 119–22, 201
Sununu, John E., 107–8, 114, 191, 196, 196n, 216
Swett, Dick, 114
Swift, Jane, 98
Sytek, Donna, 196

Taft, William Howard, 18, 28, 60
Taiwan, 217
Tea Party, 15, 60, 72, 74, 116, 195, 256
Thomas, Stephanie, 233
Thomas B. Fordham Institute, 179–81
Thoreau, Henry David, 169
Thurber, Harris E., 151
ticket splitting, 61–64, 75, 104, 106
Tocqueville, Alexis de, 3, 9, 169, 252
Tong, William, 220
Torkildsen, Peter, 96
Town Meeting model, 168–71, 180–81
township and town meetings, 3, 8–9, 252–53
Trahan, David, 66
Trotter, William Monroe, 210
Trujillo, Rafael, 213
Truman, Harry S., 22, 24, 82
Trump, Donald J.: big lie, 116; in Connecticut, 53; extremism of, 15; Latinos and, 216; and LePage, 5; loss of state power and, 38; in Maine, 63, 69, 71, 186; in Massachusetts, 92, 96; in New Hampshire, 104, 108–10, 115, 117, 119–20, 191–92, 195–97, 202, 253; in Rhode Island, 131, 137; traditional Republicans and, 44–45; in Vermont, 156, 159, 197n
Truth, Sojourner, 210
Tsongas, Paul, 96
Tuttle, Fred, 157
Twilight, Alexander, 212n

Uncle Tom's Cabin (Stowe), 254
Union Leader, 108

Van Buren, Martin, 17–18
Vanderbeck, Robert M., 7
Varnum, Joseph, 21
Venezuelans, 214
Vermont: African Americans in, 213; Asian community of, 221; campaign financing, 89; civics education, 180; civil unions and gay marriages, 160; congressional elections in, 152–53; convenience voting, 177; Democratic Party in, 148, 150–55, 157; diversity in, 160–61, 221, 235; electoral competition and, 242; environmental policies, 160; farmer Fred Tuttle's candidacy, 157; felon voting rights, 175, 181; geography and demography of, 148, 159–60; gubernatorial elections, 152; gun control in, 154; identification requirements, 177–78; Independent candidates and voters, 148, 158; infrastructure modernization, 150–51; Irish immigrants in, 208; legislative professionalism in, 239–40, 244; legislative redistricting, 151; local contested elections, 172; "Mountain Rule," 149; nonpartisan primaries in, 159; political culture of, 148; poverty rate for non-whites, 221; presidential elections, 155–57; progressive purity of, 5; registration deadlines, 174; Republican Party in, 147–50, 152; rural nature of, 208; senate elections in, 153, 157; tilting left, 6; town meetings in, 170; unusual election rules, 158–59; voter registration online and automatic, 176; white population of, 8; women in government office, 154, 158, 230, 232; women in state legislature, 233, 237–38
voter access: convenience voting, 173, 176–77; expansion or restrictions, 167–69, 252; felon voting rights, 175; identification requirements, 177–78; registration deadlines, 173–74, 175f; same-day registration, 168–69, 174, 176, 181; voter registration online and automatic, 176
Voting Rights Act (1965), 15n

Warren, Elizabeth, 3, 93, 96–97, 200, 228
Washington Examiner, 196
Washington Post, 128
Watergate hearings, 50
Weicker, Lowell, 49–51
Welch, Peter, 157–59
Weld, William, 84–85, 91–92
Wendlandt, Dalila Argaez, 216
Whig Party, 16–17
Whitehouse, Sheldon, 134
Williams, Roger, 126, 143, 254
Williamson, Marianne, 201
Wilson, Woodrow, 18–19, 28, 60
Wirt, William, 17
women in government offices: diversity and, 232, 234f, 235; electoral competition and,

240–42, 243f, 244; ethnic makeup of, 228; executive officers, 232; importance of, 229–30; legislative professionalism, 238–40, 244, 245f, 246; longitudinal study of, 236–37; progress of, 138–39; state legislatures and, 9, 228, 233, 234f, 237–38, 253; variations between states, 238–39, 246–47; Vermont's first woman governor, 154
Wong, Lisa, 219
Wood, Gordon, 126
Woodard, Colin, 9

Woodrum, Clifton, 22
Working Families Party (WFP), 139
Wright, Jim, 22
Wu, Michelle, 219

Yankees and Yankeeism, 7, 83–85, 252–53, 256
York, Byron, 196
York, Myrth, 138

Zimmerman, Joseph, 170
Zippia (website), 81
Zuckerman, Michael, 170

AMY FRIED is professor emerita of Political Science at the University of Maine. Professor Fried's recent scholarly book, *At War With Government: How Conservatives Weaponized Distrust from Goldwater to Trump*, is co-authored with Douglas B. Harris in 2021. She is also the author of *Pathways to Polling: Crisis, Cooperation, and the Making of Public Opinion Professions* in 2012, *Muffled Echoes: Oliver North and the Politics of Public*, and many shorter works in scholarly edited volumes and journals. She also provides analysis to a wide range of media outlets and writes a biweekly column for the *Bangor Daily News*. Professor Fried won the 2019 Rising Tide Career Recognition Award, the 2016 Presidential Public Service Award from the University of Maine, and in 2015 was named the Outstanding faculty member in Service and Outreach by the College of Liberal Arts and Sciences. Professor Fried is serving as president of the New England Political Science Association 2024–2025.

ERIN O'BRIEN is a proud "Bostonian with Buckeye flair." She earned her PhD from American University in Washington, DC and is professor of Political Science at UMass Boston. O'Brien's research appears in top journals including *American Journal of Political Science, Perspectives on Politics, Political Research Quarterly*, and *Women & Politics*. She is also author of three books: *The Politics of Massachusetts Exceptionalism: Reputation Meets Reality* (University of Massachusetts Press, co-edited), *The Politics of Identity: Solidarity Building among America's Working Poor* (State University of New York Press) and *Diversity in Contemporary American Politics and Government* (Pearson-Longman, co-edited). O'Brien's commentary appears in outlets including All Thing Considered (NPR), *The Atlantic*, the Associated Press (AP), *The Economist*, Marketplace (NPR), *Newsweek*, the *New York Times*, PBS Newshour, the *Wall Street Journal*, and the *Washington Post*. Locally, she is a regular commentator for Boston25, GBH, and NBC10 Boston. O'Brien is winner of best paper honors from both the Midwest and New England Political Science Associations. She enjoys open water swimming and can be frequently found taking orders from her dog Reilley, who excels at unplanned zoom appearances.